low-fat no-fat
THAI

low-fat no-fat
THAI

Over 190 delicious and authentic recipes from Thailand, Burma, Indonesia, Malaysia and the Philippines

Jane Bamforth

LORENZ BOOKS

This edition is published by Lorenz Books

Lorenz Books is an imprint of Anness Publishing Ltd
Hermes House, 88–89 Blackfriars Road, London SE1 8HA
tel. 020 7401 2077; fax 020 7633 9499
www.lorenzbooks.com; www.annesspublishing.com

If you like the images in this book and would like to investigate
using them for publishing, promotions or advertising, please visit
our website www.practicalpictures.com for more information.

© Anness Publishing Ltd 2006

UK agent: The Manning Partnership Ltd
tel. 01225 478444; fax 01225 478440

UK distributor: Grantham Book Services Ltd
tel. 01476 541080; fax 01476 541061

North American agent/distributor: National Book Network
tel. 301 459 3366; fax 301 429 5746

Australian agent/distributor: Pan Macmillan Australia
tel. 1300 135 113; fax 1300 135 103

New Zealand agent/distributor: David Bateman Ltd
tel. (09) 415 7664; fax (09) 415 8892

Publisher: Joanna Lorenz
Editorial Director: Helen Sudell
Editor: Joy Wotton
Recipes: Judy Bastyra, Jane Bamforth, Mridula Baljekar, Jenni
Fleetwood, Yasuko Fukuoka, Christine Ingram, Becky Johnson, Kathy
Man, Sallie Morris, Kate Whiteman
Home Economists: Annabel Ford, Becky Johnson, Lucy McKelvie,
Bridget Sargeson, Helen Trent
Photographers: Martin Brigdale, Nicky Dowey, Janine Hosegood, Becky
Johnson, Dave King, William Lingwood, Craig Robertson
Designer: Nigel Partridge
Production Controller: Wendy Lawson

10 9 8 7 6 5 4 3 2 1

NOTES

Bracketed terms are intended for American readers.

For all recipes, quantities are given in both metric and imperial measures
and, where appropriate, in standard cups and spoons. Follow one set,
but not a mixture, because they are not interchangeable.

Standard spoon and cup measures are level. 1 tsp = 5ml,
1 tbsp = 15ml, 1 cup = 250ml/8fl oz.

Australian standard tablespoons are 20ml. Australian readers should
use 3 tsp in place of 1 tbsp for measuring small quantities of
gelatine, flour, salt, etc.

American pints are 16fl oz/2 cups. American readers should use
20fl oz/2.5 cups in place of 1 pint when measuring liquids.

Electric oven temperatures in this book are for conventional ovens.
When using a fan oven, the temperature will probably need to be
reduced by about 10–20°C/20–40°F. Since ovens vary, you should
check with your manufacturer's instruction book for guidance.

The nutritional analysis given for each recipe is calculated per portion
(i.e. serving or item), unless otherwise stated. If the recipe gives a
range, such as Serves 4–6, then the nutritional analysis will be for the
smaller portion size, i.e. 6 servings. Measurements for sodium do not
include salt added to taste.

Medium (US large) eggs are used unless otherwise stated.

Each recipe title is followed by a symbol that indicates the following:
★ = 5g of fat or less per serving
★★ = 10g of fat or less per serving
★★★ = 15g of fat or less per serving

Main front cover image shows Stir-fried Baby Squid with Ginger
– for recipe see page 112

CONTENTS

INTRODUCTION   6

THE LOW-FAT THAI AND
SOUTH-EAST ASIAN KITCHEN   8

    HEALTHY EATING GUIDELINES   10
    PLANNING A LOW-FAT DIET   12
    FAT-FREE COOKING METHODS   13
    VEGETABLES   14
    FRUIT, NUTS AND SEEDS   16
    HERBS AND SPICES   17
    RICE   18
    NOODLES AND WRAPPERS   20
    TOFU AND SOYA PRODUCTS   22
    MEAT AND POULTRY   23
    FISH AND SHELLFISH   24
    FAT AND CALORIE
       CONTENTS OF FOOD   26

SOUPS   28

APPETIZERS AND LIGHT BITES   56

VEGETARIAN MAIN DISHES   82

FISH AND SHELLFISH   100

CHICKEN AND DUCK   128

MEAT DISHES   150

RICE AND NOODLES   176

VEGETABLES AND SALADS   198

DESSERTS   228

GLOSSARY   250

MAP   251

INDEX   252

INTRODUCTION

The majority of people living in Thailand and South-east Asia have a very healthy diet, which is low in fat, high in fibre, with plenty of vegetables and relatively small amounts of meat. Much of their protein comes from fish and tofu, both of which are low-fat foods. Noodles and rice form the bulk of most meals, and processed foods are seldom eaten. In part, this diet evolved through necessity. Subsistence workers could not afford to eat large quantities of meat on a daily basis, even though pork, duck and chickens were – and still remain – an important part of the diet.

The food of Thailand and South-east Asia is a joy to the senses, combining the refreshing aroma of lemon grass and kaffir lime leaves with the pungency of brilliant red chillies and the magical flavours of coconut milk and fresh basil. The curries of the region follow this tradition for flavourings, and are very different from their Indian counterparts: Indian curries are traditionally slow-cooked for a rich, creamy taste, while Thai and South-east Asian dishes are famously quick and easy to prepare.

Exotic cuisines are increasingly popular in the West, and enthusiastic cooks are keen to reproduce them in their own kitchens. This book, with its extensive and wide-ranging collection of recipes from Thailand, Vietnam, Cambodia, Indonesia and the Philippines, will supply delicious ideas for new gastronomic discoveries.

Thailand and South-east Asia are a great source of healthy, low-fat recipes. Asian cooks are fussy about what they eat, and ingredients are chosen with considerable care. Visit any open-air market and you will see cooks sifting through piles of gourds to choose one that is at just the right state of ripeness for the meal they have planned. Meat and fish must be very fresh, a fact that can be a bit daunting to the visitor invited to

Right: Noodles add bulk and extra flavour to dishes without having a significant impact on fat levels. Fresh or dried egg noodles are available in various widths.

choose their meal while the fish is still swimming in a tank, but this is a method which proves beyond any doubt that the item in question will not have far to travel to their table. This passion for freshness is particularly apparent – and important – if the fish is to be eaten raw.

A HEALTHY WAY OF COOKING

Steaming and stir-frying are two of the most popular cooking methods in Thailand and South-east Asia. Both these methods are ideal for the low-fat cook, since they require little or no oil to be used. The wok is the principal utensil. This extraordinarily versatile pan, with its rounded bottom, was originally designed to fit snugly on a traditional Asian brazier or stove. Modern versions have flatter bases, to prevent wobble on electric stoves, but are still very efficient in the even way

they conduct and retain heat. The sloping sides mean that the food always returns to the centre, where the heat is most intense.

Many of the woks on sale today are non-stick. Although traditional carbonized steel woks are the ones purists choose, because they are so efficient, non-stick woks are better for low-fat cooking, since they make it possible to stir-fry with the smallest amount of oil.

When stir-frying, the best technique is to place the wok over the heat without any oil. When the pan is hot, dribble drops of oil, necklace fashion, on to the inner surface just below the rim. As the drops slither down the pan, they coat the sides, then puddle on the base. You can get away with using just about a teaspoon of oil if you follow this method. Add the food to be cooked when the oil is very hot, and keep it

Above: Tiny bird's eye chillies are thin-fleshed and very hot. They give many Thai dishes their characteristic fiery flavour without adding any fat to the finished dish.

moving. This is often done with a pair of chopsticks, but the easiest way is to use two spatulas or spoons, as when tossing a salad.

Add a metal trivet to a wok and it becomes a steamer. Better still, use a bamboo steamer. These attractive-looking utensils look rather like hat boxes, and come with tightly fitting domed lids. You can stack several tiers on top of each other over a wok partly filled with water. No fat will be needed and the food will taste delicious, with just a hint of fragrance from the bamboo.

A HEALTHY LIFESTYLE

Most of us eat fats in some form or another every day and we all need a small amount of fat in our diet to maintain a healthy, balanced eating plan. However, many of us eat far too much fat, and we should all be looking to reduce our overall fat intake, especially of saturated fats, and choosy the healthier unsaturated fats.

Regular exercise is also an important factor in a healthy lifestyle, and we should all be aiming to exercise three times a week for a minimum of half an hour each session. Swimming, brisk walking, jogging, dancing, skipping and cycling are all good forms of aerobic exercise promoting a healthy heart.

ABOUT THIS BOOK

This cookbook brings together, from many regions of Thailand and South-east Asia, a wide selection of delicious and nutritious dishes, all of which are low in fat, and are ideal to include as part of an everyday healthy and low-fat eating plan.

The book includes plenty of useful and informative advice. A succinct introduction gives a blueprint for healthy eating and has helpful hints and tips on low-fat and fat-free ingredients and cooking techniques. There are plenty of practical tips for reducing fat, especially saturated fat, in your diet, and the section on ingredients provides an insight into fruits, vegetables, flavourings and other essentials used in Thai and South-east Asian cooking.

The tempting recipes – all 150 of them – will be enjoyed by the whole family. They range from soups and appetizers to desserts and there are lots of delicious main course dishes for meat eaters and vegetarians. The emphasis throughout the book is on good food with maximum taste, and if you don't let on that the dishes are also low in fat, nobody is likely to guess.

THE LOW-FAT RECIPES

Each recipe includes a nutritional breakdown, proving an at-a-glance guide to calorie and fat content (including saturates and polyunsaturates content) per serving, as well as other key components such as protein, carbohydrate, calcium, cholesterol, fibre and sodium. All the recipes in this

Above: Dry and wet spices, aromatics and herbs are often pounded together to form spice pastes. Strong-tasting shrimp paste may be added.

collection are low in fat. Many contain less than five grams of total fat or less per serving, and a few are even lower in fat, with under one gram per serving. One or two classic recipes, such as Marinated Duck Curry and Stir-fried Beef in Oyster Sauce, contain slightly more fat, but even these contain less than in the traditional versions.

For ease of reference, all recipes with a single * after the recipe title contain a maximum of five grams of total fat, those with ** contain a maximum of 10 grams of total fat and those with *** contain up to 15 grams of total fat per portion. Each recipe also has a complete breakdown of the energy, protein, carbohydrate, cholesterol, calcium, fibre and sodium values of the food.

Although the recipes are low in fat, they lose nothing in terms of flavour. This practical cookbook will enable you to enjoy healthy Thai and South-east Asian food with a clear conscience. All the recipes are easy to cook and many are so quick that you'll have supper on the table in less time than it would have taken to collect a take-away.

Left: Woks may have flat or rounded bases and one or two handles. They are an important piece of equipment in any Thai kitchen and are used for low-fat stir-frying and steaming.

THE LOW-FAT THAI AND SOUTH-EAST ASIAN KITCHEN

Cooks in Thailand and South-east Asia have much to teach us about low-fat cooking. Their traditional diet is largely composed of vegetables, with a healthy proportion of carbohydrate in the form of noodles or rice, protein in the form of tofu or only small amounts of meat or fish. Suggestions for using tofu and other ingredients typical of the region are given in this section, which also includes valuable advice about planning and maintaining a healthy low-fat diet.

HEALTHY EATING GUIDELINES

A healthy diet provides us with all the nutrients we need. By eating the right types, balance and proportions of foods, we are more likely to have more energy and a higher resistance to diseases and illnesses such as heart disease, cancers, bowel disorders and obesity.

By choosing a variety of foods every day, you are supplying your body with all the essential nutrients it needs. To get the balance right, it is important to know just how much of each type of food you should be eating.

Of the five main food groups, it is recommended that we eat at least five portions of fruit and vegetables a day, not including potatoes; carbohydrate foods such as noodles, cereals, rice and potatoes; moderate amounts of fish, poultry and dairy products; and small amounts of foods containing fat or sugar. A dish like Thai Fried Rice fits the prescription perfectly, with its balance of rice, chicken fillets, (bell) peppers and corn.

THE ROLE OF FAT IN THE DIET

Fats shouldn't be cut out of our diets completely, as they are a valuable source of energy and make foods more palatable. However, lowering the fats, especially saturated fats, in your diet, may help you to lose weight, as well as reducing your risk of developing diseases.

Aim to limit your daily intake of fats to no more than 30–35 per cent of the total number of calories you consume. Each gram of fat provides nine calories, so a person eating 2,000 calories a day should not eat more than 70g/2¾oz of fat. Saturated fat should not comprise more than 10 per cent of the total calorie intake.

TYPES OF FAT

All fats in our foods are made up of building blocks of fatty acids and glycerol, and their properties vary according to each combination.

The two main types of fat are saturated and unsaturated. The unsaturated group is divided into two further categories – polyunsaturated and monounsaturated fats. There is usually a combination of these types of unsaturated fat in foods that contain fat, but the amount of each type varies from one kind of food to another.

SATURATED FATS

These fats are usually hard at room temperature. They are not essential in the diet, and should be limited, as they are implicated in raising the level of cholesterol in the blood, which can increase the likelihood of heart disease.

The main sources of saturated fats are animal products, such as fatty cuts of meat and meat products; spreading fats that are solid at room temperature, such as butter, lard and margarine; and

Below: Thai and South-east Asian cooking makes use of a wide variety of herbs, spices and flavourings, including cinnamon, root ginger, garlic, lemon grass and kaffir limes.

Above: Asian cooks have a wonderful assortment of shellfish, such as mussels, from the sea, lakes, rivers and canals.

Above: Rice noodles and rice vermicelli form an integral part of the Thai and South-east Asian cuisine. Easily reconstituted, they are virtually fat free.

Above: Naturally low in fat, such fresh green vegetables as these snake or yard-long beans form a healthy part of the Thai diet.

full-fat dairy products such as cream and cheese. Aside from meat, these ingredients are seldom found in Thai and South-east Asian recipes, but it is also important to avoid coconut and palm oil, which are saturated fats of vegetable origin. More insidious are those fats which, when processed, change the nature of the fat from unsaturated fatty acids to saturated ones. These are called "hydrogenated" fats, and should be strictly limited, so look out for that term on food labels.

Saturated fats are also found in many processed foods, such as chips (French fries) and savoury snacks, as well as cookies, pastries and cakes.

POLYUNSATURATED FATS

Small amounts of polyunsaturated fats are essential for good health, as they provide energy, can help to reduce cholesterol levels and enable the absorption of the fat-soluble vitamins A and D. The body can't manufacture polyunsaturated fatty acids, so they must be obtained from food. There are two types: those of vegetable or plant origin, known as Omega-6, which are found in sunflower oil, soft margarine, nuts and seeds; and Omega-3 fatty acids, which come from oily fish such

as tuna, salmon, herring, mackerel and sardines as well as walnuts, soya beans, wheatgerm and rapeseed (canola) oil.

MONOUNSATURATED FATS

The best known monounsaturated fat is olive oil. This is not used in Asian cooking, but another monounsaturated oil, groundnut (peanut) oil, is a popular choice. It is ideal for stir-frying and gives food a delicious flavour. Monounsaturated fatty acids are also found in nuts such as almonds, and oily fish. They are thought to have the beneficial effect of reducing blood cholesterol levels.

THE CHOLESTEROL QUESTION

Cholesterol is a fat-like substance that occurs naturally in the body, and which we also acquire from food. It has a vital role, since it is the material from which many essential hormones and vitamin D are made. Cholesterol is carried around the body, attached to proteins called high density lipoproteins (HDLs), low density lipoproteins (LDLs) and very low density lipoproteins (VLDLs or triglycerides).

Eating too much saturated fat encourages the body to make more cholesterol than it can use or can rid itself of. After food has been consumed, the LDLs carry the fat in the blood to

the cells where it is required. Any surplus should be excreted from the body, but if there are too many LDLs in the blood, some of the fat will be deposited on the walls of the arteries. This furring up gradually narrows the arteries and is one of the most common causes of heart attacks and strokes.

By way of contrast, HDLs appear to protect against heart disease. Whether high triglyceride levels are risk factors remains unknown.

CUTTING DOWN ON FATS AND SATURATED FATS IN THE DIET

It is relatively easy to cut down on obvious sources of fat in the diet, like butter, oils, margarine, cream, whole milk and full-fat cheese, but it is also important to know about and check consumption of "hidden" fats.

By educating yourself and being aware of which foods are high in fats, and by making simple changes, you can reduce the total fat content of your diet quite considerably. Choose low-fat alternatives when selecting items like coconut milk, milk, cheese and salad dressings. Fill up with very low-fat foods, such as fruits and vegetables, and foods that are high in carbohydrates, such as bread, potatoes, rice or noodles.

PLANNING A LOW-FAT DIET

Cutting down on fat on an everyday basis means we need to keep a close eye on the fat content of everything we eat. These general guidelines on reducing fat are applicable to all cuisines.

CUTTING DOWN ON FAT IN THE DIET

Most of us eat far more fat than we require – consuming about 115g/4oz of fat every day. Yet just 10g/¼oz, the amount in a single packet of crisps (US potato chips) or a thin slice of Cheddar cheese, is all that we actually need.

Current nutritional thinking is more lenient than this and suggests an upper daily limit of about 70g/2¾oz total fat.

Using low-fat recipes helps to reduce the overall daily intake of fat, but there are also lots of other ways of reducing the fat in your diet. Just follow the "eat less, try instead" suggestions below to discover how easy it can be.

• Eat less butter, margarine, other spreading fats and cooking oils. Try reduced-fat spreads, low-fat spreads or fat-free spreads. Butter or hard margarine should be softened at room temperature so that they can be spread thinly. Try low-fat cream cheese or low-fat soft cheese for sandwiches and toast.

Above: For fat-free snacks that are always available, keep an exotic supply of fresh fruit to hand including star fruit (carambola), papaya and lychees.

• Eat less full-fat dairy products such as whole milk, cream, butter, hard margarine, crème fraîche, whole-milk yogurts and hard cheese. Try instead semi-skimmed (low-fat) or skimmed milk, low-fat or reduced-fat milk products, such as low-fat yogurts and soft cheeses, reduced-fat hard cheeses such as Cheddar, and reduced-fat crème fraîche.
• Silken tofu can be used instead of cream in soups and sauces. It is a good source of calcium and an excellent protein food.
• Eat fewer fatty cuts of meat and high-fat meat products, such as pâtés, burgers, pies and sausages. Try instead naturally low-fat meats such as skinless chicken and turkey, ostrich and venison. When cooking lamb, beef or pork, use only the leanest cuts. Always cut away any visible fat and skin from meat before cooking. Try substituting low-fat protein ingredients like dried beans, lentils or tofu for some or all of the meat in a recipe.
• Eat more fish. It is easy to cook, tastes great, and if you use a steamer, you won't need to add any extra fat at all.
• Eat fewer hard cooking fats, such as lard or hard margarine. Try instead polyunsaturated or monounsaturated oils, such as sunflower or corn oil, and don't use too much.
• Eat fewer rich salad dressings and less full-fat mayonnaise. Try reduced-fat or fat-free dressings, or just a squeeze of lemon juice. Use a reduced-fat mayonnaise and thin it with puréed silken tofu for an even greater fat saving.
• Eat less fried food. Try fat-free cooking methods like steaming, grilling (broiling), baking or microwaving. Use non-stick pans with spray oil. When roasting or grilling meat, place it on a rack and drain off excess fat frequently.
• Eat fewer deep-fried or sautéed potatoes. Boil or bake them instead, or use other carbohydrates. Avoid chow-mein noodles, which are high in fat.

Above: Tuna and salmon are good sources of Omega-3 fatty acids, phytochemicals and antioxidants, which work together for a healthy heart.

• Cut down on oil when cooking. Drain fried food on kitchen paper to remove as much oil as possible. Choose heavy, good-quality non-stick pans and use spray oil for the lightest coverage. Moisten food with fat-free or low-fat liquids such as fruit juice, defatted stock, wine or even beer.
• Eat fewer high-fat snacks, such as chocolate, cookies, chips (French fries) and crisps. Try instead a piece of fruit, some vegetable crudités or some home-baked low-fat fruit cake.

Below: Choose lean cuts of meat and naturally low-fat meats such as skinless chicken and turkey.

FAT-FREE COOKING METHODS

Thai and South-east Asian cooking uses a variety of low-fat and fat-free cooking methods, and by incorporating recipes from this region into your daily diet it is easy to bring down your total fat consumption. Where possible, steam, microwave or grill (broil) foods, without adding extra fat. Alternatively, braise in a defatted stock, wine or fruit juice, or stir-fry with just a spray of vegetable oil.

• By choosing a good quality, non-stick wok, such as the one above, you can keep the amount of fat needed for cooking foods to the absolute minimum. When cooking meat in a regular pan, dry-fry the meat to brown it, then tip it into a sieve (strainer) and drain off the excess fat before returning it to the pan and adding the other ingredients. If you do need a little fat for cooking, choose an oil high in unsaturates, such as sunflower or corn oil and use a spray where possible.

• Eat less meat and more vegetables and noodles or other forms of pasta. A good method for making a small amount of meat such as beef steak go a long way is to place it in the freezer for 30 minutes and then slice it very thinly with a sharp knife. Meat prepared this way will cook very quickly with very little fat.

• When baking chicken or fish, wrap it in a loose package of foil or baking parchment, with a little wine or fruit juice. Add some fresh herbs or spices before sealing the parcel, if you like.

• It is often unnecessary to add fat when grilling (broiling) food. If the food shows signs of drying, lightly brush or spray it with a little unsaturated oil, such as sunflower, corn or olive oil. Microwaved foods seldom need the addition of fat, so add herbs or spices for extra flavour and colour.

• Steaming is the ideal way of cooking fish. If you like, arrange the fish on a bed of aromatic flavourings such as lemon or lime slices and sprigs of herbs. Alternatively, place finely shredded vegetables or seaweed in the base of the steamer to give the fish extra flavour.

• If you do not own a steamer, cook vegetables in a covered pan over low heat with just a little water, so that they cook in their own juices.
• Vegetables can be braised in the oven in low-fat or fat-free stock, wine or a little water with some chopped fresh or dried herbs.
• Try poaching foods such as chicken, fish or fruit in low-fat or fat-free stock or fruit juice.
• Plain rice or noodles make a very good low-fat accompaniment to most Thai and South-east Asian dishes.

• The classic Asian technique of adding moisture and flavour to chicken by marinating it in a mixture of soy sauce and rice wine, with a little sesame oil, can be used with other meats too. You can also use a mixture of alcohol, herbs and spices, or vinegar or fruit juice. The marinade will also help to tenderize the meat and any remaining marinade can be used to baste the food while it is cooking.
• When serving vegetables, resist the temptation to add butter. Instead, sprinkle with chopped fresh herbs.

Low-fat spreads in cooking
A huge variety of low-fat and reduced-fat spreads is available in supermarkets, along with some spreads that are very low in fat. Generally speaking, any very low-fat spreads with a fat content of around 20 per cent or less have a high water content. These are unsuitable for cooking and can only be used for spreading.

VEGETABLES

Naturally low in fat and bursting with vitamins and minerals, vegetables are one food group that should ideally make up the bulk of our daily diet. In Thailand and South-east Asia cooks use vegetables freely in stir-fries and braised dishes, and have evolved a wide range of delicious vegetarian main courses to make the most of the abundant choice of vegetables on sale in markets.

Many of these vegetables are now commonplace in other parts of the world. Chinese leaves (Chinese cabbage), pak choi (bok choy) and beansprouts are usually available in supermarkets, and other greens, such as mizuna, Chinese mustard greens and Chinese broccoli, are often grown by small producers and can be found at farmers' markets.

CHINESE LEAVES

Also known as Chinese cabbage or Napa cabbage, this vegetable has pale green, crinkly leaves with long, wide, white ribs. It is pleasantly crunchy, has a sweet, nutty flavour and tastes wonderful raw or cooked. When buying Chinese leaves, look out for firm, slightly heavy heads with pale green leaves without blemishes or bruises. To prepare, peel off the outer leaves, cut off the root and slice the cabbage thinly or thickly. When stir-fried, Chinese leaves lose their subtle cabbage taste and take on the flavour of other ingredients in the dish.

Below: Chinese leaves have a mild, delicate flavour.

Right: Pak choi tastes similar to spinach.

PAK CHOI

Another member of the brassica family, pak choi (bok choy) has lots of noms-de-plume, including horse's ear, Chinese cabbage and Chinese white cabbage. There are several varieties, and one or other is usually on sale at the supermarket. Unlike Chinese leaves, pak choi doesn't keep well, so plan to use it within a day or two of purchase. The vegetable is generally cooked, although very young and tender pak choi can be eaten raw. The stems – regarded by many as the best part – need slightly longer cooking than the leaves.

CHOI SUM

Often sold in bunches, choi sum is a brassica with bright green leaves and thin, pale, slightly grooved stems. It has a pleasant aroma and mild taste, and remains crisp and tender if properly cooked. The leaves can be sliced, but are more often steamed whole. Choi sum will keep for a few days in the salad drawer, but is best used as soon as possible after purchase.

CHINESE BROCCOLI

With its somewhat straggly appearance, this brassica looks more like purple sprouting broccoli than prim Calabrese. Every part of Chinese broccoli is edible, and each has its own inimitable taste. To prepare, remove the tough outer leaves, then cut off the leaves. If the stems are tough, peel them. It is usual to blanch the vegetable briefly in salted boiling water or stock before stir-frying.

AUBERGINES

Popular throughout Thailand and South-east Asia, aubergines (eggplants) come in a variety of shapes, sizes and colours. They have a smoky, slightly bitter taste and spongy flesh that readily absorbs other flavours and oils. To avoid the absorption of too much fat, cut the aubergine into slices, and dry-fry these in a wok over medium heat for 4–5 minutes. They can also be braised, stuffed or baked.

MOOLI

Also known as daikon, this Asian vegetable looks rather like a parsnip, but is actually related to the radish. The flavour is milder than that of most radishes, however, although the texture is similar: crisp and crunchy. Treat it like a carrot, scraping or peeling the outer skin and then slicing it in rounds or batons. It can be eaten raw or cooked.

BAMBOO SHOOTS

Fresh bamboo shoots are quite hard to buy outside Asia, but you may find them in big-city Asian markets. They must be parboiled before being cooked, as the raw vegetable contains a highly toxic oil. Remove the base and the hard outer leaves, then cut the core into chunks. Boil these in salted water for 30 minutes, then drain, rinse under cold water and drain again. Cut into slices, shreds or cubes for further cooking. Dried bamboo slices must be soaked in water for 2–3 hours before use. Canned bamboo shoots only need rinsing before being used.

Below: Choi sum is often used in stir-fries.

Above: Thai cooking uses green apple aubergines and purple long aubergines.

WATER CHESTNUTS

Fresh, crisp water chestnuts are the corms of a plant that grows on the margins of rivers and lakes. Their snow-white flesh stays crunchy even after long cooking. Fresh water chestnuts are often available from Asian markets. They keep well in a paper bag in the refrigerator. Once released from their dark brown jackets, they must be kept submerged in water in a covered container and used within one week. Canned water chestnuts should be rinsed before being used.

Below: Mooli has a crisp, crunchy texture and is delicious raw.

BEANSPROUTS

Mung beans and soy beans are the varieties of beansprout most often used, and they are an important ingredient in the Asian kitchen. It is important to use them as fresh as possible. Better still, sprout the beans yourself. Before use, rinse them to remove the husks and tiny roots. Use them in salads or stir-fries, but take care not to overcook them, or they will become limp and tasteless.

SPRING ONIONS

Slender and crisp, spring onions (scallions) are appreciated by Asian cooks not only for their aroma and flavour, but also for their perceived cooling qualities. Use spring onions raw in salads or lightly cooked in stir-fries. They need very little preparation. Just trim off the roots, strip off the wilted outer leaves and separate the white and green parts. Spring onion green is sometimes used in Asian dishes as ribbon, to tie tiny parcels of food, in which case it is first blanched so that it becomes more flexible.

MUSHROOMS

Several types of mushrooms are used in Asian cooking, and many of these are now available in Western supermarkets.

Shiitake mushrooms are prized in Asia, both for their flavour and their medicinal qualities. They have a slightly acidic taste and a meaty, slippery texture. They contain twice as much protein as button mushrooms and their robust flavour makes them the ideal partner for noodles and rice.

To prepare fresh shiitake mushrooms, remove the stems. The caps can be left whole, or sliced. If they are to be used in a salad, cook them briefly in low-fat stock first. Dried shiitake mushrooms must be reconstituted before being used. Soak them in cold water overnight, or in a bowl of warm water for at least 30 minutes before using, then strain the soaking liquid. Remove the stems before use.

Right: Spring onions are used raw in salads.

Oyster mushrooms have a mild flavour and are pastel-coloured in shades of pink, yellow or pearl grey. They need gentle handling. Tear, rather than cut, large specimens and don't overcook them, or they will become rubbery.

Enokitake mushrooms are tiny, with bud-like caps at the end of long, slender stems. To appreciate their crisp texture and sweet flavour, use them raw in salads.

SHALLOTS

Although they belong to the same family as garlic, leeks, chives and onions – and look suspiciously like baby onions – shallots are very much their own vegetable. Sometimes called bunching onions, they have bulbs that multiply to produce clusters joined at the root end.

Shallots tend to be sweeter and much milder than large onions. Some Thai varieties are sweet enough to be used in desserts.

Indispensable in South-east Asian kitchens, shallots are far more popular than both regular onions and spring onions (scallions) for everyday use. Ground with garlic, ginger and other aromatics, shallots form the standard marinade and are also an essential ingredient in curry pastes and satay sauce. Dried shallots (hanh huong) are a popular alternative in Vietnam.

Preparation and cooking techniques: Trim the shallots, peel off the skin, then prise the bulbs apart. Leave these whole for braising, or chop as required. Thinly-sliced shallot rings are sometimes dry-fried until crisp, then used as a garnish.

Shallots will keep for several months in a cool, dry place.

FRUIT, NUTS AND SEEDS

When embarking on a low-fat eating plan, it is all too easy to concentrate solely on the fat content of foods while ignoring the amount of sugar they contain. Avoid following a sensible main course with a sugary dessert. Instead, end a meal with a piece of fresh fruit or a few nuts. The latter can be high in fat, but, with the exception of brazil nuts and coconuts, the fat in nuts is monounsaturated or polyunsaturated, and cholesterol-free.

LYCHEES

These moist fruits need no preparation once you have cracked the shells and peeled off the scaly red skin. The pearly white flesh inside can be sliced and used in a fruit salad or savoury dish. South-east Asian cooks like to pair lychees with pork. For a delectable sorbet, try puréed lychees with elderflower syrup. When buying fresh lychees, choose ones with pink or red shells; brown fruit are past their prime.

PINEAPPLES

The raw fruit and juice are very popular in Thailand, but pineapple is also used in cooked sweet and savoury dishes. Fresh pineapple will keep in a cool place for up to a week. To prepare pineapple, cut off the leaves, then quarter lengthways or cut in slices. Remove the skin and "eyes".

MANGOES

Most mangoes are oval in shape with blushed gold or pink skin. The easiest way to obtain mango chunks is to cut a thick lengthways slice off each side of the unpeeled fruit. Score the flesh on each slice with criss-cross lines. Fold these slices inside out and slice off the flesh.

PAPAYAS

Papayas or paw-paws can be small and round, but are usually pear-shaped. When ripe, the flesh is eaten as it is or used in fruit salads and other desserts. Papayas that are not too ripe can be added to soups, curries or seafood dishes. Unripe green papayas are served raw in salads and made into pickles. The juice and skins are used to tenderize meat.

LIME

These small, green and very sour citrus fruits are used extensively throughout the region. Fresh lime juice is served as a drink, with salt and sugar, and is also used in salad dressings.

COCONUT MILK AND CREAM

Coconut milk is high in fat but there is a version that is 88 per cent fat free. Coconut milk and cream are both made from the grated flesh of the coconut, and in the East, one can buy bags of freshly grated coconut for just this purpose. Warm water is added and the coconut is squeezed until the mixture is cloudy. When strained, this is coconut milk. If the milk is left to stand, coconut cream will float to the surface.

Left: Canned and fresh lychees have a wonderful scented aroma.

STAR FRUIT

The correct name for this fruit is carambola. Cylindrical in shape, the bright yellow waxy-looking fruit has five distinctive "wings" or protuberances which form the points of the star shapes revealed when the fruit is sliced. The flavour varies: fruits picked straight from the tree in Asia are inevitably sweet and scented, but those that have travelled long distances in cold storage can be disappointing.

PEANUTS

One of the most important flavourings in Thai cooking, peanuts are not especially low in fat but a small amount can make all the difference to the character of a dish. Raw peanuts have little smell, but once cooked they have a powerful aroma, a crunchy texture and a distinctive flavour. Peanuts play an important role in Asian cuisine. The smaller ones are used for making oil, while the larger, less oily nuts are widely eaten, both as a snack food and as ingredients in salads and main courses.

SESAME SEEDS

These tiny seeds are flat and pear-shaped. Raw sesame seeds have very little aroma and they are almost tasteless until they are roasted or dry-fried, which brings out their distinctive nutty flavour and aroma.

LOTUS SEEDS

Fresh lotus seeds are used as a snack food. The dried seeds must be soaked in water before use. The seeds are prized for their texture and ability to absorb other flavours. They are often added to soups.

HERBS AND SPICES

The principal flavourings favoured in South-east Asia have made a tremendous contribution to global cuisine. Ingredients like fresh ginger, lemon grass and kaffir lime now feature on menus the world over, not just in recipes that reflect their origin, but also in fusion food. Fish sauce is an essential seasoning for Thai and Vietnamese cooking, in much the same way that soy sauce is important to the Chinese and Japanese.

GARLIC

Often used with spring onions (scallions) and ginger, garlic is a vital ingredient in Thai and South-east Asian dishes. The most common variety has a purple skin, a fairly distinctive aroma and a hint of sweetness. Garlic may dominate a dish, but it may also impart a mild flavour, as when a garlic clove is heated in oil and then removed from the pan.

GALANGAL

Galangal is slightly harder than ginger, but used in much the same way. When young, the skin is creamy white with pink sprouts and the flavour is lemony. As galangal matures, the flavour intensifies and becomes more peppery.

GINGER

Valued not just as an aromatic, but also for its medicinal qualities, ginger is used throughout Asia. When young, ginger is juicy and tender, with a sharp flavour suggestive of citrus. At this stage it can easily be sliced, chopped or pounded to a paste. Older roots are tougher and may need to be peeled and grated. Pickled ginger is delicious. It can be served as a side dish, or combined with other ingredients such as beef or duck.

CHILLIES

Although they did not originate in South-east Asia, chillies have been embraced so fervently by Thailand that they are now irrevocably associated with the area. They are an essential ingredient in a variety of South-east Asian cuisines. But it is for their flavour rather than their fire that they are most valued. Be careful when you handle chillies. They contain a substance called capsaicin, which is a powerful irritant. If this comes into contact with delicate skin or the eyes, it can cause considerable pain. Wear gloves when handling chillies or wash your hands thoroughly in hot soapy water afterwards.

LEMON GRASS

A perennial tufted plant with a bulbous base, lemon grass looks like a plump spring onion (scallion). When the stalk is cut or bruised, the lively citrus aroma becomes evident. There are two main ways of using lemon grass. The stalk can be kept whole, bruised, then cooked slowly in liquid until it releases its flavour and is removed, or the tender lower portion of the stalk can be sliced or finely chopped and then stir-fried.

KAFFIR LIME LEAVES

These fruit are not true limes, but belong to a subspecies of the citrus family. Native to South-east Asia, they have green knobbly skins. The fruit is not edible, but the rind is sometimes used

Left: Red and green chillies

in cooking, but it is the leaves that are most highly prized. Kaffir lime leaves are synonymous with Thai cooking. The leaves are torn or finely shredded and used in soups and curries. Finely grated rind is added to fish or chicken dishes.

BASIL

Three types of basil are grown in Thailand, each with a slightly different appearance, flavour and use. Thai basil has a sweet, anise flavour and is used in red curries. Holy basil is pungent and tastes like cloves. Lemon basil is used in soups and is sprinkled on salads.

CORIANDER/CILANTRO

The entire coriander plant is used in Thai cooking – roots, stems, leaves and seeds. The fresh, delicate leaves are used in sauces, curries and for garnishes. The roots and stems are crushed and used for marinades. The seeds are ground to add flavour to various curry pastes.

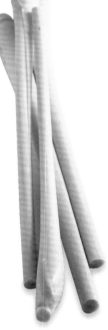

Above: Lemon grass

FISH SAUCE

Thai *nam pla* or fish sauce has a slightly stronger flavour and aroma than the Vietnamese or Chinese versions. It is used in Asia as a seasoning in all kinds of savoury dishes. It is also blended with extra flavourings such as finely chopped garlic and chillies, and sugar and lime juice to make a dipping sauce.

CURRY PASTES

Most Thai curries are based on "wet" spice mixtures, made by grinding spices and aromatics in a heavy mortar with a rough surface. Red curry paste is used in beef dishes and robust chicken dishes. Green curry paste, made from herbs and fresh green chillies, is used for chicken curries. Yellow curry paste and, the mildest of all, Mussaman curry paste are used for chicken and beef curries.

RICE

This low-fat high carbohydrate food is immensely important in Thai and South-east Asian cooking. When Thais are called to the table, the phrase used – *gkin kao* – literally translates as "a time to eat rice". All the other foods that make up a meal – meat, fish and vegetables – are regarded as accompaniments and are referred to as *ghap kao* or "things eaten with rice".

Rice is a non-allergenic food, rich in complex carbohydrates and low in salts and fats. It contains small amounts of easily digestible protein, together with phosphorous, magnesium, potassium and zinc. Brown rice, which retains the bran, yields vitamin E and some B-group vitamins, and is also a source of fibre. Although it is healthier than white rice, it is the latter that is preferred in South-east Asia.

The average Thai eats 158kg/350lb of rice every year, which is almost a pound a day. It is consumed in various forms, from basic steamed rice to rice noodles, crackers and cakes.

Two distinct types of rice are popular in Thailand. The first is a delicately scented long grain variety, which is used as a staple with all meals. It comes in several qualities, and is white and fluffy with separate grains when cooked. In northern Thailand, a starchy glutinous rice is preferred. When cooked, the grains stick together.

There are thousands of varieties of rice, many of which are known only in the areas where they are cultivated. The simplest method of classification is by the length of the grain, which can be long, medium or short. Long grain rice is three or four times as long as it is wide.

Rice Mother
The traditional rice-growing communities in Thailand have a high regard for *Mae Pra Posop*, the "Rice Mother". Elaborate ceremonies are performed in her name during various stages of rice cultivation so that she may bless the fields with bountiful harvests from year to year.

Above: Jasmine or Thai fragrant rice has tender, aromatic grains and is popular throughout central and southern Thailand and much of South-east Asia. It is widely available in supermarkets and Asian stores in the West.

JASMINE RICE

Also known as fragrant or scented rice, this long grain variety is the staple food of the central and southern parts of Thailand. As the name suggests, jasmine rice has a delicate aroma. The flavour is slightly nutty, and it resembles Basmati rice from India. The uncooked grains are translucent and, when cooked, the rice is fluffy and white. Most of the crop comes from a region between central and north-eastern Thailand where the soil is a combination of clay and sand. Newly harvested rice from this region is prized for the delicate texture of the grains.

GLUTINOUS RICE

Commonly referred to as sweet or sticky rice, glutinous rice is the mainstay of the diet in the northern and north-eastern regions of Thailand. It is delicious and very filling. The name is derived entirely from its sticky texture, as rice does not contain any gluten. Easily cultivated on the hillsides and high plateaux of these regions, glutinous rice requires less water during the growing period than the wet rice of the central lowlands.

Glutinous rice comes in both short or round grain and long grain varieties. Thai people prefer the long grain

Below: Glutinous rice, which may be black (although, more accurately, it is a very dark red), white or a hybrid known as "jasmine sweet", is most widely used in north and north-east Thailand.

Above: Rice is best cooked using the absorption method. Cook the rice with water in a tightly covered pan, then leave for 5 minutes until tender before serving.

variety; the short grain rice is more commonly used in Japanese and Chinese cooking. Some of the long grain varieties have a delicate, aromatic flavour, and these high-grade hybrids are sometimes labelled "jasmine sweet" or "jasmine glutinous rice", the adjective "jasmine" echoing the description used for their fragrant cousins in the non-glutinous rice family.

What makes this type of rice unusual is the way in which the grains clump together when cooked, enabling it to be eaten with the hands. Bitesize chunks of cooked rice are pulled off, one at a time, and rolled to a ball between the fingers and palm of the right hand. The ball is then dunked in a sauce or stew before being eaten. The process is not as messy as it sounds; if it is done correctly, then the grains stick to each other but not to the fingers or the palm. At the end of a meal, rolling the last piece of rice can actually have a cleansing effect, as the rice mops up any remaining juices or grease on the hand.

The starchiness of glutinous rice gives the uncooked grain a distinct opaque white colour, which is different from the more translucent appearance

of regular rice grains. When soaked and steamed, however, the reverse is true. Glutinous rice becomes translucent, while regular rice turns opaque.

Although it is in the north and the north-eastern regions of Thailand that glutinous rice is most popular, it is also eaten elsewhere in the country, most frequently in sweet snacks or desserts. The rice is sweetened and flavoured with coconut milk, and is especially popular in the mango and durian season, when huge amounts of the coconut-flavoured rice are sold to eat with these precious fruits. Use low-fat coconut milk to keep the fat content as low as possible.

BLACK GLUTINOUS RICE

This wholegrain rice – that is, with only the husk removed – has a rich, nutty flavour that is distinctly different from the more subtle taste of white glutinous rice. It is generally sweetened with coconut milk and sugar and eaten as a snack or dessert, rather than being used as the staple of a savoury meal. Reduced-fat coconut milk makes an excellent substitute. It does tend to be quite heavy, filling and indigestible if eaten in quantity, so it is usually nibbled as a sweetmeat snack in the mid-afternoon or later in the evening, after the evening meal has been digested. A popular version of roasted glutinous rice, flattened into a cake, is *khao mow rang*, which is sold at all markets throughout Thailand.

In spite of its name, black rice isn't actually black in colour. If the grains are soaked in water for a few hours, the water will turn a deep burgundy red, showing the rice's true colour.

RICE PRODUCTS

Throughout Thailand and South-east Asia, rice, the staple carbohydrate, is used in many different ways.

Rice Flour

This flour may be made from either glutinous or non-glutinous raw rice that has been very finely ground. It is used to make the dough for fresh rice noodles and is also used to make

Above: Rice flour is finely ground and thoroughly pulverized. As a result, it has a very light texture and is used for fresh rice noodles.

desserts such as pancakes. Rice flour is readily available in Asian food stores. When the source is non-glutinous rice it is called *paeng khao jao* and when it is made from glutinous rice it is known as *paeng khao niao*. Store it as you would wheat flour.

Fermented Rice

Made by fermenting cooked glutinous rice, this is a popular sweetmeat, sold on market stalls and by street vendors.

Rice-pot Crust

In several cultures, the crust that forms on the base of the pan when rice is cooked in a particular way is highly prized. In Thailand, the crust is lifted off the base of the pan in sheets and is then dried out in the sun before being sold. *Khao tang* is lightly toasted or fried before being eaten.

To make *khao tang* at home, spread a layer of cooked rice about 5mm/¼in thick on a lightly greased baking sheet. Dry it out in a low oven, 140°C/275°F/ Gas 1, for several hours. Leave to cool, then break into pieces. Deep-fry for just a few seconds until puffed, but not browned. Lift out using a slotted spoon and drain on kitchen paper.

NOODLES AND WRAPPERS

Second only to rice in importance in the Thai diet, noodles and wrappers are cooked in a vast number of ways. Noodles are eaten at any time of day, including breakfast, and if hunger strikes unexpectedly, one of the many roadside noodle carts will furnish a tasty snack. For the local population, soup noodles are easily the most popular dish, but tourists tend to plump for *Pad Thai* (fried noodles). Wrappers are wrapped around all kinds of fillings.

NOODLES

There are basically five main varieties of noodles used in Thai cooking: *sen ya*, *ba mee*, *sen mee*, *sen lek* and *wun sen*. Most can be bought fresh in Asian stores, but it is more likely that you will find them dried. Noodles come in several sizes, from tiny transparent threads to large sheets. Many of them are made from rice, which serves to further emphasize the importance of the grain in the Thai diet. Other types of noodles are based on wheat flour or flour made from ground mung beans.

Unfortunately, the names of noodles are not standardized and the same type of noodle may go under several different names, depending on the manufacturer or which part of the country they come from. Noodles made without eggs are often labelled "imitation noodles" or "alimentary paste".

Noodle know-how

Both dried and fresh noodles have to be cooked in boiling water before use – or soaked in boiling water until pliable. How long for depends on the type of noodle, their thickness and whether or not the noodles are going to be cooked again in a soup or sauce. As a rule, once they have been soaked, dried noodles require about 3 minutes' cooking, while fresh ones will often be ready in less than a minute and may need to be rinsed under cold water to prevent them from overcooking.

Below: Dried vermicelli rice noodles should be soaked, not boiled.

RICE NOODLES

Both fresh and dried rice noodles are available in Thai markets. Fresh noodles are highly perishable, and they must be cooked as soon as possible after purchase. Rice noodles are available in a wide range of shapes and widths from fine vermicelli to thick, round rice noodle nests.

Vermicelli Rice Noodles

These noodles are usually sold dried and must be soaked in boiling water before use. When dried, rice vermicelli are known as rice stick noodles.

Medium Rice Noodles

Resembling spaghetti, these noodles are usually sold dried. The city of Chanthaburi in Thailand is famous for *sen lek* noodles, which are sometimes called *Jantoboon* noodles after the nickname for the town.

Rice Stick Noodles

Also known as rice river noodles, these noodles are sold both dried and fresh, although the latter form is more popular. When fresh rice stick noodles tend to be rather sticky and need to be separated before being cooked.

Rice Noodle Nests

Although the Thai name of these fresh thick round rice noodles means Chinese noodles, these are actually a Thai speciality, made of rice flour. In the Lacquer Pavilion of Suan Pakkad Palace there is a panel showing the making of *khanom chine* as part of the preparations for the Buddha's last meal.

Khanom chine are white and the strands are a little thicker than spaghetti. At most markets in Thailand, nests of these noodles are a familiar sight. They are sold freshly cooked. You buy them by the hundred nests and should allow four or five nests per person. Buy the cheaper ones, because they taste better although they are not so white as the more expensive noodle nests. Fresh noodles are highly perishable, so, even though they are cooked, it makes sense to buy them early in the day, and steam them again when you get them home.

Fresh noodles are delicious when served with *nam ya*, *nam prik*, *sow nam* and a variety of curries.

Below: Rice stick noodles are flat, not unlike Italian tagliatelle.

Preparing rice noodles is a simple matter. They need only to be soaked in hot water for a few minutes to soften them before serving. Add the noodles to a large bowl of just-boiled water and leave for 5–10 minutes, or until they soften, stirring occasionally to separate the strands. Their dry weight will usually double after soaking, so 115g/4oz dry noodles will produce about 225g/8oz after soaking.

Rice stick noodles puff up and become wonderfully crisp when they are deep-fried. Just a few deep-fried noodles sprinkled over a dish of boiled or reconstituted noodles will wonderfully enhance the flavour without seriously raising the fat content.

To prepare deep-fried rice noodles, place the noodles in a large mixing bowl and soak in cold water for 15 minutes. Drain them and lay them on kitchen paper to dry.

Then heat about 1.2 litres/2 pints/5 cups vegetable oil in a large, high-sided frying pan or wok to 180°C/350°F. To test if the oil is ready, carefully drop in a couple of noodle strands. If they puff and curl up immediately, the oil is hot enough. Very carefully, add a handful of dry noodles to the hot oil. As soon as they puff up, after about 2 seconds, flip

Below: Egg noodles are available, dried and fresh, in a wide variety of widths.

Right: Spring roll wrappers are made from a wheat and water dough.

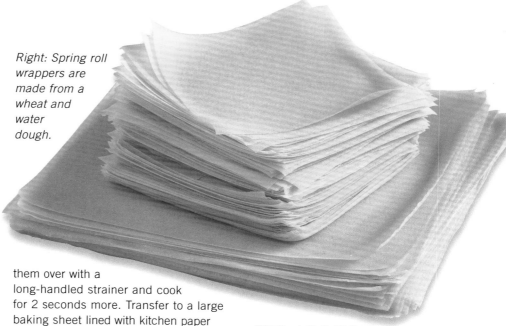

them over with a long-handled strainer and cook for 2 seconds more. Transfer to a large baking sheet lined with kitchen paper and leave to cool. When the fried noodles are cold they can be transferred to a sealed plastic bag and will stay crisp for about 2 days.

EGG NOODLES

These noodles owe their yellow colour to the egg used in their manufacture. Sold fresh in nests, they must be shaken loose before being cooked. They come in both flat and round shapes. Very thin noodles are known as egg thread noodles. The flat type of noodles are generally used for soups and the rounded type are preferred for stir-frying. Egg noodles freeze well, provided that they are correctly wrapped. Thaw them thoroughly before using them in soup or noodles dishes.

Egg noodles should be cooked in boiling water for 4–5 minutes, or according to the packet instructions. Drain and serve.

CELLOPHANE NOODLES

These thin, wiry noodles, also called glass, jelly or bean thread noodles, are made from mung beans. They are the same size as ordinary egg noodles but they are transparent, resembling strips of cellophane or glass. They are only available dried.

Cellophane noodles are never served on their own, but always as an ingredient in a dish. Soak them in hot water for 10–15 minutes to soften them, then drain and cut into shorter strands.

WRAPPERS

These are made from wheat or rice flour and are used throughout Thailand and South-east Asia to wrap around a filling. Some may be eaten fresh while others are deep-fried.

WONTON WRAPPERS

Originally Chinese, these thin yellow pastry squares are made from egg and wheat flour and can be bought fresh or frozen. Fresh wrappers will last for about five days, double-wrapped and stored in the refrigerator. Simply peel off the number you require. Frozen wrappers should be thawed before use.

RICE PAPER

These brittle, semi-transparent, paper-thin sheets are made from a mixture of rice flour, water and salt, rolled out by a machine until very thin and then dried in the sun. Packets of 50–100 sheets are available. Store in a cool, dry place. Before use, dip in water until pliable, then wrap around a filling to make fresh spring rolls.

SPRING ROLL WRAPPERS

These wafer-thin wrappers are used to make classic spring rolls. The sizes available range from 8cm/3¼in to 30cm/12in square, and they usually come in packets of 20. Once opened, spring roll wrappers will dry out quickly, so peel off one at a time and keep the rest of the wrappers covered.

TOFU AND SOYA PRODUCTS

Tofu is a very versatile ingredient and, depending upon the texture, it can be cooked by almost every conceivable method, including stir-frying, steaming and poaching. It can be used with a vast array of ingredients, both sweet and savoury. As a low-fat ingredient, tofu is freely used as a meat replacement.

Made from soya beans, tofu (also widely known as beancurd) is popular throughout South-east Asia and one of the cheapest sources of protein in the world. Highly nutritious and low in fat and sugar, tofu is a much healthier food than either meat or fish, at a fraction of the cost. Tempeh is similar to tofu, but has a nuttier, more savoury flavour.

The nutritional value of tofu cannot be stressed too highly. As a vegetable protein, it contains the eight essential amino acids plus vitamins A and B. Tofu is free from cholesterol, and is regarded as an excellent food for anyone with heart disease or high blood pressure. In addition, it is very easy to digest, and this makes it an ideal food for infants, invalids and the elderly.

Although tofu is bland, it picks up the flavours of other foods when marinaded. It is important to cook it with such strongly flavoured seasonings as garlic, ginger, spring onions (scallions), chillies, soy sauce, oyster sauce, shrimp paste, fermented black beans, salted yellow beans, or sesame

oil. Tofu tastes very good with meat. It is often cooked with either pork or beef, but seldom with chicken. It goes well with fish and shellfish.

Two basic types of fresh tofu are widely available in the West: soft or silken tofu, and a firm type, called *momen*. Both kinds are creamy white in colour and are either packed in water or sold in vacuum packs. Several other tofu products are also popular in Thai and South-east Asian cooking.

PRESSED TOFU

This is a fresh bean curd cake that has had almost all the moisture squeezed out of it, leaving a solid block with a smooth texture. Brown outside and white inside, it is often seasoned with soy sauce and may also be smoked. You can press your own cakes of tofu by placing the bean curd between two plates. Weigh down the top one. Tilt the plates slightly to allow the liquid to drain off. Pressed tofu can be sliced and stir-fried.

DRIED BEAN CURD SKIN

This can also be purchased at Asian food stores. It consists of thin sheets of curd that are skimmed off simmering soya milk and dried. They are sold flat or rolled to form bean curd sticks. The skins can be used in casseroles, soups or stir-fries, and the sticks are popular in vegetarian dishes.

Above: Tempeh, a solid bean curd originally from Indonesia, is now popular in Thai cooking.

Dried bean curd skins need to be soaked in cold water before they can be used. The sheets require 1–2 hours, but the sticks should be soaked for several hours, preferably overnight.

DEEP-FRIED TOFU

Although deep-fried tofu is not especially low in fat, when used in small quantities it can significantly enhance the flavour of a dish without greatly increasing the fat content. When tofu is deep-fried in hot oil, it puffs up and turns golden brown, the flavour intensifies and the texture becomes chewy. Cubes of deep-fried tofu are sold in Asian markets. Store in the refrigerator and use within 3 days.

PICKLED TOFU OR BEAN PASTE

This product is made by fermenting fresh tofu, then drying it in the sun before marinating it in an alcohol mixture. The curd can be red or white and the flavour is extremely powerful. The best pickled bean curd comes from China and is sold in bottles or jars.

TEMPEH

This solid bean curd is an Indonesian speciality made by fermenting cooked soya beans with a cultured starter. It resembles firm tofu, but has a slightly nutty, more savoury taste. It benefits from a marinade.

Above: (clockwise from top) Pressed, silken and firm tofu. All are naturally low in fat and absorb the flavours of the ingredients with which they are cooked.

MEAT <u>AND</u> POULTRY

It is traditional in Thailand and South-east Asia for the meat element in a dish to be a relatively small percentage of the whole, with vegetables and noodles or rice making up the major portion. This is good news for anyone on a low-fat diet. When meat is included, it is usually used in stir-fries, soups and braised or grilled (broiled) dishes, none of which require much additional fat. Chicken is immensely popular and is the leanest meat. Pork, which comes a close second, is not quite such a healthy choice, although the breeding of new and leaner animals has reduced the fat content of pork in recent years. Lamb is not widely eaten, but there's a burgeoning interest in beef, partly because of the proliferation of fast-food restaurants in major cities.

Below: A whole raw chicken

CHICKEN

A whole chicken is a popular purchase almost everywhere in South-east Asia. The breast portion will be sliced or diced for a stir-fry; the rest of the meat will be carefully cut off the carcass and used in a red-cooked dish or a curry and the bones will be simmered in water to make a stock or soup. The giblets are also valued, as are the feet.

DUCK

Much higher in saturated fat than chicken, especially if you eat the skin, duck is best kept for very occasional treats, or used in small quantities to flavour a substantial broth. When buying duck, look for a bird with a long body and a plump breast. The skin should be unmarked and should look creamy and slightly waxy. The healthiest way of cooking duck breast fillets is to steam them for about an hour, having first removed the skin. The meat can then be sliced and moistened with a little of the water from the steamer. Duck cooked this way is delicious in a salad.

PORK

The leanest cut of pork is fillet (tenderloin). There's very little waste with this cut, and it is perfect for stir-frying. Choose fillets that are pale pink all over. The flesh should be fairly firm, and should be slightly moist to the touch. Avoid any meat with discoloured areas. To prepare pork fillet, pull away the membrane that surrounds the meat, removing any fat at the same time. The sinew, which looks like a tougher strip of membrane, must be sliced away.

BEEF

In much of Thailand and South-east Asia, the cow was for many centuries regarded solely as a beast of burden, thus too precious to be slaughtered for food. Today, however, thanks to the fast-food industry, beef consumption is on the increase all over China, and even in Japan, which was for centuries a Buddhist (and therefore vegetarian) culture. When buying beef, look for deep red meat. For slow-cooked dishes, a generous marbling of fat is required, but if the meat is to be stir-fried, a leaner cut such as fillet (tenderloin) or rump (round) steak should be used.

LAMB

Although not as popular as pork or beef, lamb is nevertheless an important ingredient in some classic Asian dishes, particularly those that originated in Mongolia or Tibet. Remove any visible fat before cooking, and use sparingly, padding out the meal with vegetables or carbohydrates.

Above: Choose lean meat and cut off any visible fat.

Gluten – an alternative protein

Also known as "mock meat", gluten is another excellent source of vegetarian protein. Gluten is made from a mixture of wheat flour, salt and water, from which all the starch has been washed out. What remains when this has been done is a sponge-like gluten. Its Chinese name literally means "muscle or sinew of flour".

Like tofu, gluten has no aroma nor flavour of its own, but it has a much firmer texture, and can be shaped, coloured and flavoured to resemble meat, poultry or fish.

Unlike tofu, which is often cooked with meat and fish, gluten is regarded as a pure Buddhist ingredient, and as such, no non-vegetarian item may be mixed with it. This does not prevent accomplished Asian cooks from using a bit of sleight of hand, however, and gluten is often used with tofu to produce dishes such as "mock chicken", "mock abalone", "vegetarian duck" or "Buddhist pork" – which are all said to look and taste very much like the real thing.

Although gluten can be made at home, the task is too time-consuming to contemplate. Flavoured and cooked gluten is available in cans from Asian stores. It only needs to be reheated before being served.

Once opened, it will keep in the refrigerator for up to a week.

FISH AND SHELLFISH

Fish is an extremely important source of protein throughout Thailand and South-east Asia, whose many coastal waters, rivers and lakes provide an abundant harvest. From a healthy eating perspective, bass and sea bass, cod, sea bream, sole and plaice are excellent low-fat protein foods, but the darker-fleshed oily fish like tuna, salmon, carp, trout, mackerel, sardines and herring excite even more interest to those in search of a healthy diet. The Omega-3 fatty acids these fish contain benefit the heart. Scientific research has proved that they can help lower cholesterol and triglyceride levels and reduce the risk of high blood pressure. Scallops and squid are also a good source of Omega-3 fatty acids, and these, along with prawns (shrimp), crab and clams are used to great effect by Thai and South-east Asian cooks, whether steamed, poached, baked or fried.

CARP

This freshwater fish is widely farmed in Asia. It has meaty, moist flesh that can taste a little muddy to those unfamiliar with the distinctive taste. When buying carp, ask the fishmonger to remove the scales and strong dorsal fins. A favourite way of cooking carp is to stuff it with ginger and spring onions (scallions) and serve it with a sweet pickle sauce.

Above: Lobster and scallops are good, low-fat health choices.

MUSSELS

This shellfish is widely used in Thai and Asian cooking. Farmed mussels are now readily available and they are usually relatively free of barnacles. They are generally sold in quantities of 1kg/2¼lb, sufficient for a main course for two or three people. Look for good-size specimens with glossy shells. Discard any that are not closed, or which fail to shut when tapped. Use the back of a short stout knife to scrape away any barnacles, pull away the hairy "beards", then wash the shellfish thoroughly. The best way to cook mussels is to steam them in a small amount of flavoured liquor in a large lidded pan for 3–4 minutes until the shells open. Use finely chopped fresh root ginger, lemon grass, torn lime leaves and some fish sauce to add flavouring to the mussels.

LOBSTER

This luxury shellfish is usually served as a restaurant dish. To cook a live lobster, put it in a pan of ice cold water, cover the pan tightly and bring the water to the boil. The shell will turn bright red and the flesh will be tender and succulent when the lobster is cooked. If you buy a ready-cooked lobster the tail should spring back into a curl when pulled out straight. Try eating lobster with a dip of soy sauce with grated ginger.

Right from top: Freshwater carp, mackerel and grey mullet.

SALMON

The finest wild salmon has a superb flavour and is an excellent low-fat choice being full of Omega-3 acids. It is a costly fish, however, and so it may not be affordable on a regular basis. Responsibly farmed salmon is more economical to buy, and although the flavour is not quite as good as that of wild salmon, it is still delicious. The rosy flesh is beautifully moist and responds very well to being poached or baked, either on its own or with herbs and spices or aromatics. Salmon can take quite robust flavours. Try it with sweet soy sauce and noodles for a quick supper. When buying fresh salmon, have a good fishmonger cut you a chunk from a large salmon for really excellent results; do not use ready-cut steaks.

CRAB

Several varieties of crab are found in Asian waters. Off the coast of Vietnam and Cambodia, the saltwater variety can grow huge, at least 60cm/2ft in diameter. Crab meat has a distinctive taste that goes well with Thai and South-east Asian flavours. A popular Thai soup combines crab with asparagus, and a Vietnamese dish involves steaming lobster and crabs in beer.

Above: Raw, unshelled prawns

SCALLOPS

The tender, sweet flesh of this seafood needs very little cooking. Whenever possible, buy scallops fresh. If they are to be used for sashimi, the coral (roe), black stomach and frill must be removed first. In cooked dishes, the coral can be retained and is regarded as a delicacy.

SEA BASS

Characterized by the delicate flavour of its flesh, sea bass is enjoyed throughout Asia. It holds its shape when cooked, and can be grilled (broiled), steamed, baked or barbecued whole. Sea bass fillets taste delicious when they have been marinated, then cooked on a ridged griddle pan. Chunks or strips make a sensational stir-fry.

SHRIMPS AND PRAWNS

If you ask for shrimp in Britain, then you will be given tiny crustaceans, while in the United States, the term is used to describe the larger shellfish which the British refer to as prawns. However, Asian cooks use both words fairly

Right: Cooked prawns are a way of adding protein to a meal without adding fat.

indiscriminately, so check what a recipe requires. Buy raw shellfish whenever possible, and then cook it yourself. This applies to fresh and frozen mixed seafood. If the shellfish are frozen, thaw them slowly and pat them dry before cooking. Since they are low in fat, they are one of the healthiest forms of protein.

SQUID

The cardinal rule with squid is to either cook it very quickly, or simmer it for a long time. Anything in between will result in seafood that is tough and rubbery. Squid is an ideal candidate for stir-frying with flavours like ginger, garlic, spring onion (scallion) and chilli, and it will also make an interesting salad. For a slow-cooked dish, try squid cooked in a clay pot with chillies and noodles.

TUNA

This very large fish is usually sold as steaks, which can be pink or red, depending on the variety. Avoid steaks with heavy discoloration around the bone, or which are brownish and dull-looking. The flesh should be solid and compact. Tuna loses its colour and can become dry when overcooked, so cook it only briefly over high heat, or stew it gently with moist ingredients like tomatoes and peppers.

Fantail prawns/shrimp

1 Remove the heads from the prawns and peel away most of the body shell. Leave a little of the shell to keep the tail intact.

2 Make a tiny incision in the back of each prawn and remove the black intestinal cord.

3 Hold the prepared prawns by the tails and dip lightly in seasoned cornflour (cornstarch), and then in a frothy batter before cooking them in hot oil until the tails, which are free from batter, turn red.

Butterfly prawns/shrimp

Prawns (shrimp) prepared this way cook quickly and curl attractively.

1 Remove the heads and body shells, but leave the tails. Pull out the intestinal cords using tweezers.

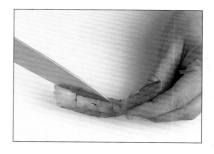

2 Make a cut through the belly of each prawn.

3 Gently open out the two halves of the prawn so that they will look like butterfly wings.

FAT AND CALORIE CONTENTS OF FOOD

The figures show the weight of fat (g) and the energy content per 100g (3½oz) of each of the following typical foods used in Thai and South-east Asian cooking. Use the table to help work out the fat content of favourite dishes.

MEATS	fat (g)	Energy kcals/kJ
Beef minced (ground), raw	16.2	225kcal/934kJ
Beef, rump (round) steak, lean only	4.1	125kcal/526kJ
Beef, fillet (tenderloin) steak	8.5	191kcal/799kJ
Chicken, minced (ground), raw	8.5	106kcal/449kJ
Chicken fillet, raw	1.1	106kcal/449kJ
Chicken thighs, without skin, raw	6.0	126kcal/530kJ
Duck, without skin, cooked	9.5	182kcal/765kJ
Lamb leg, lean, cooked	6.3	198kcal/831kJ
Liver, lamb's, raw	6.2	137kcal/575kJ
Pork, average, lean, raw	4.0	123kcal/519kJ
Pork, lean roast	4.0	163kcal/685kJ
Pork, minced (ground), raw	4.0	123kcal/519kJ
Pork, ribs, raw	10.0	114kcal/480kJ
Turkey, meat only, raw	1.6	105kcal/443kJ
Turkey, minced (ground), raw	6.5	170kcal/715kJ

FISH AND SHELLFISH	fat (g)	Energy kcals/kJ
Cod, raw	0.7	80kcal/337kJ
Crab meat, raw	0.5	54kcal/230kJ
Mackerel, raw	16.0	221kcal/930kJ
Monkfish, raw	1.5	76kcal/320kJ
Mussels, raw, weight without shells	1.8	74kcal/312kJ
Mussels, raw, weight with shells	0.6	24kcal/98kJ
Oysters, raw	4.2	120kcal/508kJ
Prawns (shrimp)	1.0	76kcal/320kJ
Salmon, steamed	13.0	200kcal/837kJ
Scallops, raw	1.6	105kcal/440kJ
Sardine fillets, grilled	10.4	195kcal/815kJ
Sardines, grilled, weight with bones	6.3	19kcal/497kJ
Sea bass, raw	2.0	97kcal/406kJ
Squid, boiled	1.0	79kcal/330kJ
Swordfish, grilled	5.1	155kcal/649kJ
Tuna, grilled	6.3	184kcal/770kJ

VEGETABLES	fat (g)	Energy kcals/kJ
Asparagus	0.0	12.5kcal/52.5kJ
Aubergine (eggplant)	0.4	15kcal/63kJ
Bamboo shoots	0.0	29kcal/120kJ
Beansprouts	1.6	10kcal/42kJ
(Bell) peppers	0.4	32kcals/128kJ
Beans, fine green	0.0	7kcal/29kJ
Beetroot (beets)	0.1	36kcal/151kJ
Broccoli	0.9	33kcal/138kJ
Carrot	0.3	35kcal/156kJ
Celery	0.2	7kcal/142kJ
Chilli, fresh	0.0	30kcal/120kJ
Chinese leaves (Chinese cabbage)	0.0	8kcal/35kJ
Courgettes (zucchini)	0.4	18kcal/74kJ
Cucumber	0.1	10kcal/40kJ
Leek	0.3	20kcal/87kJ
Lotus root, raw	0.0	74kcal/310kJ
Mangetouts (snow peas)	0.4	81kcal/339kJ
Mung beans, cooked	0.1	70kcal/295kJ
Mushrooms, button (white)	0.5	24kcal/100kJ
Mushrooms, shiitake	0.2	55kcal/230kJ
Mushrooms, dried	0.0	56kcal/240kJ
Onion	0.2	36kcal/151kJ
Pak choi (bok choy)	0.0	13kcal/53kJ
Spinach (fresh, cooked)	0.0	20kcal/87kJ
Spring onion (scallion)	0.0	17kcal/83kJ
Sweet potato (peeled, boiled)	0.0	84kcal/358kJ
Water chestnuts	0.0	98kcal/410kJ

NUTS AND SEEDS	fat (g)	Energy kcals/kJ
Cashew nuts	48.0	573kcal/2406kJ
Chestnuts	2.7	169kcal/714kJ
Peanuts	26.9	586kcal/2464kJ
Sesame seeds	47.0	507kcal/2113kJ

Below: Red meat such as beef, lamb and pork have a higher quantity of fat per 100g than white meat.

Below: Seafood is a good source of vitamins, minerals and protein. Oily fish contains high levels of Omega-3 fatty acids.

FRUIT	fat (g)	Energy kcals/kJ
Apples, eating	0.1	47kcal/199kJ
Bananas	0.3	95kcal/403kJ
Grapefruit	0.1	30kcal/126kJ
Grapes (green)	0.0	56kcal/235kJ
Lychees	0.1	58kcal/248kJ
Mangoes	0.0	60Kcal/251kJ
Nectarine	0.0	40kcal/169kJ
Oranges	0.1	37kcal/158kJ
Papayas	0	36kcal/153kJ
Peaches	0.0	31kcal/132kJ
Pineapple, fresh	0.0	50Kcal/209kJ
Pineapple, canned chunks	0.2	63Kcal/264kJ
Raspberries	0.0	28Kcal/117kJ
Star fruit (carambola)	0.0	25Kcal/105kJ
Strawberries	0.0	27kcal/113kJ
Watermelon	0.0	23kcal/95kJ

BEANS, NOODLES, RICE AND TOFU	fat (g)	Energy kcals/kJ
Aduki beans, cooked	0.2	123kcal/525kJ
Noodles, cellophane	trace	351kcal/1468kJ
Noodles, egg	0.5	62kcal/264kJ
Noodles, plain wheat	2.5	354kcal/1190kJ
Noodles, rice	0.1	360kcal/1506kJ
Noodles, soba	0.1	99kcal/414kJ
Rice, brown, uncooked	2.8	357kcal/1518kJ
Rice, white, uncooked	3.6	383kcal/1630kJ
Tofu, firm	4.2	73kcal/304kJ
Tofu, silken	2.5	55kcal/230kJ

BAKING AND PANTRY	fat (g)	Energy kcals/kJ
Cornflour (cornstarch)	0.7	354kcal/1508kJ
Flour, plain (all-purpose) white	1.3	341kcal/1450kJ
Flour, self-raising (self-rising)	1.2	330kcal/1407kJ
Flour, wholemeal (whole-wheat)	2.2	310kcal/1318kJ
Tapioca	0.0	28kcal/119kJ
Honey	0.0	288kcal/1229kJ
Soy sauce, per 5ml/1 tsp	0.0	9kcal/40kJ
Sugar, white	0.3	94kcal/1680kJ

FATS, OILS AND EGGS	fat (g)	Energy kcals/kJ
Butter	81.7	737kcal/3031kJ
Low-fat spread	40.5	390kcal/1605kJ
Very low-fat spread	25.0	273kcal/1128kJ
Oil, corn, per 1 tbsp/15ml	13.8	124kcal/511kJ
Oil, groundnut (peanut), per 1 tbsp/15ml	14.9	134kcal/552kJ
Oil, sesame seed, per 1 tbsp/15ml	14.9	134kcal/552kJ
Oil, sunflower, per 1 tbsp/15ml	13.8	124kcal/511kJ
Eggs	10.8	147kcal/612kJ
Coconut milk	17.0	225kcal/944kJ
Coconut milk, reduced-fat	8.6	137kcal/575kJ
Coconut cream	68.8	669kcal/2760kJ

DAIRY PRODUCTS	fat (g)	Energy kcals/kJ
Cheese, hard	34.4	412kcal/1708kJ
Cheese, hard, reduced fat	15.0	261kcal/1091kJ
Cheese, cottage	3.9	98kcal/413kJ
Cheese, cream	47.4	439kcal/1807kJ
Cream, double (heavy)	48.0	449kcal/1849kJ
Cream, reduced-fat double (heavy)	24.0	243kcal/1002kJ
Cream, single (light)	19.1	198kcal/817kJ
Cream, whipping	39.3	373kcal/1539kJ
Crème fraîche	40.0	379kcal/156kJ
Crème fraîche, reduced fat	15.0	165kcal/683kJ
Fromage frais, plain	7.1	113kcal/469kJ
Fromage frais, very low-fat	0.2	58kcal/247kJ
Milk, full cream (whole)	3.9	66kcal/275kJ
Milk, semi-skimmed (low-fat)	1.5	35kcal/146kJ
Milk, skimmed	0.1	33kcal/130kJ
Yogurt, low-fat natural (plain)	0.8	56kcal/236kJ
Yogurt, Greek (US strained plain)	9.1	115kcal/477kJ

Below: Vegetables are very low in fat. Eat them raw for a filling snack, or steam them to retain maximum nutritional value.

Below: Soya products, such as tofu, soya milk and soya beans, contain isoflavones that are thought to lower cholesterol levels.

SOUPS

In Thailand and South-east Asian countries such as Indonesia and Malaysia soups are more often than not served throughout the meal. They offer a healthy, low-fat flavoursome choice that provides the palate with tastes and textures that complement or contrast with main dishes. Any of these soups are also ideal served for a light lunch or supper — from Hot and Sweet Vegetable and Tofu Soup and Thai Fish Broth to Piquant Prawn Laksa and Beef Noodle Soup there's something for everyone.

SPICY GREEN BEAN SOUP ★

THE BALINESE BASE THIS POPULAR SOUP ON BEANS, BUT ANY SEASONAL VEGETABLES CAN BE ADDED OR SUBSTITUTED. THE RECIPE ALSO INCLUDES SHRIMP PASTE, WHICH IS KNOWN LOCALLY AS TERASI.

2 Finely grind the chopped garlic, macadamia nuts or almonds, shrimp paste and the coriander seeds to a paste using a pestle and mortar or in a food processor.

3 Heat the oil in a wok, and fry the onion until transparent. Remove with a slotted spoon. Add the nut paste to the wok and fry it for 2 minutes without allowing it to brown.

4 Add the reserved vegetable water to the wok and stir well. Add the reduced-fat coconut milk to the wok, bring to the boil and add the bay leaves. Cook the soup, uncovered, for 15–20 minutes.

5 Just before serving, reserve a few green beans, fried onions and beansprouts for garnish and stir the rest into the soup and heat through. Add the lemon wedges, lemon juice and seasoning; stir well. Pour into individual soup bowls and serve, garnished with reserved green beans, onion and beansprouts.

SERVES EIGHT

INGREDIENTS
225g/8oz green beans
1.2 litres/2 pints/5 cups lightly
  salted water
1 garlic clove, roughly chopped
2 macadamia nuts or 4 almonds,
  finely chopped
1cm/1/2 in cube shrimp paste
10–15ml/2–3 tsp coriander seeds,
  dry fried
15ml/1 tbsp sunflower oil
1 onion, finely sliced
400ml/14fl oz can reduced-fat
  coconut milk
2 bay leaves
225g/8oz/4 cups
  beansprouts
8 thin lemon wedges
30ml/2 tbsp lemon juice
salt and ground black pepper

1 Trim the beans, then cut them into small pieces. Bring the lightly salted water to the boil, add the beans to the pan and cook for 3–4 minutes. Drain, reserving the cooking water. Set the beans aside.

COOK'S TIP
Dry fry the coriander seeds for about 2 minutes until the aroma is released.

Energy 51kcal/212kJ; Protein 2.2g; Carbohydrate 5.2g, of which sugars 4.2g; Fat 2.5g, of which saturates 0.4g, of which polyunsaturates 1.2g; Cholesterol 3mg; Calcium 43mg; Fibre 1.2g; Sodium 84mg.

CELLOPHANE NOODLE SOUP ★

THE NOODLES USED IN THIS SOUP GO BY VARIOUS NAMES: GLASS NOODLES, CELLOPHANE NOODLES, BEAN THREAD OR TRANSPARENT NOODLES. THEY ARE ESPECIALLY VALUED FOR THEIR BRITTLE TEXTURE.

SERVES FOUR

INGREDIENTS

4 large dried shiitake mushrooms
15g/½oz dried golden needles
  (lily buds)
½ cucumber, coarsely chopped
2 garlic cloves, halved
90g/3½oz white cabbage, chopped
1.2 litres/2 pints/5 cups boiling water
115g/4oz cellophane noodles
30ml/2 tbsp soy sauce
15ml/1 tbsp palm sugar or light
  muscovado (brown) sugar
90g/3½oz block silken tofu, diced
fresh coriander (cilantro) leaves,
  to garnish

1 Soak the shiitake mushrooms in warm water for 30 minutes. In a separate bowl, soak the dried golden needles in warm water, also for 30 minutes.

2 Meanwhile, put the cucumber, garlic and cabbage in a food processor and process to a smooth paste. Scrape the mixture into a large pan and add the measured boiling water.

3 Bring to the boil, then reduce the heat and cook for 2 minutes, stirring occasionally. Strain this stock into another pan, return to a low heat and bring to simmering point.

4 Drain the golden needles, rinse under cold running water, then drain again. Cut off any hard ends. Add to the stock with the noodles, soy sauce and sugar and cook for 5 minutes more.

5 Strain the mushroom soaking liquid into the soup. Discard the mushroom stems, then slice the caps. Divide them and the tofu among four bowls. Pour the soup over, garnish and serve.

Energy 148kcal/618kJ; Protein 4.1g; Carbohydrate 29.7g, of which sugars 5.7g; Fat 1.1g, of which saturates 0.1g, of which polyunsaturates 0.5g; Cholesterol 0mg; Calcium 139mg; Fibre 0.7g; Sodium 546mg.

OMELETTE SOUP ★

A VERY SATISFYING BUT HEALTHY SOUP THAT IS QUICK AND EASY TO PREPARE. IT IS VERSATILE, TOO, IN THAT YOU CAN VARY THE VEGETABLES ACCORDING TO WHAT IS AVAILABLE.

SERVES FOUR

INGREDIENTS
1 egg
5ml/1 tsp sunflower oil
900ml/1½ pints/3¾ cups
   vegetable stock
2 large carrots, finely diced
4 leaves pak choi (bok choy),
   shredded
30ml/2 tbsp soy sauce
2.5ml/½ tsp granulated sugar
2.5ml/½ tsp ground black pepper
fresh coriander (cilantro) leaves,
   to garnish

VARIATION
Use Savoy cabbage instead of pak choi. In Thailand there are about forty different types of pak choi, including miniature versions.

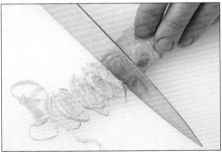

1 Put the egg in a bowl and beat lightly with a fork. Heat the oil in a small frying pan until it is hot, but not smoking. Pour in the egg and swirl the pan so that it coats the base evenly. Cook over a medium heat until the omelette has set and the underside is golden. Slide it out of the pan and roll it up like a pancake. Slice into 5mm/¼in rounds and set aside for the garnish.

2 Put the stock into a large pan. Add the carrots and pak choi and bring to the boil. Reduce the heat and simmer for 5 minutes, then add the soy sauce, granulated sugar and pepper.

3 Stir well, then pour into warmed bowls. Lay a few omelette rounds on the surface of each portion and complete the garnish with the coriander leaves.

Energy 52kcal/217kJ; Protein 3.4g; Carbohydrate 4.1g, of which sugars 3.8g; Fat 2.6g, of which saturates 0.6g, of which polyunsaturates 0.9g; Cholesterol 48mg; Calcium 100mg; Fibre 1.7g; Sodium 628mg.

CRAB AND ASPARAGUS SOUP ★

THE VIETNAMESE OFTEN COMBINE ASPARAGUS WITH CRAB AND MAKE A DELICIOUS LOW-FAT SOUP.
SERVE THIS SOUP AS A LIGHT LUNCH OR SUPPER WITH PLAIN NOODLES.

SERVES SIX

INGREDIENTS
    350g/12oz asparagus spears,
      trimmed and halved
    900ml/1½ pints/3¾ cups chicken
      stock, preferably home-made
    15ml/1 tbsp sunflower oil
    6 shallots, chopped
    115g/4oz crab meat, fresh or
      canned, chopped
    15ml/1 tbsp cornflour (cornstarch),
      mixed to a paste with water
    30ml/2 tbsp Thai fish sauce
    1 egg, lightly beaten
    chopped chives, plus extra chives
      to garnish
    salt and ground black pepper to taste

1 Cook the asparagus spears in the chicken stock for 5–6 minutes until tender. Drain, reserving the stock.

2 Heat the oil and stir-fry the shallots for 2 minutes. Add the asparagus spears, crab meat and chicken stock.

3 Bring the mixture to the boil and cook for 3 minutes, then remove the wok or pan from the heat and spoon some of the liquid into the cornflour mixture. Return this to the wok or pan and stir until the soup begins to thicken slightly.

4 Stir in the fish sauce, with salt and pepper to taste, then pour the beaten egg into the soup, stirring briskly so that the egg forms threads. Finally, stir the chopped chives into the soup and serve immediately, garnished with chives.

COOK'S TIP
If fresh asparagus isn't available, use 350g/12oz can asparagus. Drain and halve the spears.

Energy 75kcal/313kJ; Protein 6.6g; Carbohydrate 5.2g, of which sugars 2.4g; Fat 3.3g, of which saturates 0.6g, of which polyunsaturates 1.4g; Cholesterol 46mg; Calcium 49mg; Fibre 1.2g; Sodium 476mg.

HOT AND SWEET VEGETABLE AND TOFU SOUP ★

AN INTERESTING COMBINATION OF HOT, SWEET AND SOUR FLAVOURS THAT MAKES FOR A SOOTHING,
LOW-FAT SOUP. IT TAKES ONLY MINUTES TO MAKE AS THE SPINACH AND SILKEN TOFU ARE SIMPLY
PLACED IN BOWLS AND COVERED WITH THE FLAVOURED HOT STOCK.

SERVES FOUR

INGREDIENTS

1.2 litres/2 pints/5 cups
   vegetable stock
5–10ml/1–2 tsp Thai red
   curry paste
2 kaffir lime leaves, torn
40g/1½oz/3 tbsp palm sugar or light
   muscovado (brown) sugar
30ml/2 tbsp soy sauce
juice of 1 lime
1 carrot, cut into thin batons
50g/2oz baby spinach leaves, any
   coarse stalks removed
225g/8oz block silken tofu, diced

1 Heat the stock in a large pan, then add the red curry paste. Stir constantly over a medium heat until the paste has dissolved. Add the lime leaves, sugar and soy sauce and bring to the boil.

2 Add the lime juice and carrot to the pan. Reduce the heat and simmer for 5–10 minutes. Place the spinach and tofu in four individual serving bowls and pour the hot stock on top to serve.

Energy 98kcal/412kJ; Protein 5.3g; Carbohydrate 12.7g, of which sugars 12.3g; Fat 3.3g, of which saturates 0.4g, of which polyunsaturates 1.7g; Cholesterol 0mg; Calcium 318mg; Fibre 0.6g; Sodium 558mg.

TOFU SOUP WITH MUSHROOMS AND TOMATO ★

THIS LIGHT, CLEAR THAI BROTH IS PERFECT TO BALANCE A MEAL THAT MAY INCLUDE SOME HEAVIER MEAT OR POULTRY DISHES. AS THE SOUP IS RELIANT ON AN AROMATIC BROTH, THE BASIC STOCK NEEDS TO BE RICH IN TASTE. THE TOFU AND MUSHROOMS ABSORB ALL THE DELICIOUS FLAVOURS.

SERVES FOUR

INGREDIENTS

    115g/4oz/scant 2 cups dried shiitake
      mushrooms, soaked in water for
      20 minutes
    5ml/1 tsp sunflower oil
    2 shallots, halved and sliced
    2 Thai chillies, seeded and sliced
    4cm/1½in fresh root ginger, peeled
      and grated or finely chopped
    15ml/1 tbsp *nuoc mam*
    350g/12oz tofu, rinsed, drained
      and cut into bitesize cubes
    4 tomatoes, skinned, seeded and
      cut into thin strips
    salt and ground black pepper
    1 bunch coriander (cilantro),
      stalks removed, finely chopped,
      to garnish
For the stock
    1 meaty chicken carcass
    25g/1oz dried squid or shrimp,
      soaked in water for 15 minutes
    2 onions, peeled and quartered
    2 garlic cloves, crushed
    7.5cm/3in fresh root ginger,
      chopped
    15ml/1 tbsp *nuoc mam*
    6 black peppercorns
    2 star anise
    4 cloves
    1 cinnamon stick
    sea salt

1 To make the stock, put the chicken carcass in a deep pan. Drain and rinse the dried squid or shrimp. Add to the pan with the remaining stock ingredients, except the salt, and pour in 2 litres/3½ pints/8 cups water. Bring to the boil, and boil for a few minutes, skim off any foam, then reduce the heat and simmer with the lid on for 1½–2 hours.

2 Remove the lid and continue simmering the stock for a further 30 minutes to reduce. Skim off any fat, season, then strain and measure out 1.5 litres/2½ pints/6¼ cups.

3 Squeeze dry the soaked shiitake mushrooms, remove the stems and slice the caps into thin strips. Heat the oil in a large pan or wok and stir in the shallots, chillies and ginger. As the fragrance begins to rise, stir in the *nuoc mam*, followed by the stock.

4 Add the tofu, mushrooms and tomatoes and bring to the boil. Reduce the heat and simmer for 5–10 minutes. Season to taste and sprinkle the finely chopped fresh coriander over the top. Serve piping hot.

Energy 100kcal/418kJ; Protein 8.8g; Carbohydrate 5.2g, of which sugars 4.5g; Fat 5g, of which saturates 0.7g, of which polyunsaturates 2.6g; Cholesterol 0mg; Calcium 480mg; Fibre 1.8g; Sodium 32mg.

MIXED VEGETABLE SOUP ★

IN THAILAND, THIS TYPE OF SOUP IS USUALLY MADE IN LARGE QUANTITIES AND THEN REHEATED FOR CONSUMPTION OVER SEVERAL DAYS. IF YOU WOULD LIKE TO DO THE SAME, DOUBLE OR TREBLE THE QUANTITIES. CHILL LEFTOVER SOUP RAPIDLY AND REHEAT THOROUGHLY BEFORE SERVING.

SERVES FOUR

INGREDIENTS
    15ml/1 tbsp sunflower oil
    15ml/1 tbsp magic paste (see
      Cook's Tip)
    90g/3½oz Savoy cabbage or
      Chinese leaves (Chinese cabbage),
      finely shredded
    90g/3½oz mooli (daikon),
      finely diced
    1 medium cauliflower,
      coarsely chopped
    4 celery sticks, coarsely chopped
    1.2 litres/2 pints/5 cups
      vegetable stock
    130g/4½oz fried tofu, cut into
      2.5cm/1in cubes
    5ml/1 tsp palm sugar or light
      muscovado (brown) sugar
    45ml/3 tbsp light soy sauce

1 Heat the sunflower oil in a large, heavy pan or wok. Add the magic paste and cook over a low heat, stirring frequently, until it gives off its aroma. Add the shredded Savoy cabbage or Chinese leaves, mooli, cauliflower and celery. Pour in the vegetable stock, increase the heat to medium and bring to the boil, stirring occasionally. Gently stir in the tofu cubes.

2 Add the sugar and soy sauce. Reduce the heat and simmer for 15 minutes, until the vegetables are cooked and tender. Taste and add a little more soy sauce if needed. Serve hot.

COOK'S TIP
Magic paste is a mixture of crushed garlic, white pepper and coriander (cilantro). Look for it at Thai markets.

Energy 75kcal/311kJ; Protein 3.6g; Carbohydrate 4g, of which sugars 3.8g; Fat 5g, of which saturates 0.6g, of which polyunsaturates 3g; Cholesterol 0mg; Calcium 196mg; Fibre 1g; Sodium 825mg.

BROTH WITH STUFFED CABBAGE LEAVES ★

A SUBTLY SPICY FILLING OF PRAWNS, PORK AND VEGETABLES IS FLAVOURED WITH TRADITIONAL THAI INGREDIENTS. THE HEALTHY LOW-FAT FILLING IS WRAPPED IN CABBAGE LEAVES AND SIMMERED IN A WONDERFULLY AROMATIC CHICKEN STOCK FOR FULL FLAVOUR WITHOUT FAT.

SERVES FOUR

INGREDIENTS
  10 Chinese leaves (Chinese cabbage)
    or Savoy cabbage leaves, halved,
    main ribs removed
  4 spring onions (scallions),
    green tops left whole, white
    part finely chopped
  5–6 dried cloud ear (wood ear)
    mushrooms, soaked in hot water
    for 15 minutes
  115g/4oz minced (ground) lean pork
  115g/4oz prawns (shrimp), shelled,
    deveined and finely chopped
  1 Thai chilli, seeded and chopped
  30ml/2 tbsp *nuoc mam*
  15ml/1 tbsp soy sauce
  4cm/1½in fresh root ginger, peeled
    and very finely sliced
  chopped fresh coriander (cilantro),
    to garnish
For the stock
  1 meaty chicken carcass
  2 onions, peeled and quartered
  4 garlic cloves, crushed
  4cm/1½in fresh root ginger,
    chopped
  30ml/2 tbsp *nuoc mam*
  30ml/2 tbsp soy sauce
  6 black peppercorns
  a few sprigs of fresh thyme
  sea salt

1 To make the chicken stock, put the chicken carcass into a deep pan. Add all the other stock ingredients except the sea salt and pour over 2 litres/3½ pints/8 cups of water. Bring to the boil, and boil for a few minutes, skim off any foam, then reduce the heat and simmer gently with the lid on for 1½–2 hours.

2 Remove the lid and simmer for a further 30 minutes to reduce the stock. Skim off any fat, season with sea salt, then strain the stock and measure out 1.5 litres/2½ pints/6¼ cups. It is important to skim off any froth or fat, so that the broth is light and fragrant.

3 Blanch the cabbage leaves in boiling water for about 2 minutes, or until tender. Remove with a slotted spoon and refresh under cold water. Add the green tops of the spring onions to the boiling water and blanch for a minute, or until tender, then drain and refresh under cold water. Carefully tear each piece into five thin strips and set aside.

4 Squeeze dry the cloud ear mushrooms, then trim and finely chop and mix with the pork, prawns, spring onion whites, chilli, *nuoc mam* and soy sauce. Lay a cabbage leaf flat on a surface and place a teaspoon of the filling about 1cm/½in from the bottom edge – the edge nearest to you.

5 Fold this bottom edge over the filling, and then fold in the sides of the leaf to seal it. Roll all the way to the top of the leaf to form a tight bundle. Wrap a piece of blanched spring onion green around the bundle and tie it so that it holds together. Repeat with the remaining leaves and filling.

6 Bring the stock to the boil in a wok or deep pan. Stir in the finely sliced ginger, then reduce the heat and drop in the cabbage bundles. Bubble very gently over a low heat for about 20 minutes to ensure that the filling is thoroughly cooked. Serve immediately, ladled into bowls with a sprinkling of fresh coriander leaves.

Energy 80kcal/334kJ; Protein 12.7g; Carbohydrate 3.9g, of which sugars 3.7g; Fat 1.5g, of which saturates 0.5g, of which polyunsaturates 0.4g; Cholesterol 74mg; Calcium 68mg; Fibre 1.4g; Sodium 891mg.

PIQUANT PRAWN LAKSA ★

THIS SPICY SOUP TASTES JUST AS GOOD WHEN MADE WITH FRESH CRAB MEAT OR ANY FLAKED COOKED FISH. IF YOU ARE SHORT OF TIME OR CAN'T FIND ALL THE SPICY PASTE INGREDIENTS, BUY READY-MADE LAKSA PASTE, WHICH IS AVAILABLE FROM MANY ASIAN STORES.

2 To make the spicy paste, place the freshly prepared chopped lemon grass, seeded and chopped red chillies, sliced fresh root ginger, shrimp paste, chopped garlic cloves, ground turmeric and tamarind paste in a mortar and pound with a pestle to form a paste. Alternatively, put the ingredients in a food processor and whizz until a smooth paste is formed.

3 Heat the vegetable oil in a large pan, add the spicy paste and fry, stirring constantly, for a few moments to release all the flavours, but be careful not to let it burn.

SERVES THREE

INGREDIENTS
115g/4oz rice vermicelli or noodles
10ml/2 tsp vegetable oil
750ml/1¼ pints/3 cups fish stock
200ml/7fl oz/scant 1 cup coconut milk
30ml/2 tbsp Thai fish sauce
½ lime
18 cooked peeled prawns (shrimp)
salt and cayenne pepper
60ml/4 tbsp fresh coriander (cilantro)
    sprigs, chopped, to garnish
For the spicy paste
2 lemon grass stalks, finely chopped
2 fresh red chillies, seeded
    and chopped
2.5cm/1in piece fresh root ginger,
    peeled and sliced
2.5ml/½ tsp dried shrimp paste
2 garlic cloves, chopped
2.5ml/½ tsp ground turmeric
30ml/2 tbsp tamarind paste

1 Cook the rice vermicelli or noodles in a large pan of boiling salted water according to the instructions on the packet. Tip the vermicelli or noodles into a large strainer, then rinse them under cold water until the liquid runs clear and drain. Keep warm.

VARIATION
Replace the rice vermicelli or noodles with fresh egg noodles for a more substantial soup.

4 Add the fish stock and coconut milk and bring to the boil. Stir in the fish sauce, then simmer for 5 minutes. Season with salt and cayenne to taste, adding a squeeze of lime. Add the prawns and heat through for a few seconds.

5 Divide the noodles among three soup plates. Pour over the soup, making sure that each portion includes an equal number of prawns. Garnish with coriander and serve piping hot.

Energy 224kcal/939kJ; Protein 15.7g; Carbohydrate 33.7g, of which sugars 3.6g; Fat 2.9g, of which saturates 0.5g, of which polyunsaturates 1.4g; Cholesterol 130mg; Calcium 108mg; Fibre 0.5g; Sodium 206mg

COCONUT AND SEAFOOD SOUP ★

THE LONG LIST OF INGREDIENTS COULD MISLEAD YOU INTO THINKING THAT THIS SOUP IS COMPLICATED AND VERY TIME-CONSUMING TO PREPARE. IN FACT, IT IS EXTREMELY EASY TO PUT TOGETHER AND THE MARRIAGE OF FLAVOURS WORKS BEAUTIFULLY.

SERVES FOUR

INGREDIENTS
  750ml/1¼ pints/3 cups fish stock
  5 thin slices fresh root ginger
  2 lemon grass stalks, chopped
  3 kaffir lime leaves, shredded
  bunch garlic chives,
    about 25g/1oz
  small bunch fresh coriander
    (cilantro), about 15g/½oz
  5ml/1 tsp sunflower oil
  4 shallots, chopped
  250ml/8fl oz/1 cup reduced-fat
    coconut milk
  30–45ml/2–3 tbsp Thai fish sauce
  45ml/3 tbsp Thai green curry paste
  350g/12oz raw large prawns
    (shrimp), peeled and deveined
  350g/12oz prepared squid
  a little fresh lime juice (optional)
  salt and ground black pepper
  30ml/2 tbsp crisp fried shallot
    slices, to serve

1 Pour the fish stock into a large pan and add the slices of ginger, the chopped lemon grass and half the shredded kaffir lime leaves.

VARIATIONS
• Instead of squid, you could add 400g/ 14oz firm white fish, such as monkfish, cut into small pieces.
• You could also replace the squid with mussels. Steam 675g/1½lb live mussels in a tightly covered pan for 3–4 minutes, or until they have opened. Discard any that remain shut, then remove them from their shells and add to the soup.

2 Reserve a few garlic chives for the garnish, then chop the remainder. Add half the chopped garlic chives to the pan. Strip the coriander leaves from the stalks and set the leaves aside. Add the stalks to the pan. Bring to the boil, reduce the heat to low and cover the pan, then simmer gently for 20 minutes. Strain the stock into a bowl.

3 Rinse and dry the pan. Add the oil and shallots. Cook over a medium heat for 5–10 minutes, until the shallots are just beginning to brown.

4 Stir in the strained stock, coconut milk, the remaining kaffir lime leaves and 30ml/2 tbsp of the fish sauce. Heat gently until simmering and cook over a low heat for 5–10 minutes.

5 Stir in the curry paste and prawns, then cook for 3 minutes. Add the squid and cook for a further 2 minutes. Add the lime juice, if using, and season, adding more fish sauce to taste. Stir in the remaining chives and the reserved coriander leaves. Serve in bowls and sprinkle each portion with fried shallots and whole garlic chives.

Energy 164kcal/692kJ; Protein 29.7g; Carbohydrate 4.5g, of which sugars 3.4g; Fat 3.1g, of which saturates 0.7g, of which polyunsaturates 1.2g; Cholesterol 368mg; Calcium 137mg; Fibre 0.5g; Sodium 363mg.

PUMPKIN AND COCONUT SOUP ★

IN THIS LOVELY LOOKING SOUP, THE NATURAL SWEETNESS OF THE PUMPKIN IS HEIGHTENED BY THE ADDITION OF A LITTLE SUGAR, BUT THIS IS BALANCED BY THE CHILLIES, SHRIMP PASTE AND DRIED SHRIMP. REDUCED-FAT COCONUT MILK BLURS THE BOUNDARIES BEAUTIFULLY.

SERVES SIX

INGREDIENTS
  450g/1lb pumpkin
  2 garlic cloves, crushed
  4 shallots, finely chopped
  2.5ml/½ tsp shrimp paste
  1 lemon grass stalk, chopped
  2 fresh green chillies, seeded
  15ml/1 tbsp dried shrimp soaked
    for 10 minutes in warm water
    to cover
  600ml/1 pint/2½ cups
    chicken stock
  600ml/1 pint/2½ cups reduced-fat
    coconut milk
  30ml/2 tbsp Thai fish sauce
  5ml/1 tsp granulated sugar
  115g/4oz small cooked shelled
    prawns (shrimp)
  salt and ground black pepper
To garnish
  2 fresh red chillies, seeded and
    thinly sliced
  10–12 fresh basil leaves

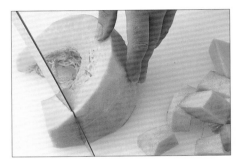

1 Peel the pumpkin and cut it into quarters with a sharp knife. Scoop out the seeds with a teaspoon and discard. Cut the flesh into chunks about 2cm/¾in thick and set aside.

2 Put the garlic, shallots, shrimp paste, lemon grass, green chillies and salt to taste in a mortar. Drain the dried shrimp, discarding the soaking liquid, and add them, then use a pestle to grind the mixture into a paste. Alternatively, place all the ingredients in a food processor and process to a paste.

3 Bring the chicken stock to the boil in a large pan. Add the ground paste and stir well to dissolve.

4 Add the pumpkin chunks and bring to a simmer. Simmer for 10–15 minutes, or until the pumpkin is tender.

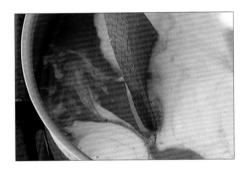

5 Stir in the coconut milk, then bring the soup back to simmering point. Do not let it boil. Add the fish sauce, sugar and ground black pepper to taste.

6 Add the prawns and cook for a further 2–3 minutes, until they are heated through. Serve in warm soup bowls, garnished with chillies and basil leaves.

COOK'S TIP
Shrimp paste is made from ground shrimp fermented in brine.

Energy 63kcal/269kJ; Protein 6g; Carbohydrate 9g, of which sugars 8.2g; Fat 0.7g, of which saturates 0.3g, of which polyunsaturates 0.1g; Cholesterol 50mg; Calcium 101mg; Fibre 1g; Sodium 611mg.

PRAWN AND PORK SOUP WITH RICE STICKS ★

THIS LOW-FAT AND HEALTHY SOUP IS A SPECIALITY OF HO CHI MINH CITY (FORMERLY SAIGON), WHERE THE PORK STOCK IS ENHANCED WITH THE INTENSE SWEET AND SMOKY FLAVOUR OF DRIED SQUID. IT IS ALSO A POPULAR EVERYDAY SOUP IN CAMBODIA.

SERVES FOUR

INGREDIENTS
225g/8oz lean pork tenderloin
225g/8oz dried rice sticks
    (vermicelli), soaked in lukewarm
    water for 20 minutes
20 prawns (shrimp), shelled
    and deveined
115g/4oz/½ cup beansprouts
2 spring onions (scallions),
    finely sliced
2 green or red Thai chillies, seeded
    and finely sliced
1 garlic clove, finely sliced
1 bunch each coriander (cilantro)
    and basil, stalks removed, leaves
    roughly chopped
1 lime, cut into quarters, and
    nuoc cham, to serve
For the stock
25g/1oz dried squid
450g/1lb pork ribs
1 onion, peeled and quartered
225g/8oz carrots, peeled and cut
    into chunks
15ml/1 tbsp *nuoc mam*
15ml/1 tbsp soy sauce
6 black peppercorns
salt

1 To make the stock, soak the dried squid in water for 30 minutes, rinse and drain. Put the ribs in a large pan and cover with approximately 2.5 litres/4½ pints/10 cups water. Bring to the boil, skim off any fat, and add the dried squid with the remaining stock ingredients. Cover the pan and simmer for 1 hour, then skim off any foam or fat and continue to simmer, uncovered, for a further 1½ hours.

2 Strain the stock and check the seasoning. You should have roughly 2 litres/3½ pints/8 cups.

COOK'S TIP
To serve the soup on its own, add bitesize pieces of soaked dried shiitake mushrooms or cubes of firm tofu.

3 Pour the stock into a wok or deep pan and bring to the boil. Reduce the heat, add the pork tenderloin and simmer for 25 minutes. Lift the tenderloin out of the stock, place it on a board and cut it into thin slices. Meanwhile, keep the stock simmering gently over a low heat.

4 Bring a pan of water to the boil. Drain the rice sticks and add to the water. Cook for about 5 minutes, or until tender, separating them with chopsticks if they stick together. Drain the rice sticks and divide them among four warm bowls.

5 Drop the prawns into the simmering stock for 1 minute. Lift them out with a slotted spoon and layer them with the slices of pork on top of the rice sticks. Ladle the hot stock over them and sprinkle with beansprouts, spring onions, chillies, garlic and herbs. Serve each bowl of soup with a wedge of lime to squeeze over it and *nuoc cham* to splash on top.

Energy 234kcal/981kJ; Protein 26.2g; Carbohydrate 24.8g, of which sugars 1.6g; Fat 3.3g, of which saturates 1g, of which polyunsaturates 0.6g; Cholesterol 137mg; Calcium 84mg; Fibre 1.1g; Sodium 681mg.

NORTHERN PRAWN AND SQUASH SOUP ★

AS THE TITLE OF THE RECIPE SUGGESTS, THIS COMES FROM NORTHERN THAILAND. IT IS QUITE HEARTY, SOMETHING OF A CROSS BETWEEN A SOUP AND A STEW. THE BANANA FLOWER ISN'T ESSENTIAL, BUT IT DOES ADD A UNIQUE AND AUTHENTIC FLAVOUR.

SERVES FOUR

INGREDIENTS

1 butternut squash, about 300g/11oz
1 litre/1¾ pints/4 cups
   vegetable stock
90g/3½oz/scant 1 cup green beans,
   cut into 2.5cm/1in pieces
45g/1¾oz dried banana
   flower (optional)
15ml/1 tbsp Thai fish sauce
225g/8oz raw prawns (shrimp)
small bunch fresh basil
cooked rice, to serve
For the chilli paste
   115g/4oz shallots, sliced
   10 drained bottled green peppercorns
   1 small fresh green chilli, seeded and
      finely chopped
   2.5ml/½ tsp shrimp paste

1 Peel the squash and cut it in half. Scoop out the seeds and discard, then cut the flesh into neat cubes. Set aside.

2 Make the chilli paste by pounding the sliced shallots, peppercorns, chilli and shrimp paste together using a mortar and pestle or puréeing them in a spice blender.

3 Heat the **vegetable** stock gently in a large pan, then stir in the chilli paste. Add the squash, beans and banana flower, if using. Bring to the boil and cook for 15 minutes.

4 Add the fish sauce, prawns and basil. Simmer for 3 minutes. Serve in warmed bowls, accompanied by rice.

Energy 73kcal/307kJ; Protein 11.8g; Carbohydrate 5.2g, of which sugars 3.9g; Fat 0.7g, of which saturates 0.2g, of which polyunsaturates 0.2g; Cholesterol 113mg; Calcium 90mg; Fibre 1.7g; Sodium 669mg.

HOT-AND-SOUR FISH SOUP ★

This tangy soup is found throughout Asia — with the balance of hot, sweet and sour flavours varying from Cambodia to Vietnam. Chillies provide the heat, tamarind produces the tartness and the delicious sweetness comes from pineapple.

SERVES FOUR

INGREDIENTS

1 catfish, sea bass or red snapper, about 1kg/2¼lb, filleted
30ml/2 tbsp *nuoc mam*
2 garlic cloves, finely chopped
25g/1oz dried squid, soaked in water for 30 minutes
10ml/2 tsp vegetable oil
2 spring onions (scallions), sliced
2 shallots, sliced
4cm/1½in fresh root ginger, peeled and chopped
2–3 lemon grass stalks, cut into strips and crushed
30ml/2 tbsp tamarind paste
2–3 Thai chillies, seeded and sliced
15ml/1 tbsp sugar
30–45ml/2–3 tbsp *nuoc mam*
225g/8oz fresh pineapple, peeled and diced
3 tomatoes, skinned, seeded and roughly chopped
50g/2oz canned sliced bamboo shoots, drained
1 small bunch fresh coriander (cilantro), stalks removed, leaves finely chopped
salt and ground black pepper
115g/4oz/½ cup beansprouts and 1 bunch dill, fronds roughly chopped, to garnish
1 lime, cut into quarters, to serve

1 Cut the fish into bitesize pieces, mix with the *nuoc mam* and garlic and leave to marinate. Save the head, tail and bones for the stock. Drain and rinse the soaked dried squid.

2 Heat the oil in a deep pan and stir in the spring onions, shallots, ginger, lemon grass and dried squid. Add the reserved fish head, tail and bones, and sauté them gently for a minute or two. Pour in 1.2 litres/2 pints/5 cups water and bring to the boil. Reduce the heat and simmer for 30 minutes.

3 Strain the stock into another deep pan and bring to the boil. Stir in the tamarind paste, chillies, sugar and *nuoc mam* and simmer for 2–3 minutes. Add the pineapple, tomatoes and bamboo shoots and simmer for a further 2–3 minutes. Stir in the fish pieces and the chopped fresh coriander, and cook until the fish turns opaque.

4 Season to taste and ladle the soup into hot bowls. Garnish with beansprouts and dill, and serve with the lime quarters to squeeze over.

VARIATIONS
• Depending on your mood, or your palate, you can adjust the balance of hot and sour by adding more chilli or tamarind to taste. Enjoyed as a meal in itself, the soup is usually served with plain steamed rice but in Ho Chi Minh City in Vietnam it is served with chunks of fresh baguette, which are perfect for soaking up the spicy, fruity, tangy broth.
• Other fresh herbs, such as chopped mint and basil leaves, also complement this soup.

Energy 166kcal/704kJ; Protein 23.1g; Carbohydrate 10.9g, of which sugars 10g; Fat 3.7g, of which saturates 0.6g, of which polyunsaturates 1.7g; Cholesterol 51mg; Calcium 113mg; Fibre 3g; Sodium 116mg.

THAI FISH BROTH ★

LEMON GRASS, CHILLIES AND GALANGAL ARE AMONG THE FLAVOURINGS USED IN THIS FRAGRANT SOUP.

SERVES THREE

INGREDIENTS
    1 litre/1¾ pints/4 cups fish or
       light chicken stock
    4 lemon grass stalks
    3 limes
    2 small fresh hot red chillies,
       seeded and thinly sliced
    2cm/¾in piece fresh galangal,
       peeled and thinly sliced
    6 fresh coriander (cilantro) stalks
    2 kaffir lime leaves,
       finely chopped
    350g/12oz monkfish fillet, skinned
       and cut into 2.5cm/1in pieces
    15ml/1 tbsp rice vinegar
    45ml/3 tbsp Thai fish sauce
    30ml/2 tbsp chopped coriander
       (cilantro) leaves, to garnish

1 Pour the stock into a pan and bring it to the boil. Meanwhile, slice the bulb end of each lemon grass stalk diagonally into pieces about 3mm/⅛in thick. Peel off four wide strips of lime rind with a potato peeler, taking care to avoid the white pith underneath which would make the soup bitter. Squeeze the limes and reserve the juice.

2 Add the sliced lemon grass, lime rind, chillies, galangal and coriander stalks to the stock, with the kaffir lime leaves. Simmer for 1–2 minutes.

VARIATIONS
Prawns (shrimp), scallops, squid or sole can be substituted for the monkfish. If you use kaffir lime leaves, you will need the juice of only 2 limes.

3 Add the monkfish, rice vinegar and Thai fish sauce, with half the reserved lime juice. Simmer for about 3 minutes, until the fish is just cooked. Lift out and discard the coriander stalks, taste the broth and add more lime juice if necessary; the soup should taste quite sour. Sprinkle with the coriander leaves and serve very hot.

Energy 88kcal/373kJ; Protein 19.2g; Carbohydrate 1.5g, of which sugars 1.3g; Fat 0.6g, of which saturates 0.1g, of which polyunsaturates 0.2g; Cholesterol 16mg; Calcium 40mg; Fibre 0.4g; Sodium 1112mg

BAMBOO SHOOT, FISH <u>AND</u> RICE SOUP ★

THIS IS A REFRESHING SOUP MADE WITH FRESHWATER FISH SUCH AS CARP OR CATFISH.

SERVES FOUR

INGREDIENTS

75g/3oz/scant ½ cup long grain rice,
  well rinsed
250ml/8fl oz/1 cup reduced-fat
  coconut milk
30ml/2 tbsp *tuk prahoc*
2 lemon grass stalks, trimmed
  and crushed
25g/1oz galangal, thinly sliced
2–3 Thai chillies
4 garlic cloves, crushed
15ml/1 tbsp palm sugar
1 fresh bamboo shoot, peeled,
  boiled in water for 10 minutes,
  and sliced
450g/1lb freshwater fish fillets,
  such as carp or catfish, skinned
  and cut into bitesize pieces
1 small bunch fresh
  basil leaves
1 small bunch fresh coriander
  (cilantro), chopped, and 1 chilli,
  finely sliced, to garnish
rice or noodles, to serve
For the stock
  450g/1lb pork ribs
  1 onion, quartered
  225g/8oz carrots, cut
    into chunks
  25g/1oz dried squid or dried shrimp,
    soaked in water for 30 minutes,
    rinsed and drained
  15ml/1 tbsp *nuoc mam*
  15ml/1 tbsp soy sauce
  6 black peppercorns
  salt

1 To prepare the stock, put the ribs in a large pan and cover with 2.5 litres/ 4¼ pints/10 cups water. Bring to the boil, skim off any fat, and add the remaining stock ingredients. Cover the pan and simmer for 1 hour, then skim off any foam or fat.

2 Simmer the stock, uncovered, for a further 1–1½ hours, until it has reduced. Check the seasoning and strain the stock into another pan. There should be approximately 2 litres/3½ pints/7¾ cups of stock.

3 Bring the pan of stock to the boil. Stir in the rice and reduce the heat. Add the coconut milk, *tuk prahoc*, lemon grass, galangal, chillies, garlic and sugar. Simmer for about 10 minutes to let the flavours mingle. The rice should be just cooked, with bite to it.

4 Add the sliced bamboo shoot and the pieces of fish. Simmer for 5 minutes, until the fish is cooked. Check the seasoning and stir in the basil leaves. Ladle the soup into bowls, garnish with the chopped coriander and chilli, and serve with the rice or noodles.

Energy 269kcal/1130kJ; Protein 35.5g; Carbohydrate 23.2g, of which sugars 7.9g; Fat 3.8g, of which saturates 1.1g, of which polyunsaturates 0.9g; Cholesterol 87mg; Calcium 109mg; Fibre 2.6g; Sodium 214mg

good

GINGER, CHICKEN AND COCONUT SOUP ★

THIS AROMATIC SOUP IS RICH WITH COCONUT MILK AND INTENSELY FLAVOURED WITH GALANGAL, LEMON GRASS AND KAFFIR LIME LEAVES.

SERVES SIX

INGREDIENTS
    4 lemon grass stalks, roots trimmed
    2 × 400ml/14fl oz cans reduced-fat
        coconut milk
    475ml/16fl oz/2 cups chicken stock
    2.5cm/1in piece galangal, peeled and
        thinly sliced
    10 black peppercorns, crushed
    10 kaffir lime leaves, torn
    300g/11oz chicken breast fillets,
        cut into thin strips
    115g/4oz/1 cup button (white)
        mushrooms
    50g/2oz/½ cup baby corn cobs,
        quartered lengthways
    60ml/4 tbsp lime juice
    45ml/3 tbsp Thai fish sauce
    fresh red chillies, spring onions and
        fresh coriander (cilantro), to garnish

1 Cut off the lower 5cm/2in from each lemon grass stalk and chop it finely. Bruise the remaining pieces of stalk. Bring the coconut milk and chicken stock to the boil in a large pan. Add all the lemon grass, the galangal, peppercorns and half the lime leaves, lower the heat and simmer gently for 10 minutes. Strain into a clean pan.

2 Return the soup to the heat, then add the chicken, mushrooms and corn. Simmer for 5–7 minutes or until the chicken is cooked.

3 Stir in the lime juice and Thai fish sauce, then add the remaining lime leaves. Serve hot, garnished with chopped chillies, spring onions and coriander.

HOT-AND-SOUR PRAWN SOUP ★

THIS IS A CLASSIC THAI SEAFOOD SOUP — TOM YAM KUNG — AND IT IS PROBABLY THE MOST POPULAR AND WELL-KNOWN SOUP FROM THAT COUNTRY.

SERVES SIX

INGREDIENTS
    450g/1lb raw king prawns (jumbo
        shrimp), thawed if frozen
    1 litre/1¾ pints/4 cups chicken
        stock or water
    3 lemon grass stalks, root trimmed
    10 kaffir lime leaves, torn in half
    225g/8oz can straw mushrooms
    45ml/3 tbsp Thai fish sauce
    60ml/4 tbsp lime juice
    30ml/2 tbsp chopped spring onion
        (scallion)
    15ml/1 tbsp fresh coriander
        (cilantro) leaves
    4 fresh red chillies, seeded
        and thinly sliced
    salt and ground black pepper

1 Shell the prawns, putting the shells in a colander. Devein and set aside.

2 Rinse the shells under cold water to remove all grit and sand, then put in a large pan with the chicken stock or water. Bring to the boil.

3 Bruise the lemon grass stalks with a pestle or mallet and add them to the stock with half the lime leaves. Simmer gently for 5–6 minutes, until the stock is fragrant.

4 Strain the stock, return it to the clean pan and reheat. Add the drained mushrooms and the prawns, then cook until the prawns turn pink.

5 Stir in the Thai fish sauce, lime juice, spring onion, coriander, chillies and the remaining lime leaves. Taste and adjust the seasoning. The soup should be sour, salty, spicy and hot.

Top: Energy 90kcal/383kJ; Protein 13.2g; Carbohydrate 7.4g, of which sugars 7.2g; Fat 1.1g, of which saturates 0.4g, of which polyunsaturates 0.2g; Cholesterol 35mg; Calcium 44mg; Fibre 0.3g; Sodium 807mg.
Bottom: Energy 69kcal/292kJ; Protein 14.5g; Carbohydrate 1.1g, of which sugars 1g; Fat 0.8g, of which saturates 0.1g, of which polyunsaturates 0.2g; Cholesterol 146mg; Calcium 81mg; Fibre 0.9g; Sodium 682mg.

CHICKEN RICE SOUP WITH LEMON GRASS ★

THIS IS CAMBODIA'S ANSWER TO THE CHICKEN NOODLE SOUP THAT IS POPULAR IN THE WEST. LIGHT AND FAT-FREE, THIS TANGY AND DELICIOUS SOUP IS THE PERFECT CHOICE FOR A HOT DAY, AS WELL AS A GREAT PICK-ME-UP WHEN YOU ARE FEELING LOW OR TIRED.

SERVES FOUR

INGREDIENTS
    2 lemon grass stalks, trimmed,
      cut into 3 pieces, and lightly
      bruised
    15ml/1 tbsp Thai fish sauce
    90g/3½oz/½ cup short grain
      rice, rinsed
    1 small bunch coriander (cilantro)
      leaves, finely chopped, and 1
      green or red chilli, seeded
      and cut into thin strips,
      to garnish
    1 lime, cut in wedges, to serve
    sea salt
    ground black pepper
For the stock
    1 small chicken or 2 meaty
      chicken legs
    1 onion, quartered
    2 cloves garlic, crushed
    25g/1oz fresh root ginger,
      sliced
    2 lemon grass stalks, cut in half
      lengthways and bruised
    2 dried red chillies
    30ml/2 tbsp *nuoc mam*

1 Put the chicken into a deep pan. Add all the other stock ingredients and pour in 2 litres/3½ pints/7¾ cups water. Bring to the boil for a few minutes, then reduce the heat and simmer gently with the lid on for 2 hours.

2 Skim off any fat from the stock, strain and reserve. Remove the skin from the chicken and shred the meat. Set aside.

3 Pour the stock back into the deep pan and bring to the boil. Reduce the heat and stir in the lemon grass stalks and fish sauce. Stir in the rice and simmer, uncovered, for about 40 minutes. Add the shredded chicken and season to taste.

4 Ladle the piping hot soup into warmed individual bowls, garnish with chopped coriander and the thin strips of chilli and serve with lime wedges to squeeze over.

COOK'S TIPS
• The fresh, citrus aroma of lemon grass and lime, combined with the warmth of the chillies, is invigorating and awakens the senses. However, many Vietnamese and Cambodians often spike the soup with additional chillies as a garnish, or served on the side.
• Variations of this soup crop up all over Cambodia and Vietnam, where it is often served as a meal in itself.

Energy 194kcal/817kJ; Protein 26.2g; Carbohydrate 18.4g, of which sugars 0.3g; Fat 1.6g, of which saturates 0.3g, of which polyunsaturates 0.2g; Cholesterol 70mg; Calcium 36mg; Fibre 0.6g; Sodium 268mg.

AROMATIC BROTH WITH ROAST DUCK, PAK CHOI AND EGG NOODLES ★

SERVED ON ITS OWN, THIS CHINESE-INSPIRED DUCK AND NOODLE SOUP MAKES A DELICIOUS AUTUMN OR WINTER MEAL. IN A VIETNAMESE HOUSEHOLD, A BOWL OF WHOLE FRESH OR MARINATED CHILLIES MIGHT BE PRESENTED AS A FIERY SIDE DISH TO CHEW ON.

SERVES SIX

INGREDIENTS
    5ml/1 tsp sunflower oil
    2 shallots, thinly sliced
    4cm/1½in fresh root ginger,
      peeled and sliced
    15ml/1 tbsp soy sauce
    5ml/1 tsp five-spice powder
    10ml/2 tsp sugar
    175g/6oz pak choi (bok choy)
    450g/1lb fresh egg noodles
    225g/8oz roast duck, thinly sliced
    sea salt
For the stock
    1 chicken carcass
    2 carrots, peeled and quartered
    2 onions, peeled and quartered
    4cm/1½in fresh root ginger, peeled
      and cut into chunks
    2 lemon grass stalks, chopped
    30ml/2 tbsp *nuoc mam*
    15ml/1 tbsp soy sauce
    6 black peppercorns
For the garnish
    4 spring onions (scallions), sliced
    1–2 red Serrano chillies, seeded and
      finely sliced
    1 bunch each coriander (cilantro) and
      basil, stalks removed, leaves
      chopped

1 To make the stock, put the chicken carcass into a deep pan. Add all the other stock ingredients and pour in 2.5 litres/4½ pints/10¼ cups water. Bring to the boil, and boil for a few minutes, skim off any foam, then reduce the heat and simmer gently with the lid on for 2–3 hours. Remove the lid and continue to simmer for a further 30 minutes to reduce the stock. Skim off any fat, season with salt, then strain the stock. Measure out 2 litres/3½ pints/8 cups.

2 Heat the oil in a wok or deep pan and stir in the shallots and ginger. Add the soy sauce, five-spice powder, sugar and stock and bring to the boil. Season with a little salt, reduce the heat and simmer for 10–15 minutes.

3 Meanwhile, cut the pak choi diagonally into wide strips and blanch in boiling water to soften them. Drain and refresh under cold running water to prevent them cooking any further. Bring a large pan of water to the boil, then add the fresh noodles. Cook for 5 minutes, then drain well.

4 Divide the noodles among six soup bowls, lay some of the pak choi and sliced duck over them, and then ladle over generous amounts of the simmering broth. Garnish with the spring onions, chillies and herbs, and serve immediately.

COOK'S TIP
If you can't find fresh egg noodles, substitute dried egg noodles instead. Soak the dried noodles in lukewarm water for 20 minutes, then cook, one portion at a time, in a sieve (strainer) lowered into the boiling water. Use a chopstick to untangle them as they soften. Ready-cooked egg noodles are also available in supermarkets.

Energy 337kcal/1411kJ; Protein 12.1g; Carbohydrate 62.5g, of which sugars 1.1g; Fat 3.3g, of which saturates 0.8g, of which polyunsaturates 0.9g; Cholesterol 41mg; Calcium 66mg; Fibre 0.7g; Sodium 269mg.

CRISPY WONTON SOUP ★

THE FRESHLY COOKED CRISP WONTONS ARE SUPPOSED TO SIZZLE AND "SING" IN THE HOT SOUP AS THEY ARE TAKEN TO THE TABLE. ALTHOUGH IT CONTAINS WONTONS THIS RECIPE IS VERY LOW IN FAT.

2 Place the wonton wrappers under a slightly dampened dish towel so that they do not dry out. Next, dampen the edges of a wonton wrapper. Place about 5ml/1 tsp of the filling in the centre of the wrapper. Gather it up like a purse and pinch together well. Fill the remaining wontons in the same way.

3 Make the soup. Drain the cloud ears, trim away any rough stems, then slice thinly. Bring the stock to the boil, add the ginger and the spring onions and simmer for 3 minutes. Add the sliced cloud ears, shredded spring greens, bamboo shoots and soy sauce. Simmer for 10 minutes, then stir in the sesame oil. Season to taste with salt and pepper, cover and keep hot.

4 Meanwhile, preheat the oven to 240°C/475°F/Gas 9. Lightly whisk the egg white with the sunflower oil and water. Brush the wontons generously with egg white and place them on a non-stick baking sheet. Bake for about 5 minutes, until browned and crisp. Ladle the soup into six warmed soup bowls and share the wontons among them. Serve immediately.

SERVES SIX

INGREDIENTS
- 2 cloud ear (wood ear) mushrooms, soaked for 30 minutes in warm water to cover
- 1.2 litres/2 pints/5 cups home-made chicken stock
- 2.5cm/1in piece fresh root ginger, peeled and grated
- 4 spring onions (scallions), chopped
- 2 rich-green inner spring greens (collards) leaves, finely shredded
- 50g/2oz drained canned bamboo shoots, sliced
- 25ml/1½ tbsp dark soy sauce
- 2.5ml/½ tsp sesame oil
- salt and ground black pepper

For the filled wontons
- 2.5ml/½ tsp sesame oil
- ½ small onion, finely chopped
- 10 drained canned water chestnuts, finely chopped
- 115g/4oz minced (ground) lean pork
- 24 wonton wrappers
- 1 egg white
- 5ml/1 tsp sunflower oil

1 Make the filled wontons. Heat the sesame oil in a small pan. When hot, add the finely chopped onion and water chestnuts and the lean pork and cook, stirring often, until the meat is no longer pink but not overbrown. Tip the mixture into a bowl, season to taste and leave to cool.

VARIATION
For a delicious soup that is even lower in fat, replace the pork with an equivalent quantity of minced (ground) lean chicken or turkey breast fillets. Season well with freshly ground black pepper.

COOK'S TIP
The wontons can be sprinkled with 5ml/1 tsp toasted sesame seeds for extra flavour and crunch. To toast sesame seeds, put them in a dry frying pan and place over a medium heat until the seeds change colour. Shake the pan constantly so that the seeds brown evenly and do not burn.

Energy 132kcal/554kJ; Protein 8.4g; Carbohydrate 17g, of which sugars 3.4g; Fat 3.9g, of which saturates 0.7g, of which polyunsaturates 1.9g; Cholesterol 12mg; Calcium 140mg; Fibre 2.7g; Sodium 332mg.

HOT AND SOUR SOUP ★

ONE OF ASIA'S MOST POPULAR SOUPS, THIS IS FAMED FOR ITS CLEVER BALANCE OF FLAVOURS. THE "HOT" COMES FROM PEPPER; THE "SOUR" FROM VINEGAR. OTHER RECIPES USE CHILLIES AND LIME JUICE.

SERVES SIX

INGREDIENTS
    4–6 Chinese dried mushrooms
    2–3 small pieces of cloud ear (wood
        ear) mushrooms and a few golden
        needles (lily buds), optional
    115g/4oz lean pork fillet, cut into
        fine strips
    45ml/3 tbsp cornflour (cornstarch)
    150ml/¼ pint/⅔ cup water
    15ml/1 tbsp sunflower oil
    1 small onion, finely chopped
    1.5 litres/2½ pints/6¼ cups good
        quality beef or chicken stock, or
        2 × 300g/11oz cans consommé
        made up to the full quantity
        with water
    150g/5oz drained fresh firm
        tofu, diced
    60ml/4 tbsp rice vinegar
    15ml/1 tbsp light soy sauce
    1 egg, beaten
    salt and ground white or
        black pepper
    2–3 spring onions (scallions),
        shredded, to garnish

2 Lightly dust the strips of pork fillet with some of the cornflour; mix the remaining cornflour to a smooth paste with the measured water.

3 Heat the oil in a wok or pan and fry the onion until soft. Increase the heat and fry the pork until it changes colour. Add the stock or consommé, mushrooms, soaking water, and cloud ears and golden needles, if using. Bring to the boil, then simmer for 15 minutes.

4 Discard the golden needles, lower the heat and stir in the cornflour paste to thicken. Add the tofu, vinegar, soy sauce, and salt and pepper.

5 Bring the soup to just below boiling point, then drizzle in the beaten egg by letting it drop from a balloon whisk (or to be authentic, from the fingertips) so that it forms threads in the gently simmering soup. Serve immediately, garnished with spring onion shreds.

1 Place the dried mushrooms in a bowl, with the pieces of cloud ear and the golden needles, if using. Add sufficient warm water to cover and leave to soak for about 30 minutes. Drain the mushrooms, reserving the soaking water. Cut off and discard the mushroom stems and slice the caps finely. Trim away any tough stem from the cloud ears, then chop them finely. Using kitchen string, tie the golden needles into a bundle.

Energy 102kcal/426kJ; Protein 7.7g; Carbohydrate 8g, of which sugars 0.8g; Fat 4.8g, of which saturates 1g, of which polyunsaturates 2g; Cholesterol 44mg; Calcium 140mg; Fibre 0.2g; Sodium 273mg.

BEEF NOODLE SOUP ★

Some would say that this classic noodle soup is Vietnam in a bowl. Made with beef or chicken, it is Vietnamese fast food, street food, working men's food and family food. It is nutritious, particularly low in fat, and makes an intensely satisfying meal.

SERVES SIX

INGREDIENTS
    250g/9oz beef sirloin, trimmed
    500g/1¼lb dried noodles, soaked in
      lukewarm water for 20 minutes
    1 onion, halved and finely sliced
    6–8 spring onions (scallions),
      cut into long pieces
    2–3 red Thai chillies, seeded and
      finely sliced
    115g/4oz/½ cup beansprouts
    1 large bunch each fresh coriander
      (cilantro) and mint, stalks removed,
      leaves chopped
    2 limes, cut in wedges, and hoisin
      sauce, *nuoc mam* or *nuoc cham*
      to serve
For the stock
    1.5kg/3lb 5oz oxtail, trimmed of fat
      and cut into thick pieces
    1kg/2¼lb beef shank or brisket
    2 large onions, peeled and quartered
    2 carrots, peeled and cut into chunks
    7.5cm/3in fresh root ginger,
      cut into chunks
    6 cloves
    2 cinnamon sticks
    6 star anise
    5ml/1 tsp black peppercorns
    30ml/2 tbsp soy sauce
    45–60ml/3–4 tbsp *nuoc mam*
    salt

1 To make the stock, put the oxtail into a large, deep pan and cover it with water. Bring it to the boil and blanch the meat for about 10 minutes. Drain the meat, rinsing off any scum, and clean out the pan. Put the blanched oxtail back into the pan with the other stock ingredients, apart from the *nuoc mam* and salt, and cover with about 3 litres/5¼ pints/12 cups water. Bring it to the boil, reduce the heat and simmer, covered, for 2–3 hours.

2 Remove the lid and simmer for another hour, until the stock has reduced to about 2 litres/3½ pints/ 8 cups. Skim off any fat and then strain the stock into another pan.

3 Cut the beef sirloin across the grain into thin pieces, the size of the heel of your hand. Bring the stock to the boil once more, stir in the *nuoc mam*, season to taste, then reduce the heat and leave the stock simmering until ready to use.

4 Meanwhile, bring a pan filled with water to the boil, drain the rice sticks and add to the water. Cook for about 5 minutes or until tender – you may need to separate them with a pair of chopsticks if they look as though they are sticking together.

5 Drain the noodles and divide them equally among six wide soup bowls. Top each serving with the slices of beef, onion, spring onions, chillies and beansprouts.

6 Ladle the hot stock over the top of these ingredients, top with the fresh herbs and serve with the lime wedges to squeeze over. Pass around the hoisin sauce, *nuoc mam* or *nuoc cham* for those who like a little sweetening, fish flavouring or extra fire.

COOK'S TIPS
• The key to this soup is a tasty, light stock flavoured with ginger, cinnamon, cloves and star anise, so it is worth cooking it slowly and leaving it to stand overnight to allow the flavours to develop.
• To enjoy this dish, use your chopsticks to lift the noodles through the layers of flavouring and slurp them up. This is the essence of Vietnam.

Energy 391kcal/1633kJ; Protein 14.9g; Carbohydrate 70.5g, of which sugars 1.9g; Fat 4.3g, of which saturates 1.6g, of which polyunsaturates 0.3g; Cholesterol 24mg; Calcium 41mg; Fibre 1.1g; Sodium 398mg.

APPETIZERS AND LIGHT BITES

Follow the low-fat recipes in this section and treat your

party guests to such delicious healthy snacks as Corn Fritters,

Fish Cakes with Cucumber Relish and succulent Salt and

Pepper Prawns. Traditional street fare such as spring rolls,

fritters and samosas can be amazingly low in cholesterol

and prove a healthy-eating choice. Garlic, ginger, coriander,

chillies and vegetables combine to make appetizers and light

bites that are both irresistible and delicious.

POTATO, SHALLOT AND GARLIC SAMOSAS WITH GREEN PEAS ★

MOST SAMOSAS ARE DEEP-FRIED. THESE THAI SNACKS ARE BAKED, MAKING THEM A HEALTHIER OPTION. THEY ARE PERFECT FOR PARTIES, SINCE THE PASTRIES NEED NO LAST-MINUTE ATTENTION.

MAKES TWENTY-FIVE

INGREDIENTS
1 large potato, about 250g/
    9oz, diced
15ml/1 tbsp sunflower oil
2 shallots, finely chopped
1 garlic clove, finely chopped
60ml/4 tbsp reduced-fat
    coconut milk
5ml/1 tsp Thai red or green
    curry paste
75g/3oz/¾ cup peas
juice of ½ lime
25 samosa wrappers or 10 x 5cm/
    4 x 2in strips of filo pastry
salt and ground black pepper
oil, for brushing

1 Preheat the oven to 220°C/425°F/ Gas 7. Bring a small pan of water to the boil, add the diced potato, cover and cook for 10–15 minutes, until tender. Drain and set aside.

2 Meanwhile, heat the sunflower oil in a large frying pan and cook the shallots and garlic over a medium heat, stirring occasionally, for 4–5 minutes, until softened and golden.

COOK'S TIP
Many Asian food stores sell what is described as a samosa pad. This is a packet, usually frozen, containing about 50 oblong pieces of samosa pastry. Filo pastry, cut to size, can be used instead.

3 Add the drained diced potato, coconut milk, red or green curry paste, peas and lime juice to the frying pan. Mash together coarsely with a wooden spoon. Season to taste with salt and pepper and cook over a low heat for 2–3 minutes, then remove the pan from the heat and set aside until the mixture has cooled a little.

4 Lay a samosa wrapper or filo strip flat on the work surface. Brush with a little oil, then place a generous teaspoonful of the potato mixture in the middle of one end. Turn one corner diagonally over the filling to meet the long edge.

5 Continue folding over the filling, keeping the triangular shape as you work down the strip. Brush with a little more oil if necessary and place on a baking sheet. Prepare all the other samosas in the same way.

6 Bake for 15 minutes, or until the pastry is golden and crisp. Leave to cool slightly before serving.

Energy 42kcal/178kJ; Protein 1.2g; Carbohydrate 8.5g, of which sugars 0.6g; Fat 0.6g, of which saturates 0.1g, of which polyunsaturates 0.4g; Cholesterol 0mg; Calcium 14mg; Fibre 0.5g; Sodium 4mg.

CRISPY MIXED VEGETABLE <u>AND</u> GINGER SAMOSAS ★

SURPRISINGLY LOW IN FAT, SAMOSAS ARE SOLD BY STREET VENDORS THROUGHOUT THE EAST. BAKING THE SAMOSAS HELPS KEEP THE FAT CONTENT TO A MINIMUM.

MAKES ABOUT TWENTY

INGREDIENTS
   1 packet 25cm/10in square spring
      roll wrappers, thawed if frozen
   30ml/2 tbsp plain (all-purpose) flour,
      mixed to a paste with water
   about 15ml/1 tbsp sunflower oil
   coriander (cilantro) leaves, to garnish
   cucumber, carrot and celery, cut into
      matchsticks, to serve (optional)
For the filling
   15ml/1 tbsp sunflower oil
   1 small onion, finely chopped
   1cm/½in piece fresh root ginger,
      peeled and chopped
   1 garlic clove, crushed
   2.5ml/½ tsp chilli powder
   1 large potato, about 225g/8oz,
      cooked until just tender and
      finely diced
   50g/2oz/½ cup cauliflower florets,
      lightly cooked, finely chopped
   50g/2oz/½ cup frozen peas, thawed
   5–10ml/1–2 tsp garam masala
   15ml/1 tbsp chopped fresh coriander
      (cilantro) leaves and stems
   squeeze of lemon juice
   salt

2 Preheat the oven to 200°C/400°F/ Gas 6. Cut the spring roll wrappers into three strips (or two for larger samosas). Brush the edges with a little flour paste. Place a small spoonful of filling about 2cm/¾in in from the edge of one strip.

3 Fold one corner over the filling to make a triangle and continue this folding until the entire strip has been used and a triangular pastry has been formed. Seal any open edges with flour and water paste, adding more water if the paste is thick.

4 Place the samosas on a non-stick baking sheet and brush with oil. Bake for about 10 minutes, until crisp. Serve hot garnished with coriander leaves and accompanied by cucumber, carrot and celery matchsticks, if you like.

COOK'S TIP
Filo pastry can be used instead of spring roll wrappers. Cut the pastry into 8.5cm/ 3in wide strips.

1 Heat the oil in a large wok and fry the onion, ginger and garlic for 5 minutes until the onion has softened. Add the chilli powder, cook for 1 minute, then stir in the potato, cauliflower and peas. Sprinkle with garam masala and set aside to cool. Stir in the chopped coriander, lemon juice and salt.

Energy 44kcal/186kJ; Protein 1.2g; Carbohydrate 8.3g, of which sugars 0.6g; Fat 0.9g, of which saturates 0.1g, of which polyunsaturates 0.5g; Cholesterol 0mg; Calcium 17mg; Fibre 0.6g; Sodium 2mg.

CORN FRITTERS ★

SOMETIMES IT IS THE SIMPLEST DISHES THAT TASTE THE BEST. THESE LOW-FAT FRITTERS, PACKED WITH CRUNCHY CORN, FRESH CORIANDER AND CHILLI AND ACCOMPANIED WITH DELICIOUS SWEET CHILLI SAUCE, ARE VERY EASY TO PREPARE AND UNDERSTANDABLY POPULAR.

MAKES TWELVE

INGREDIENTS

3 corn cobs, total weight
  about 250g/9oz
1 garlic clove, crushed
small bunch fresh coriander
  (cilantro), chopped
1 small fresh red or green chilli,
  seeded and finely chopped
1 spring onion (scallion),
  finely chopped
15ml/1 tbsp soy sauce
75g/3oz/¾ cup rice flour or plain
  (all-purpose) flour
2 eggs, lightly beaten
60ml/4 tbsp water
spray oil, for shallow frying
salt and ground black pepper
sweet chilli sauce,
  to serve

1 Using a sharp knife, slice the kernels from the corn cobs and place them in a large bowl. Add the crushed garlic, chopped coriander, chopped and seeded red or green chilli, chopped spring onion, soy sauce, flour, beaten eggs and water and mix well. Season with salt and pepper to taste and mix again. The mixture should be firm enough to hold its shape, but not stiff.

2 Spray a little oil into a large non-stick frying pan. Add spoonfuls of the corn mixture, gently spreading each one out to make a roundish fritter. Cook for 1–2 minutes on each side until golden-brown and cooked through.

3 Drain on kitchen paper and keep hot while frying more fritters in the same way. Serve hot with sweet chilli sauce.

Energy 49kcal/208kJ; Protein 2.3g; Carbohydrate 7.5g, of which sugars 0.6g; Fat 1.3g, of which saturates 0.3g, of which polyunsaturates 0.2g; Cholesterol 32mg; Calcium 21mg; Fibre 0.6g; Sodium 102mg.

PORK PÂTÉ IN A BANANA LEAF ★★

THIS PÂTÉ, CHA LUA, HAS A VIETNAMESE TWIST: IT IS STEAMED IN BANANA LEAVES AND HAS A SLIGHTLY SPRINGY TEXTURE AND DELICATE FLAVOUR. BAGUETTES ARE A COMMON SIGHT ALONGSIDE THE NOODLES AND VEGETABLES IN SOUTHERN MARKETS AND FREQUENTLY EATEN SMEARED WITH PÂTÉ.

SERVES SIX

INGREDIENTS

45ml/3 tbsp *nuoc mam*
15ml/1 tbsp vegetable or sesame oil
15ml/1 tbsp sugar
10ml/2 tsp five-spice powder
2 shallots, peeled and finely chopped
2 garlic cloves, crushed
675g/1½lb/3 cups minced
  (ground) pork
25g/1oz/¼ cup potato starch
7.5ml/1½ tsp baking powder
1 banana leaf, trimmed into a strip
  25cm/10in wide
vegetable oil, for brushing
salt and ground black pepper
nuoc cham and a baguette or salad,
  to serve

1 In a bowl, beat the *nuoc mam* and oil with the sugar and five-spice powder. Once the sugar has dissolved, stir in the shallots and garlic. Add the minced pork and seasoning, and knead well until thoroughly combined. Cover and chill for 2–3 hours.

2 Knead the mixture again, thumping it down into the bowl to remove any air. Add the potato starch and baking powder and knead until smooth and pasty. Mould the pork mixture into a fat sausage, about 18cm/7in long, and place it on an oiled dish.

COOK'S TIP
You can find banana leaves in African, Caribbean and Asian markets. To prepare them, trim the leaves to fit the steamer, using a pair of scissors, making sure that there is enough to fold over the pâté. If you cannot find banana leaves, you can use large spring green (collard) leaves, or several Savoy cabbage leaves instead.

VARIATION
This pâté can also be added to noodles, soups and stir-fried dishes, in which it is complemented by fresh herbs and spices.

3 Lay the banana leaf on a flat surface, brush it with a little vegetable oil, and place the pork sausage across it. Lift up the edge of the banana leaf nearest to you and fold it over the sausage mixture, tuck in the sides, and roll it up into a firm, tight bundle. Secure the bundle with a piece of string, so that it doesn't unravel during the cooking process.

4 Fill a wok one-third full with water. Balance a bamboo steamer, with its lid on, above the level of the water. Bring to the boil, lift the lid and place the banana leaf bundle on the rack, being careful not to burn yourself. Re-cover and steam for 45 minutes. Leave the pâté to cool in the leaf, open it up and cut it into slices. Drizzle with *nuoc cham*, and serve with a baguette or salad.

Energy 187kcal/783kJ; Protein 24.5g; Carbohydrate 6.7g, of which sugars 3.2g; Fat 6.9g, of which saturates 1.9g, of which polyunsaturates 2.1g; Cholesterol 71mg; Calcium 13mg; Fibre 0.2g; Sodium 79mg.

Tung Tong ★

POPULARLY CALLED "GOLD BAGS", THESE CRISP PASTRY PURSES HAVE A CORIANDER-FLAVOURED FILLING BASED ON WATER CHESTNUTS AND CORN. THEY ARE THE PERFECT VEGETARIAN SNACK.

MAKES EIGHTEEN

INGREDIENTS
    18 spring roll wrappers, about
      8cm/3¼in square, thawed
      if frozen
    plum sauce, to serve
    1 egg white
    5ml/1 tsp sunflower oil
For the filling
    4 baby corn cobs
    130g/4½oz can water chestnuts,
      drained and chopped
    1 shallot, coarsely chopped
    1 egg, separated
    30ml/2 tbsp cornflour (cornstarch)
    60ml/4 tbsp water
    small bunch fresh coriander
      (cilantro), chopped
    salt and ground black pepper

1 Make the filling. Place the baby corn, water chestnuts, shallot and egg yolk in a food processor or blender. Process to a coarse paste.

2 Place the egg white in a cup, add the sunflower oil and 5ml/1 tsp water, and whisk it lightly with a fork.

3 Preheat the oven to 180°C/350°F/ Gas 4. Put the cornflour in a small pan and stir in the water until smooth. Add the corn mixture and chopped coriander and season with salt and pepper to taste. Cook over a low heat, stirring constantly, until the mixture boils and thickens.

4 Leave the filling for the pastry purses to cool slightly. Prepare a non-stick baking sheet or line a baking sheet with baking parchment.

5 Place 5ml/1 tsp in the centre of a spring roll wrapper. Brush the edges lightly with the beaten egg white, then gather up the points and press them firmly together to make a pouch or bag.

6 Repeat with remaining wrappers and filling. Brush each pouch generously with the egg white, and place on the baking sheet. Bake for 12–15 minutes, until golden brown. Serve hot, with the plum sauce.

VARIATION
Rice paper wrappers can be used in place of spring roll wrappers if you are following a wheatfree diet. Simply reconstitute the wrappers by brushing them on both sides with warm water to soften them immediately before you use them.

Energy 36kcal/151kJ; Protein 1.5g; Carbohydrate 6.4g, of which sugars 0.4g; Fat 0.7g, of which saturates 0.1g, of which polyunsaturates 0.2g; Cholesterol 11mg; Calcium 17mg; Fibre 0.5g; Sodium 73mg.

THAI TEMPEH CAKES WITH SWEET CHILLI ★

MADE FROM SOYA BEANS, TEMPEH IS SIMILAR TO TOFU BUT HAS A NUTTIER TASTE. HERE, IT IS COMBINED WITH A FRAGRANT BLEND OF LEMON GRASS, CORIANDER AND GINGER.

MAKES EIGHT

INGREDIENTS

1 lemon grass stalk, outer leaves removed and inside finely chopped
2 garlic cloves, chopped
2 spring onions (scallions), finely chopped
2 shallots, finely chopped
2 fresh red chillies, seeded and finely chopped
2.5cm/1in piece fresh root ginger, finely chopped
60ml/4 tbsp chopped fresh coriander (cilantro), plus extra to garnish
250g/9oz/2¼ cups tempeh, thawed if frozen, sliced
15ml/1 tbsp fresh lime juice
5ml/1 tsp granulated sugar
45ml/3 tbsp plain (all-purpose) flour
1 large (US extra large) egg, lightly beaten
salt and ground black pepper
spray vegetable oil, for frying
For the dipping sauce
45ml/3 tbsp mirin (see Cook's Tip)
45ml/3 tbsp white wine vinegar
2 spring onions (scallions), thinly sliced
15ml/1 tbsp granulated sugar
2 fresh red chillies, seeded and finely chopped
30ml/2 tbsp chopped fresh coriander (cilantro)
large pinch of salt

1 Make the dipping sauce. Mix together the mirin, vinegar, spring onions, sugar, chillies, coriander and salt in a small bowl. Cover with clear film (plastic wrap) and set aside until ready to serve.

COOK'S TIP
Mirin is a sweet rice wine from Japan. It has quite a delicate flavour and is used for cooking. Rice wine for drinking, called sake, is rather more expensive. Both mirin and sake are available from Asian food stores. If you cannot locate mirin, dry sherry can be used instead, although the results will not be quite the same.

2 Place the lemon grass, garlic, spring onions, shallots, chillies, ginger and coriander in a food processor or blender, then process to a coarse paste. Add the tempeh, lime juice and sugar and process until combined. Add the flour and egg, with salt and pepper to taste. Process again until the mixture forms a coarse, sticky paste.

3 Scrape the paste into a bowl. Take one-eighth of the mixture at a time and form it into rounds with your hands.

4 Spray a little oil in a non-stick frying pan. Fry the cakes for 5–6 minutes, turning once, until golden. Drain on kitchen paper. Transfer to a platter, garnish and serve with the sauce.

Energy 77kcal/322kJ; Protein 4.6g; Carbohydrate 8.4g, of which sugars 3.8g; Fat 2.3g, of which saturates 0.4g, of which polyunsaturates 0.8g; Cholesterol 24mg; Calcium 204mg; Fibre 1.1g; Sodium 16mg.

FISH CAKES WITH CUCUMBER RELISH ★

THESE WONDERFUL SMALL FISH CAKES ARE A VERY FAMILIAR AND POPULAR APPETIZER IN THAILAND AND INCREASINGLY THROUGHOUT SOUTH-EAST ASIA. THEY ARE USUALLY SERVED WITH THAI BEER.

MAKES ABOUT TWELVE

INGREDIENTS
5 kaffir lime leaves
300g/11oz cod, cut into chunks
30ml/2 tbsp red curry paste
1 egg
30ml/2 tbsp Thai fish sauce
5ml/1 tsp sugar
30ml/2 tbsp cornflour (cornstarch)
15ml/1 tbsp chopped fresh
  coriander (cilantro)
50g/2oz green beans, finely sliced
spray vegetable oil, for frying
Chinese mustard cress,
  to garnish
For the cucumber relish
60ml/4 tbsp coconut or rice vinegar
50g/2oz/¼ cup sugar
1 head pickled garlic
15ml/1 tbsp fresh root ginger
1 cucumber, cut into matchsticks
4 shallots, finely sliced

1 Make the cucumber relish. Bring the vinegar and sugar to the boil in a small pan with 60ml/4 tbsp water, stirring until the sugar has dissolved. Remove from the heat and cool.

2 Separate the pickled garlic into cloves. Chop these finely along with the ginger and place in a bowl. Add the cucumber and shallots, pour over the vinegar mixture and mix lightly.

3 Reserve two kaffir lime leaves for garnish and thinly slice the remainder. Put the chunks of fish, curry paste and egg in a food processor and process to a smooth paste. Transfer the mixture to a bowl and stir in the fish sauce, sugar, cornflour, sliced kaffir lime leaves, coriander and green beans. Mix well, then shape the mixture into about twelve 5mm/¼in thick cakes, measuring about 5cm/2in in diameter.

4 Spray the oil in a non-stick wok or deep-frying pan. Fry the fish cakes, a few at a time, for about 4–5 minutes until cooked and evenly brown.

5 Lift out the fish cakes and drain them on kitchen paper. Keep each batch hot while frying successive batches. Garnish with the reserved kaffir leaves and Chinese mustard cress. Serve with the cucumber relish.

Energy 54kcal/228kJ; Protein 5.4g; Carbohydrate 6.4g, of which sugars 5g; Fat 0.9g, of which saturates 0.2g, of which polyunsaturates 0.2g; Cholesterol 27mg; Calcium 12mg; Fibre 0.2g; Sodium 22mg.

GREEN CURRY PUFFS ★

SHRIMP PASTE AND GREEN CURRY SAUCE, USED JUDICIOUSLY, GIVE THESE PUFFS THEIR DISTINCTIVE,
SPICY, SAVOURY FLAVOUR, AND THE ADDITION OF CHILLI STEPS UP THE HEAT.

MAKES TWENTY-FOUR

INGREDIENTS
   24 small wonton wrappers, about
      8cm/3¼ in square, thawed if frozen
   15ml/1 tbsp cornflour (cornstarch),
      mixed to a paste with 30ml/
      2 tbsp water
   5ml/1 tsp sunflower oil
For the filling
   1 small potato, about 115g/4oz,
      boiled and mashed
   25g/1oz/3 tbsp cooked petits pois
      (baby peas)
   25g/1oz/3 tbsp cooked corn
   few sprigs fresh coriander
      (cilantro), chopped
   1 small fresh red chilli, seeded and
      finely chopped
   ½ lemon grass stalk, finely chopped
   15ml/1 tbsp soy sauce
   5ml/1 tsp shrimp paste or fish sauce
   5ml/1 tsp Thai green curry paste

1 Combine the filling ingredients. Lay out one wonton wrapper and place a teaspoon of the filling in the centre.

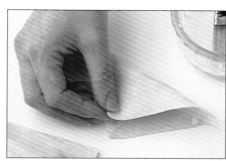

2 Brush a little of the cornflour paste along two sides of the square. Fold the other two sides over to meet them, then press together to make a triangular pastry and seal in the filling. Make more pastries in the same way, thinning the paste with a little water if it becomes too thick.

3 Preheat the oven to 240°C/475°F/ Gas 9 and prepare a non-stick baking tray or line a baking tray with baking parchment. Lightly whisk the egg white with the oil and 5ml/1 tsp water.

4 Brush the pastries generously with the egg white and place on the baking sheet. Bake for about 5–8 minutes, until browned and crisp. If you intend serving the puffs hot, place them in a low oven while cooking successive batches. The puffs also taste good cold.

COOK'S TIP
Wonton wrappers dry out quickly, so keep them covered, using clear film (plastic wrap), until you are ready to use them.

Energy 32kcal/134kJ; Protein 1g; Carbohydrate 6.7g, of which sugars 0.4g; Fat 0.3g, of which saturates 0g, of which polyunsaturates 0.1g; Cholesterol 1mg; Calcium 16mg; Fibre 0.4g; Sodium 58mg.

FIRECRACKERS ★

IT'S EASY TO SEE HOW THESE PASTRY-WRAPPED PRAWN SNACKS GOT THEIR NAME (KRATHAK IN THAI) SINCE AS WELL AS RESEMBLING FIREWORKS, THEIR CONTENTS EXPLODE WITH FLAVOUR.

2 Mix the curry paste with the fish sauce in a shallow dish. Add the prawns and turn them in the mixture until they are well coated. Cover and leave to marinate for 10 minutes.

3 Place a wonton wrapper on the work surface at an angle so that it forms a diamond shape, then fold the top corner over so that the point is in the centre. Place a prawn, slits down, on the wrapper, with the tail projecting from the folded end, then fold the bottom corner over the other end of the prawn.

4 Fold each side of the wrapper over in turn to make a tightly folded roll. Tie a noodle in a bow around the roll and set it aside. Repeat with the remaining prawns and wrappers.

5 Preheat the oven to 240°C/475°F/ Gas 9. Prepare a non-stick baking sheet or line a baking sheet with baking parchment. Lightly whisk the egg white with the oil and 5ml/1 tsp water. Brush the wrapped prawns generously with egg white, so they are well moistened, and place on the baking sheet. Bake for 5–6 minutes, until crisp and lightly browned.

MAKES SIXTEEN

INGREDIENTS
  16 large, raw king prawns (jumbo
    shrimp), heads and shells removed
    but tails left on
  5ml/1 tsp red curry paste
  15ml/1 tbsp Thai fish sauce
  16 small wonton wrappers, about
    8cm/3¼ in square, thawed if frozen
  16 fine egg noodles, soaked
    (see Cook's Tip)
  1 egg white
  5ml/1 tsp sunflower oil

1 Place the prawns on their sides and cut two slits through the underbelly of each, one about 1cm/½ in from the head end and the other about 1cm/½ in from the first cut, cutting across the prawn. This will prevent the prawns from curling when they are cooked.

COOK'S TIP
Soak the fine egg noodles used as ties for the prawn rolls in a bowl of boiling water for 2–3 minutes, until softened, then drain, refresh under cold running water and drain well again.

Energy 37kcal/155kJ; Protein 2.1g; Carbohydrate 6g, of which sugars 0.2g; Fat 0.6g, of which saturates 0.1g, of which polyunsaturates 0.2g; Cholesterol 13mg; Calcium 13mg; Fibre 0.2g; Sodium 88mg.

CHA GIO AND NUOC CHAM ★★

CHINESE SPRING ROLL WRAPPERS ARE USED HERE INSTEAD OF THE RICE PAPERS TRADITIONALLY USED IN VIETNAM AND THE PHILIPPINES. CHA GIO IS AN IMMENSELY POPULAR SNACK IN VIETNAM.

MAKES FIFTEEN

INGREDIENTS
25g/1oz cellophane noodles soaked for 10 minutes in hot water to cover
6–8 dried cloud ear (wood ear), mushrooms soaked for 30 minutes in warm water to cover
225g/8oz minced (ground) lean pork
225g/8oz fresh or canned crab meat
4 spring onions (scallions), trimmed and finely chopped
5ml/1 tsp Thai fish sauce
flour and water paste, to seal
250g/9oz packet spring roll wrappers
1 egg white
5ml/1 tsp sunflower oil
salt and ground black pepper
For the *nuoc cham* sauce
2 fresh red chillies, seeded and pounded to a paste
2 garlic cloves, crushed
15ml/1 tbsp sugar
45ml/3 tbsp Thai fish sauce
juice of 1 lime or ½ lemon

1 Make the *nuoc cham* sauce by mixing the chillies, garlic, sugar and fish sauce in a bowl and stirring in lime or lemon juice to taste. Drain the noodles and snip into 2.5cm/1in lengths. Drain the cloud ears, trim away any rough stems and slice the wood ears finely.

COOK'S TIP
Serve the rolls Vietnamese-style by wrapping each roll in a lettuce leaf with a few sprigs of fresh mint and coriander (cilantro) and a stick of cucumber.

2 Mix the noodles and the cloud ears with the pork and set aside. Remove any cartilage from the crab meat and add to the pork mixture with the spring onions and fish sauce. Season to taste, mixing well.

3 Place a spring roll wrapper in front of you, diamond-fashion. Spoon some mixture just below the centre, fold over the nearest point and roll once.

4 Fold in the sides to enclose, brush the edges with flour paste and roll up to seal. Repeat with the remaining wrappers.

5 Preheat the oven to 200°C/400F/Gas 6. Whisk the egg white with the oil and 5ml/1 tsp water. Brush the rolls generously with egg white, and place on a non-stick baking sheet. Bake for 25–30 minutes, until crisp and brown. To eat, dip the hot rolls in the *nuoc cham* sauce.

Energy 133kcal/558kJ; Protein 11.1g; Carbohydrate 10g, of which sugars 0.4g; Fat 5.7g, of which saturates 0.7g, of which polyunsaturates 2.6g; Cholesterol 36mg; Calcium 21mg; Fibre 0.5g; Sodium 211mg.

SOFT-SHELL CRABS WITH CHILLI AND SALT ★★

IF FRESH SOFT-SHELL CRABS ARE UNAVAILABLE, YOU CAN BUY FROZEN ONES IN ASIAN SUPERMARKETS. ALLOW TWO SMALL CRABS PER SERVING, OR ONE IF THEY ARE LARGE.

SERVES FOUR

INGREDIENTS
　8 small soft-shell crabs, thawed
　　if frozen
　50g/2oz/½ cup plain
　　(all-purpose) flour
　15ml/1 tbsp sunflower oil
　2 large fresh red chillies, or
　　1 green and 1 red, seeded and
　　thinly sliced
　4 spring onions (scallions) or a
　　small bunch of garlic chives,
　　chopped
　coarse sea salt and ground
　　black pepper
To serve
　shredded lettuce, mooli (daikon)
　　and carrot
　light soy sauce

1 Pat the crabs dry with kitchen paper. Season the flour with pepper and coat the crabs lightly with the mixture.

2 Heat the oil in a shallow pan until very hot, then put in the crabs (you may need to do this in two batches). Fry for 2–3 minutes on each side, until the crabs are golden brown but still juicy in the middle. Drain the cooked crabs on kitchen paper and keep hot.

3 Add the sliced chillies and spring onions or garlic chives to the oil remaining in the pan and cook gently for about 2 minutes. Sprinkle over a generous pinch of salt, then spread the mixture on to the crabs.

4 Mix the shredded lettuce, mooli and carrot together. Arrange on plates, top each portion with two crabs and serve, with light soy sauce for dipping.

Energy 133kcal/558kJ; Protein 11.1g; Carbohydrate 10g, of which sugars 0.4g; Fat 5.7g, of which saturates 0.7g, of which polyunsaturates 2.6g; Cholesterol 36mg; Calcium 21mg; Fibre 0.5g; Sodium 211mg.

SALT AND PEPPER PRAWNS ★

THESE SUCCULENT SHELLFISH BEG TO BE EATEN SIZZLINGLY HOT WITH THE FINGERS, SO PROVIDE FINGER BOWLS OR HOT CLOTHS FOR YOUR GUESTS.

SERVES FOUR

INGREDIENTS

  15–18 large raw prawns (shrimp),
    in the shell, about 450g/1lb
  15ml/1 tbsp sunflower oil
  3 shallots or 1 small onion,
    very finely chopped
  2 garlic cloves, crushed
  1cm/½in piece fresh root
    ginger, peeled and very
    finely grated
  1–2 fresh red chillies, seeded and
    finely sliced
  2.5ml/½ tsp sugar or
    to taste
  3–4 spring onions (scallions),
    shredded, to garnish
For the fried salt
  10ml/2 tsp salt
  5ml/1 tsp Sichuan peppercorns

1 Make the fried salt by dry frying the salt and peppercorns in a heavy frying pan over medium heat until the peppercorns begin to release their aroma. Leave the mixture until cool, then tip it into a mortar and crush it with a pestle.

COOK'S TIP
"Fried salt" is also known as "Cantonese salt" or simply "salt and pepper mix". It is widely used as a table condiment or as a dip for deep fried or roasted food, but can also be an ingredient in a recipe, as here. Black or white peppercorns can be substituted for the Sichuan peppercorns. For the best flavour it really is best made when required.

2 Carefully remove the heads and legs from the raw prawns and discard. Leave the body shells and the tails in place. Pat dry with sheets of kitchen paper.

3 Heat the oil in a shallow pan until very hot. Fry the prawns for 2–3 minutes each side until cooked through, then lift them out and drain thoroughly on kitchen paper.

4 Reheat the oil in the frying pan. Add the fried salt, together with the shallots or onion, garlic, ginger, chillies and sugar. Toss together for 1 minute, then add the prawns and toss them over the heat for 1 minute more until they are coated and the shells are impregnated with the seasonings. Serve immediately, garnished with the spring onions.

Energy 122kcal/514kJ; Protein 20.1g; Carbohydrate 2.7g, of which sugars 2.4g; Fat 3.5g, of which saturates 0.5g, of which polyunsaturates 1.9g; Cholesterol 219mg; Calcium 97mg; Fibre 0.3g; Sodium 1197mg.

PAN-STEAMED MUSSELS <u>WITH</u> LEMON GRASS, CHILLI <u>AND</u> THAI HERBS ★

LIKE SO MANY THAI DISHES, THIS IS VERY EASY TO PREPARE AND VERY LOW IN FAT. THE LEMON GRASS AND KAFFIR LIME LEAVES ADD A REFRESHING TANG TO THE MUSSELS.

SERVES SIX

INGREDIENTS
   500g/1¼ lb fresh mussels
   1 lemon grass stalk, finely chopped
   2 shallots, chopped
   2 kaffir lime leaves, coarsely torn
   1 fresh red chilli, sliced
   15ml/1 tbsp Thai fish sauce
   30ml/2 tbsp fresh lime juice
   thinly sliced spring onions (scallions)
      and coriander (cilantro) leaves,
      to garnish

1 Clean the mussels by pulling off the beards, scrubbing the shells well and removing any barnacles. Discard any mussels that are broken or which do not close when tapped sharply.

2 Place the mussels in a large, heavy pan and add the lemon grass, shallots, kaffir lime leaves, chilli, fish sauce and lime juice. Mix well. Cover the pan tightly and steam the mussels over a high heat, shaking the pan occasionally, for 5–7 minutes, until the shells have opened.

3 Using a slotted spoon, transfer the cooked mussels to a warmed serving dish or individual bowls. Discard any mussels that have failed to open.

4 Garnish the mussels with the thinly sliced spring onions and coriander leaves. Serve immediately.

Energy 26kcal/112kJ; Protein 4.5g; Carbohydrate 1g, of which sugars 0.8g; Fat 0.5g, of which saturates 0.1g, of which polyunsaturates 0.2g; Cholesterol 10mg; Calcium 52mg; Fibre 0.1g; Sodium 231mg.

MUSSELS <u>AND</u> CLAMS <u>WITH</u> LEMON GRASS <u>AND</u> COCONUT MILK ★

LEMON GRASS HAS AN INCOMPARABLE AROMATIC FLAVOUR AND IS WIDELY USED WITH ALL KINDS OF SEAFOOD IN THAILAND AS THE FLAVOURS MARRY SO PERFECTLY.

SERVES SIX

INGREDIENTS
900g/2lb fresh mussels
225g/8oz baby clams
120ml/4fl oz/½ cup dry white wine
1 bunch spring onions
   (scallions), chopped
1 lemon grass stalk, chopped
3 kaffir lime leaves, chopped
10ml/2 tsp Thai green curry paste
120ml/4fl oz/½ cup reduced-fat
   coconut milk
30ml/2 tbsp chopped fresh
   coriander (cilantro)
salt and ground black pepper
garlic chives, to garnish

1 Clean the mussels by pulling off the beards, scrubbing the shells well and scraping off any barnacles with the blade of a knife. Scrub the clams. Discard any mussels or clams that are damaged or broken or which do not close immediately when tapped sharply.

2 Put the wine in a large pan with the spring onions, lemon grass and lime leaves. Stir in the curry paste. Simmer until the wine has almost evaporated.

COOK'S TIPS
• In these days of marine pollution, it is unwise to gather fresh shellfish yourself. Those available from fish stores have either been farmed or have undergone a purging process to clean them.
• Depending on where you live, you may have difficulty obtaining clams. If so, use a few extra mussels instead.

3 Add the mussels and clams to the pan and increase the heat to high. Cover tightly and steam the shellfish for 5–6 minutes, until they open.

4 Using a slotted spoon, transfer the mussels and clams to a heated serving bowl, cover and keep hot. Discard any shellfish that remain closed. Strain the cooking liquid into a clean pan through a sieve lined with muslin (cheesecloth) and simmer briefly to reduce to about 250ml/8fl oz/1 cup.

5 Stir the coconut milk and chopped coriander into the sauce and season with salt and pepper to taste. Heat through. Pour the sauce over the mussels and clams, garnish with the garlic chives and serve immediately.

Energy 73kcal/309kJ; Protein 10.5g; Carbohydrate 2.1g, of which sugars 1.8g; Fat 1.2g, of which saturates 0.2g, of which polyunsaturates 0.4g; Cholesterol 26mg; Calcium 129mg; Fibre 0.7g; Sodium 271mg.

SPRING ROLLS WITH MUSHROOMS AND PORK ★

ONE OF THE MOST POPULAR FOODS THROUGHOUT VIETNAM IS THE SPRING ROLL, WHICH MAKES AN IDEAL QUICK SNACK. EVEN THOUGH THE SPRING ROLLS ARE DEEP FRIED, THE BRIEF COOKING TIME AND CAREFUL DRAINING ON KITCHEN PAPER MEANS THEY ARE VERY LOW IN FAT.

MAKES ABOUT 30

INGREDIENTS
   30 dried rice wrappers
   sunflower oil, for deep-frying
   1 bunch fresh mint, stalks removed,
     and *nuoc cham*, to serve
For the filling
   50g/2oz dried bean thread
     (cellophane) noodles, soaked in
     warm water for 20 minutes
   25g/1oz dried cloud ear (wood ear)
     mushrooms, soaked in warm water
     for 15 minutes
   2 eggs
   30ml/2 tbsp *nuoc mam*
   2 garlic cloves, crushed
   10ml/2 tsp sugar
   1 onion, finely chopped
   3 spring onions (scallions),
     finely sliced
   350g/12oz/1½ cups minced (ground)
     lean pork
   175g/6oz/1¾ cups cooked crab meat
     or raw prawns (shrimp)
   salt and ground black pepper

1 To make the filling, squeeze dry the soaked noodles and chop them into small pieces. Squeeze dry the soaked dried cloud ear mushrooms and chop them.

2 Beat the eggs in a bowl. Stir in the *nuoc mam*, garlic and sugar. Add the onion, spring onions, noodles, mushrooms, pork and crab meat or prawns. Season well with salt and ground black pepper.

COOK'S TIP
These spring rolls filled with rice noodles and served with fresh mint and *nuoc cham* are typically Vietnamese. You can substitute beansprouts for the noodles to create rolls more akin to the traditional version. Fresh mint leaves give these rolls a refreshing bite, but fresh coriander (cilantro), basil or flat leaf parsley will work just as well and give an interesting flavour. Dipped into a piquant sauce of your choice, the rolls are very moreish.

3 Have ready a damp dish towel, some clear film (plastic wrap) and a bowl of water. Dip a rice wrapper in the water and place it on the damp towel. Spoon about 15ml/1 tbsp of the spring roll filling on to the side nearest to you, just in from the edge. Fold the nearest edge over the filling, fold over the sides, tucking them in neatly, and then roll the whole wrapper into a tight cylinder. Place the roll on a plate and cover with clear film to keep it moist. Continue making spring rolls in the same way, using the remaining wrappers and filling.

4 Heat the sunflower oil in a wok or heavy pan for deep-frying. Make sure it is hot enough by dropping in a small piece of bread; it should foam and sizzle. Cook the spring rolls in batches, turning them in the oil so that they become golden all over. Drain them on kitchen paper and serve immediately with mint leaves to wrap around them and *nuoc cham* for dipping.

Energy 55kcal/232kJ; Protein 4.5g; Carbohydrate 7g, of which sugars 0.4g; Fat 0.9g, of which saturates 0.3g, of which polyunsaturates 0.1g; Cholesterol 31mg; Calcium 10mg; Fibre 0.1g; Sodium 24mg.

GRILLED PRAWNS WITH LEMON GRASS ★

Next to every fish stall in every market there is bound to be someone cooking up fragrant, citrus-scented snacks for you to eat as you wander around the market. The aromatic scent of lemon grass is hard to resist.

SERVES FOUR

INGREDIENTS

16 king prawns (jumbo shrimp),
  cleaned, with shells intact
120ml/4fl oz/½ cup *nuoc mam*
30ml/2 tbsp sugar
15ml/1 tbsp sunflower oil
3 lemon grass stalks, trimmed and
  finely chopped

1 Using a small sharp knife, carefully slice open each king prawn shell along the back and pull out the black vein, using the point of the knife. Try to keep the rest of the shell intact. Place the deveined prawns in a shallow dish and set aside.

2 Put the *nuoc mam* in a small bowl with the sugar, and beat together until the sugar has dissolved completely. Add the oil and lemon grass and mix well.

3 Pour the marinade over the prawns, using your fingers to rub it all over the prawns and inside the shells too. Cover the dish with clear film (plastic wrap) and chill for at least 4 hours.

COOK'S TIP
Big, juicy king prawns are best for this recipe, but you can use smaller ones if the large king prawns are not available.

4 Cook the prawns on a barbecue or under a conventional grill (broiler) for 2–3 minutes each side. Serve with little bowls of water for rinsing sticky fingers.

Energy 97kcal/409kJ; Protein 9.2g; Carbohydrate 8.8g, of which sugars 8.7g; Fat 3.1g, of which saturates 0.4g, of which polyunsaturates 1.8g; Cholesterol 98mg; Calcium 46mg; Fibre 0g; Sodium 897mg.

POPIAH ★

Here is the Malaysian version of the spring roll. Do not be put off by the number of ingredients; it takes a little time to get everything together but once it is all on the table the cook can retire as guests assemble their own.

MAKES ABOUT TWENTY-FOUR PANCAKES

INGREDIENTS
  40g/1¹/₂oz/¹/₃ cup cornflour
    (cornstarch)
  215g/7¹/₂oz/generous 1³/₄ cups
    plain (all-purpose) flour
  salt
  450ml/³/₄ pint/scant 2 cups water
  6 eggs, beaten
  spray sunflower oil, for frying
For the cooked filling
  15ml/1 tbsp sunflower oil
  1 onion, finely chopped
  2 garlic cloves, crushed
  115g/4oz cooked lean pork, chopped
  115g/4oz crab meat or peeled
    cooked prawns (shrimp), thawed
    if frozen
  115g/4oz drained canned bamboo
    shoot, thinly sliced
  1 small yam bean, peeled and grated
    or 12 drained canned water
    chestnuts, finely chopped
  15–30ml/1–2 tbsp yellow
    salted beans
  15ml/1 tbsp light soy sauce
  ground black pepper
For the fresh fillings
  2 hard-boiled eggs, chopped
  2 Chinese sausages, steamed
    and sliced
  115g/4oz packet fried tofu, each
    piece halved
  225g/8oz/4 cups beansprouts
  115g/4oz crab meat or peeled
    cooked prawns (shrimp)
  ¹/₂ cucumber, cut into matchsticks
  small bunch of spring onions
    (scallions), finely chopped
  20 lettuce leaves, rinsed and dried
  fresh coriander (cilantro) sprigs,
    to garnish
  selection of sauces, including bottled
    chopped chillies, bottled chopped
    garlic and hoisin sauce, to serve

COOK'S TIP
Yam beans are large tubers with a mild
sweet texture similar to water chestnuts.

1 Sift the flours and salt into a bowl. Add the measured water and eggs and mix to a smooth batter.

2 Spray a heavy non-stick frying pan with sunflower oil, then pour in just enough batter to cover the base.

3 As soon as it sets, flip and cook the other side. The pancakes should be quite thin. Repeat with the remaining batter to make 20–24 pancakes in all. Pile the cooked pancakes on top of each other, with a layer of baking parchment between each to prevent them sticking. Wrap in foil and keep warm in a low oven.

4 Make the cooked filling for the popiah. Heat the oil in a wok and stir-fry the onion and garlic together for 5 minutes until softened but not browned. Add the pork, crab meat or prawns, bamboo shoot and grated yam bean or water chestnuts. Stir-fry the mixture over a medium heat for 2–3 minutes.

5 Add the salted yellow beans and soy sauce to the wok, with pepper to taste. Cover and cook the beans gently for 15–20 minutes, adding a little boiling water if the mixture starts to dry out. Spoon into a serving bowl and allow to cool.

6 Meanwhile, arrange the chopped hard-boiled eggs, sliced Chinese sausages, sliced tofu, beansprouts, crab meat or prawns, cucumber matchsticks, finely chopped spring onions and lettuce leaves in piles on a large platter or in separate bowls. Spoon the bottled chopped chillies, bottled chopped garlic and hoisin into small bowls.

7 To serve, arrange the popiah on a large warm platter. Each person makes up his or her own popiah by spreading a very small amount of chopped chilli, garlic or hoisin sauce on a pancake, adding a lettuce leaf, a little of the cooked filling and a small selection of the fresh ingredients. The pancake wrapper should not be over-filled.

8 The ends can be tucked in and the pancake rolled up in typical spring roll fashion, then eaten in the hand. They also look attractive simply rolled with the filling showing. The popiah can be filled and rolled before guests arrive, in which case, garnish with sprigs of coriander. It is more fun though for everyone to fill and roll their own.

Energy 94kcal/396kJ; Protein 6.7g; Carbohydrate 10g, of which sugars 0.7g; Fat 3.4g, of which saturates 0.8g, of which polyunsaturates 0.8g; Cholesterol 88mg; Calcium 60mg; Fibre 0.6g; Sodium 109mg.

CRUNCHY SUMMER ROLLS ★

THESE DELIGHTFUL RICE PAPER ROLLS FILLED WITH CRUNCHY RAW SUMMER VEGETABLES AND FRESH MINT AND CORIANDER ARE LIGHT AND REFRESHING, EITHER AS A SNACK OR AN APPETIZER TO A MEAL, AND ARE ENJOYED ALL OVER VIETNAM AND CAMBODIA.

SERVES FOUR

INGREDIENTS

12 round rice papers
1 lettuce, leaves separated and
    ribs removed
2–3 carrots, cut into julienne strips
1 small cucumber, peeled, halved
    lengthways and seeded, and cut
    into julienne strips
3 spring onions (scallions), trimmed
    and cut into julienne strips
225g/8oz mung beansprouts
1 bunch fresh mint leaves
1 bunch coriander (cilantro) leaves
dipping sauce, to serve
    (see Cook's Tips)

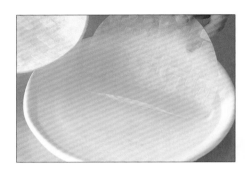

1 Pour some lukewarm water into a shallow dish. Soak the rice papers, 2–3 at a time, for about 5 minutes until they are pliable. Place the soaked papers on a clean dish towel and cover with a second dish towel to keep them moist.

2 Work with one paper at a time. Place a lettuce leaf towards the edge nearest to you, leaving about 2.5cm/1in to fold over. Place a mixture of the vegetables on top, followed by some mint and coriander leaves.

3 Fold the edge nearest to you over the filling, tuck in the sides, and roll tightly to the edge on the far side. Place the filled roll on a plate and cover with clear film (plastic wrap), so it doesn't dry out. Repeat with the remaining rice papers and vegetables. Serve with a dipping sauce of your choice. If you are making these summer rolls ahead of time, keep them in the refrigerator under a damp dish towel, so that they remain moist.

COOK'S TIPS
• In Vietnam, these crunchy filled rolls are often served with a light peanut dipping sauce. In Cambodia, they are accompanied by a dipping sauce called *tuk trey* (also the name of the national fish sauce), which is similar to the Vietnamese dipping sauce, *nuoc cham*, except that it has chopped peanuts in it. They are, in fact, delicious with any dipping sauce.
• Rice papers can be bought in Chinese and South-east Asian markets.

VARIATION
This recipe only uses vegetables, which are cut into equal lengths, but you can also add pre-cooked shredded lean chicken, pork or prawns (shrimp) to summer rolls.

Energy 107kcal/447kJ; Protein 3.9g; Carbohydrate 20.6g, of which sugars 4.4g; Fat 0.9g, of which saturates 0.1g, of which polyunsaturates 0.3g; Cholesterol 0mg; Calcium 62mg; Fibre 2.9g; Sodium 16mg.

CRISPY SPRING ROLLS ★

IT IS SAID THAT THESE FAMOUS SNACKS WERE TRADITIONALLY SERVED WITH TEA WHEN VISITORS CAME TO CALL AFTER THE NEW YEAR. AS THIS WAS SPRINGTIME, THEY CAME TO BE KNOWN AS SPRING ROLLS. BUY FRESH OR FROZEN SPRING ROLL WRAPPERS FROM ASIAN STORES.

MAKES TWELVE

INGREDIENTS
  12 spring roll wrappers, thawed
    if frozen
  30ml/2 tbsp plain (all-purpose) flour
    mixed to a paste with water
For the filling
  6 Chinese dried mushrooms,
    soaked for 30 minutes in
    warm water
  150g/5oz fresh firm tofu
  15ml/1 tbsp sunflower oil
  225g/8oz finely minced (ground)
    lean pork
  225g/8oz peeled cooked prawns
    (shrimp), roughly chopped
  2.5ml/½ tsp cornflour (cornstarch),
    mixed to a paste with 15ml/1 tbsp
    light soy sauce
  75g/3oz each shredded bamboo shoot
    or grated carrot, sliced water
    chestnuts and beansprouts
  6 spring onions (scallions) or 1 young
    leek, finely chopped
  2.5ml/½ tsp sesame oil
For the dipping sauce
  100ml/3½ fl oz/scant ½ cup
    light soy sauce
  15ml/1 tbsp chilli sauce or finely
    chopped fresh red chilli
  a little sesame oil
  rice vinegar, to taste

1 Make the filling. Drain the mushrooms. Cut off and discard the stems and slice the caps finely. Cut the tofu into slices of a similar size.

2 Heat the oil in a wok and stir-fry the pork for 2–3 minutes or until the colour changes. Add the prawns, cornflour paste and bamboo shoot or carrot. Stir in the water chestnuts.

COOK'S TIP
Thaw frozen spring roll wrappers at room temperature. Separate with a metal spatula. Cover with a damp cloth until needed.

3 Increase the heat, add the beansprouts and finely chopped spring onions or leek and toss the mixture for 1 minute. Stir in the dried Chinese mushrooms and tofu.

4 Off the heat, season the mixture to taste, and then stir in the sesame oil. Cool quickly on a large platter.

5 Separate the spring roll wrappers (see Cook's Tip). Place a wrapper on the work surface with one corner nearest you. Spoon some of the filling near the centre of the wrapper and fold the nearest corner over the filling. Smear a little of the flour paste on the free sides, turn the sides to the middle and roll up. Repeat this procedure with the remaining wrappers and filling.

6 Preheat the oven to 200°C/400°F/ Gas 6. Prepare a non-stick baking sheet or line a baking sheet with non-stick baking parchment. Lightly whisk the egg white with the oil and 5ml/1 tsp water. Generously brush the spring rolls with egg white, so they are moistened all over, and place on the baking sheet. Bake for about 20 minutes, until crisp and golden.

Energy 83kcal/349kJ; Protein 9.5g; Carbohydrate 7.9g, of which sugars 1.4g; Fat 1.7g, of which saturates 0.4g, of which polyunsaturates 0.5g; Cholesterol 48mg; Calcium 97mg; Fibre 0.5g; Sodium 645mg.

THAI SPRING ROLLS ★

CRUNCHY SPRING ROLLS ARE A POPULAR SNACK IN THAILAND. THAIS FILL THEIR VERSION WITH A DELICIOUS GARLIC, PORK AND NOODLE MIXTURE.

MAKES ABOUT TWENTY-FOUR

INGREDIENTS
24 × 15cm/6in square spring
  roll wrappers
30ml/2 tbsp plain (all-purpose) flour
1 egg white
5ml/1 tsp sunflower oil
Thai sweet chilli dipping sauce,
  to serve (optional)
For the filling
4–6 Chinese dried mushrooms,
  soaked for 30 minutes in warm
  water to cover
50g/2oz cellophane noodles
15ml/1 tbsp sunflower oil
2 garlic cloves, chopped
2 fresh red chillies, seeded
  and chopped
225g/8oz minced (ground) lean pork
50g/2oz peeled cooked prawns
  (shrimp), thawed if frozen
30ml/2 tbsp Thai fish sauce
5ml/1 tsp sugar
1 carrot, grated
50g/2oz drained canned bamboo
  shoots, chopped
50g/2oz/1 cup beansprouts
2 spring onions, finely chopped
15ml/1 tbsp chopped fresh
  coriander (cilantro)
ground black pepper

1 Drain the mushrooms. Cut off the stems and discard; chop the caps finely.

2 Place the noodles in a large bowl, cover with boiling water and soak for 10 minutes. Drain the noodles and snip them into 5cm/2in lengths.

3 Heat the oil in a wok, add the garlic and chillies and stir-fry for 30 seconds. Transfer to a plate, add the pork and cook, stirring, until it has browned and is cooked through.

4 Add the noodles, mushrooms and prawns to the wok. Stir in the Thai fish sauce and sugar, then add ground black pepper to taste.

5 Tip the noodle mixture into a bowl and stir in the grated carrot, chopped bamboo shoots, beansprouts, finely chopped spring onions and chopped coriander together with the reserved chilli and pork mixture.

COOK'S TIP
Thai fish sauce or *nam pla* is one of the most important ingredients in Thai cuisine. It is made from fish, usually anchovies, which are salted, then fermented in wooden barrels to create the thin liquid that is the basis of the sauce. The strong flavour becomes less pronounced with cooking, and does not necessarily impart a fishy flavour to the dish.

6 Unwrap the spring roll wrappers. Cover them with a dampened dish towel while you are making the rolls, so that they do not dry out. Put the flour in a small bowl and stir in a little water to make a paste. Place a spoonful of filling in the centre of a spring roll wrapper.

7 Turn the bottom edge over to cover the filling, then fold in the left and right sides. Roll the wrapper up almost to the top then brush the top edge with the flour paste and seal. Fill the remaining wrappers in the same way, thinning the paste with a little water if it is too thick.

8 Preheat the oven to 220°C/425°F/ Gas 7. Prepare a non-stick baking sheet or line a baking sheet with baking parchment. Lightly whisk the egg white with the sunflower oil and 5ml/1 tsp water. Brush the spring rolls generously with egg white, so that they are moistened all over, and place on the baking tray. Bake for about 10 minutes, until lightly browned and crisp. Serve hot with Thai sweet chilli sauce, if you like.

Energy 46kcal/193kJ; Protein 3.3g; Carbohydrate 6.9g, of which sugars 0.7g; Fat 0.6g, of which saturates 0.2g, of which polyunsaturates 0.2g; Cholesterol 10mg; Calcium 17mg; Fibre 0.4g; Sodium 15mg.

LEMON GRASS SNAILS ★

THE LIVE SNAILS SOLD IN VIETNAMESE MARKETS ARE USUALLY DESTINED FOR THIS POPULAR DELICACY. SERVED STRAIGHT FROM THE BAMBOO STEAMER, THESE LEMON GRASS-INFUSED MORSELS ARE SERVED AS AN APPETIZER, OR AS A SPECIAL SNACK, DIPPED IN NUOC CHAM.

SERVES FOUR

INGREDIENTS
  12 fresh snails in their shells
  115g/4oz lean minced (ground) pork,
    passed through the mincer twice
  2 lemon grass stalks, trimmed
    and finely chopped or ground
    (reserve the outer leaves)
  1 spring onion (scallions),
    finely chopped
  15g/½oz fresh root ginger, peeled
    and finely grated
  1 red Thai chilli, seeded and
    finely chopped
  5ml/1 tsp sesame oil
  sea salt and ground black pepper
  nuoc cham or other sauce,
    for dipping

2 Chop the snails finely and put them in a bowl. Add the minced pork, lemon grass, spring onions, ginger, chilli and oil. Season with salt and pepper and mix all the ingredients together.

3 Select the best of the lemon grass leaves and tear each one into thin ribbons, roughly 7.5cm/3in long. Bend each ribbon in half and put it inside a snail shell, so that the ends are poking out. The idea is that each diner pulls the ends of the lemon grass ribbon to gently prize the steamed morsel out of its shell.

COOK'S TIP
Freshwater snails in their shells are available in South-east Asian markets, and some supermarkets and delicatessens. The idea of eating snails may have come from the French, who colonized Vietnam and Cambodia in the 19th and 20th centuries, but the method of cooking them in Vietnam is very different. Snails are plucked live from the water, straight into the bamboo steamer. If you ask for snails in a Vietnamese restaurant, they are likely to be cooked this way.

4 Using your fingers, stuff each shell with the snail and pork mixture, gently pushing it between the lemon grass ends to the back of the shell so that it fills the shell completely.

5 Fill a wok or large pan a third of the way up with water and bring it to the boil. Arrange the snail shells, open side up, in a steamer that fits the wok or pan.

6 Place the lid on the steamer and steam for about 10 minutes, until the mixture is cooked. Serve hot with *nuoc cham* or another strong-flavoured dipping sauce of your choice, such as soy sauce spiked with chopped chillies.

1 Pull the snails out of their shells and place them in a colander. Rinse the snails thoroughly in plenty of cold water and pat dry with kitchen paper. Rinse the shells and leave to drain.

Energy 85kcal/357kJ; Protein 12g; Carbohydrate 0.4g, of which sugars 0.4g; Fat 4g, of which saturates 1.2g, of which polyunsaturates 0.9g; Cholesterol 36mg; Calcium 29mg; Fibre 0.7g; Sodium 38mg.

VEGETARIAN MAIN DISHES

Combined with nuts and tofu in moderation, vegetarian dishes

provide a healthy basis for many delicious meals. The wide

range of different vegetables, together with herbs, spices and

sauces, makes Asian cooking a real pleasure for vegetarians

trying to cut down on fat and cholesterol in their diet.

An added attraction is that most dishes are very quick and

easy to make. Aromatic vegetable curries, unusual stir-fries,

stuffed vegetables and a warming stew are included here.

STUFFED SWEET PEPPERS ★

THIS IS AN UNUSUAL RECIPE IN THAT THE STUFFED PEPPERS ARE STEAMED RATHER THAN BAKED. THE FILLING INCORPORATES TYPICAL Thai INGREDIENTS SUCH AS RED CURRY PASTE AND KAFFIR LIME LEAVES.

SERVES FOUR

INGREDIENTS
3 garlic cloves, finely chopped
2 coriander (cilantro) roots,
   finely chopped
400g/14oz/3 cups
   mushrooms, quartered
5ml/1 tsp Thai vegetarian red
   curry paste
1 egg, lightly beaten
15ml/1 tbsp light soy sauce
2.5ml/½ tsp granulated sugar
3 kaffir lime leaves, finely chopped
4 yellow (bell) peppers, halved
   lengthways and seeded

VARIATIONS
For extra colour use red or orange (bell)
peppers if you prefer, or a combination
of the two.

1 In a mortar or spice grinder pound
or blend the garlic with the coriander
roots. Scrape into a bowl.

2 Put the mushrooms in a food
processor and pulse briefly until they
are finely chopped. Add to the garlic
and coriander mixture, then stir in the
curry paste, egg, soy sauce, sugar and
lime leaves.

3 Place the pepper halves in a single
layer in two steamer baskets. Spoon the
mushroom mixture loosely into the
pepper halves. Do not pack the mixture
down tightly or the filling will dry out too
much. Bring the water in the steamer
to the boil, then lower the heat to a
simmer. Steam the peppers for
15 minutes, or until the flesh is tender.
Serve hot.

Energy 95kcal/399kJ; Protein 5.6g; Carbohydrate 12.8g, of which sugars 12g; Fat 2.8g, of which saturates 0.7g, of which polyunsaturates 0.8g; Cholesterol 48mg; Calcium 53mg; Fibre 4.5g; Sodium 301mg.

CORN AND CASHEW NUT CURRY ★★

A SUBSTANTIAL CURRY, THIS COMBINES ALL THE ESSENTIAL FLAVOURS OF SOUTHERN THAILAND. IT IS DELICIOUSLY AROMATIC, BUT THE FLAVOUR IS FAIRLY MILD.

SERVES FOUR

INGREDIENTS
5ml/1 tsp sunflower oil
4 shallots, chopped
50g/2oz/½ cup cashew nuts
5ml/1 tsp Thai vegetarian red
  curry paste
400g/14oz potatoes, peeled and cut
  into chunks
1 lemon grass stalk, finely chopped
200g/7oz can chopped tomatoes
600ml/1 pint/2½ cups boiling water
200g/7oz/generous 1 cup drained
  canned whole kernel corn
4 celery sticks, sliced
2 kaffir lime leaves, rolled into
  cylinders and thinly sliced
15ml/1 tbsp tomato ketchup
15ml/1 tbsp light soy sauce
5ml/1 tsp palm sugar or light
  muscovado (brown) sugar
4 spring onions (scallions), sliced
small bunch fresh basil, chopped

1 Heat the oil in a large, heavy pan or wok. Add the shallots and stir-fry over a medium heat for 2–3 minutes, until softened. Add the cashew nuts and stir-fry for a few minutes until golden.

2 Stir in the red curry paste. Stir-fry for 1 minute, then add the potatoes, lemon grass, tomatoes and boiling water.

3 Bring back to the boil, then reduce the heat to low, cover and simmer gently for 15–20 minutes, or until the potatoes are tender.

4 Stir the corn, celery, lime leaves, tomato ketchup, soy sauce and sugar into the pan or wok. Simmer for a further 5 minutes, until heated through, then spoon into warmed serving bowls. Sprinkle with the sliced spring onions and basil and serve.

COOK'S TIP
Rolling the lime leaves into cylinders before slicing produces very fine strips – a technique known as cutting *en chiffonnade*. Remove the central rib from the leaves before cutting them.

Energy 246kcal/1037kJ; Protein 6.9g; Carbohydrate 38.3g, of which sugars 12.7g; Fat 8.3g, of which saturates 1.6g, of which polyunsaturates 2.1g; Cholesterol 0mg; Calcium 40mg; Fibre 3.5g; Sodium 535mg.

AUBERGINE CURRY WITH COCONUT MILK ★

AUBERGINE CURRIES ARE POPULAR THROUGHOUT SOUTH-EAST ASIA, THE THAI VERSION BEING THE MOST FAMOUS. ALL ARE HOT AND AROMATIC, ENHANCED WITH REDUCED-FAT COCONUT MILK. THIS CAMBODIAN RECIPE USES THE TRADEMARK HERBAL PASTE, KROEUNG.

2 Stir in the coconut milk and stock, and add the aubergines and lime leaves.

3 Partially cover the pan and simmer over a gentle heat for about 25 minutes until the aubergines are tender. Stir in the basil and check the seasoning. Serve with jasmine rice and lime wedges.

SERVES FOUR

INGREDIENTS
    15ml/1 tbsp sunflower oil
    4 garlic cloves, crushed
    2 shallots, sliced
    2 dried chillies
    45ml/3 tbsp *kroeung*
    15ml/1 tbsp palm sugar
    300ml/½ pint/1¼ cups reduced-fat
       coconut milk
    550ml/18fl oz/2¼ cups vegetable stock
    4 aubergines (eggplants), trimmed
       and cut into bitesize pieces
    6 kaffir lime leaves
    1 bunch fresh basil, stalks removed
    jasmine rice and 2 limes, cut into
       quarters, to serve
    salt and ground black pepper

1 Heat the sunflower oil in a wok or heavy pan until sizzling. Stir in the crushed garlic cloves, sliced shallots and whole chillies and stir-fry for a few minutes until they begin to colour. Stir in the *kroeung*, and palm sugar and stir-fry until the mixture begins to darken.

Energy 80kcal/338kJ; Protein 1g; Carbohydrate 12.3g, of which sugars 11.9g; Fat 3.4g, of which saturates 0.6g, of which polyunsaturates 1.9g; Cholesterol 0mg; Calcium 47mg; Fibre 1.2g; Sodium 139mg.

GLAZED PUMPKIN IN COCONUT MILK ★

PUMPKINS, BUTTERNUT SQUASH AND WINTER MELONS CAN ALL BE COOKED IN THIS WAY. THROUGHOUT SOUTH-EAST ASIA, VARIATIONS OF THIS SWEET, MELLOW DISH ARE SERVED AS A MAIN COURSE OR AS AN ACCOMPANIMENT TO RICE OR A SPICY CURRY.

SERVES FOUR

INGREDIENTS
200ml/7fl oz/scant 1 cup
  reduced-fat coconut milk
15ml/1 tbsp *kroeung*
30ml/2 tbsp palm sugar
15ml/1 tbsp sunflower oil
4 garlic cloves, finely chopped
25g/1oz fresh root ginger, peeled and
  finely shredded
675g/1½lb pumpkin flesh, cubed
ground black pepper
a handful of curry or basil leaves,
  to garnish
fried onion rings, to garnish
plain rice, to serve

1 In a bowl, beat the coconut milk and the *kroeung* with the sugar, until it has dissolved. Set aside.

2 Heat the oil in a wok or heavy pan and stir in the garlic and ginger. Stir-fry until they begin to colour, then stir in the pumpkin cubes, mixing well.

3 Pour in the reduced-fat coconut milk and mix well. Reduce the heat, cover and simmer for about 20 minutes, until the pumpkin is tender and the sauce has reduced. Season with ground black pepper and garnish with curry or basil leaves and fried onion rings. Serve hot with plain rice.

Energy 92kcal/386kJ; Protein 1.8g; Carbohydrate 14.4g, of which sugars 13.5g; Fat 3.4g, of which saturates 0.6g, of which polyunsaturates 1.8g; Cholesterol 0mg; Calcium 93mg; Fibre 2.3g; Sodium 60mg.

TOFU AND GREEN BEAN RED CURRY ★

THIS IS ONE OF THOSE VERSATILE RECIPES THAT SHOULD BE IN EVERY COOK'S REPERTOIRE. THIS VERSION USES GREEN BEANS, BUT OTHER TYPES OF VEGETABLE WORK EQUALLY WELL. THE LOW-FAT TOFU TAKES ON THE FLAVOUR OF THE SPICE PASTE AND ALSO BOOSTS THE NUTRITIONAL VALUE.

SERVES FOUR

INGREDIENTS
    200ml/7fl oz/scant 1 cup reduced-fat
    coconut milk
    15ml/1 tbsp Thai vegetarian red
    curry paste
    10ml/2 tsp palm sugar or light
    muscovado (brown) sugar
    225g/8oz/3¼ cups button
    (white) mushrooms
    400ml/14fl oz/1⅔ cups
    vegetable stock
    115g/4oz/1 cup green beans, trimmed
    175g/6oz firm tofu, rinsed, drained
    and cut in 2cm/¾ in cubes
    4 kaffir lime leaves, torn
    2 fresh red chillies, seeded and sliced
    fresh coriander (cilantro) leaves,
    to garnish

1 Pour the reduced-fat coconut milk into a wok or pan. Cook until the coconut milk starts to separate and an oily sheen appears on the surface.

2 Add the red curry paste and sugar to the coconut milk. Mix thoroughly, then add the mushrooms. Stir and cook for 1 minute.

3 Stir in the stock. Bring back to the boil, then add the green beans and tofu cubes. Simmer gently for 4–5 minutes more.

4 Stir in the kaffir lime leaves and sliced red chillies. Spoon the curry into a serving dish, garnish with the coriander leaves and serve immediately.

Energy 67kcal/282kJ; Protein 5.3g; Carbohydrate 6.5g, of which sugars 6g; Fat 2.4g, of which saturates 0.4g, of which polyunsaturates 1.1g; Cholesterol 0mg; Calcium 253mg; Fibre 1.3g; Sodium 60mg.

SNAKE BEANS WITH TOFU ★★

ANOTHER NAME FOR SNAKE BEANS IS YARD-LONG BEANS. THIS IS SOMETHING OF AN EXAGGERATION BUT THEY DO GROW TO LENGTHS OF 40CM/16IN AND MORE. LOOK FOR THEM IN ASIAN STORES AND MARKETS, BUT IF YOU CAN'T FIND ANY, SUBSTITUTE OTHER GREEN BEANS.

SERVES FOUR

INGREDIENTS

500g/1¼lb long beans, thinly sliced
200g/7oz silken tofu, cut into cubes
2 shallots, thinly sliced
200ml/7fl oz/scant 1 cup reduced-fat
  coconut milk
25g/1oz roasted peanuts, chopped
juice of 1 lime
10ml/2 tsp palm sugar or light
  muscovado (brown) sugar
60ml/4 tbsp soy sauce
5ml/1 tsp dried chilli flakes

VARIATIONS
The sauce also works very well with mangetouts (snow peas). Alternatively, for a brightly coloured variation, stir in sliced yellow or red (bell) pepper.

1 Bring a pan of lightly salted water to the boil. Add the beans and blanch them for 30 seconds.

2 Drain the beans immediately, then refresh under cold water and drain again, shaking well to remove as much water as possible. Place in a serving bowl and set aside.

3 Put the tofu and shallots in a pan with the coconut milk. Heat gently, stirring, until the tofu begins to crumble.

4 Add the peanuts, lime juice, sugar, soy sauce and chilli flakes. Heat, stirring, until the sugar has dissolved. Pour the sauce over the beans, toss to combine and serve immediately.

Energy 167kcal/697kJ; Protein 9.9g; Carbohydrate 12.9g, of which sugars 9.3g; Fat 10g, of which saturates 1g, of which polyunsaturates 2.2g; Cholesterol 7mg; Calcium 327mg; Fibre 3.4g; Sodium 191mg.

Tofu and Vegetable Thai Curry ★★

Traditional Thai ingredients — chillies, galangal, lemon grass and kaffir lime leaves — give this curry a wonderfully fragrant aroma. The tofu needs to marinate for at least 2 hours, so bear this in mind when timing your meal.

SERVES FOUR

INGREDIENTS

  175g/6oz firm tofu
  45ml/3 tbsp dark soy sauce
  5ml/1 tsp sesame oil
  5ml/1 tsp chilli sauce
  2.5cm/1in piece fresh root ginger,
    peeled and finely grated
  1 head broccoli, about 225g/8oz
  ½ head cauliflower, about 225g/8oz
  15ml/1 tbsp sunflower oil
  1 onion, sliced
  200ml/7fl oz/scant 1 cup reduced-fat
    coconut milk
  350ml/12fl oz/1½ cups water
  1 red (bell) pepper, seeded
    and chopped
  175g/6oz/generous 1 cup green
    beans, halved
  115g/4oz/1½ cups shiitake or button
    (white) mushrooms, halved
  shredded spring onions (scallions),
    to garnish
  boiled jasmine rice or noodles,
    to serve
For the curry paste
  2 fresh red or green chillies, seeded
    and chopped
  1 lemon grass stalk, chopped
  2.5cm/1in piece fresh
    galangal, chopped
  2 kaffir lime leaves
  10ml/2 tsp ground coriander
  a few fresh coriander (cilantro)
    sprigs, including the stalks
  45ml/3 tbsp water

1 Rinse and drain the tofu. Using a sharp knife, cut it into 2.5cm/1in cubes. Place the cubes in the base of an ovenproof dish in a single layer.

2 Mix together the soy sauce, sesame oil, chilli sauce and grated ginger in a jug (pitcher) and pour over the tofu. Toss gently to coat all the cubes evenly, cover with clear film (plastic wrap) and leave to marinate for at least 2 hours or overnight if possible, turning and basting the tofu occasionally.

3 Make the curry paste. Place the chillies, lemon grass, galangal, lime leaves, ground coriander and fresh coriander in a food processor and process until well blended. Add the water and process to a thick paste.

4 Preheat the oven to 190°C/375°F/Gas 5. Cut the broccoli and cauliflower into small florets. Cut any stalks into thin slices.

5 Heat the sunflower oil in a frying pan and add the sliced onion. Cook over a low heat for about 8 minutes, until soft and lightly browned. Stir in the curry paste and the coconut milk. Add the water and bring to the boil.

6 Stir in the red pepper, green beans, broccoli and cauliflower. Transfer to a Chinese sand pot or earthenware casserole. Cover and place towards the bottom of the oven.

7 Stir the tofu and marinade, then place the dish on a shelf near the top of the oven. Cook for 30 minutes. Remove both the dish and the sand pot or casserole from the oven. Add the tofu, with any remaining marinade, to the curry, with the mushrooms, and stir well.

8 Return the sand pot or casserole to the oven, reduce the temperature to 180°C/350°F/Gas 4 and cook for about 15 minutes, or until the vegetables are tender. Garnish with the spring onions and serve with the rice or noodles.

COOK'S TIP
Tofu or beancurd is made from soya beans and is sold in blocks. It is a creamy white colour and naturally low in fat. Tofu has a bland flavour and its absorbent nature means that it takes on the flavours of marinades or other foods with which it is cooked.

Energy 155kcal/646kJ; Protein 10.9g; Carbohydrate 12.2g, of which sugars 10.5g; Fat 7.2g, of which saturates 1.1g, of which polyunsaturates 3.8g; Cholesterol 0mg; Calcium 333mg; Fibre 5.3g; Sodium 875mg.

SWEET AND SOUR VEGETABLES WITH TOFU ★

BIG, BOLD AND BEAUTIFUL, THIS IS A HEARTY STIR-FRY THAT WILL SATISFY THE HUNGRIEST GUESTS. IT IS PACKED WITH COLOURFUL VEGETABLES INCLUDING CORN COBS, RED PEPPERS AND GREEN MANGETOUTS.

SERVES FOUR

INGREDIENTS
    4 shallots
    3 garlic cloves
    15ml/1 tbsp sunflower oil
    250g/9oz Chinese leaves (Chinese
       cabbage), shredded
    8 baby corn cobs, sliced on
       the diagonal
    2 red (bell) peppers, seeded and
       thinly sliced
    200g/7oz/1¾ cups mangetouts
       (snow peas), trimmed and sliced
    250g/9oz tofu, rinsed, drained and
       cut in 1cm/½in cubes
    60ml/4 tbsp vegetable stock
    30ml/2 tbsp light soy sauce
    15ml/1 tbsp granulated sugar
    30ml/2 tbsp rice vinegar
    2.5ml/½ tsp dried chilli flakes
    small bunch coriander
       (cilantro), chopped

1 Slice the shallots thinly using a sharp knife. Finely chop the garlic.

2 Heat the oil in a wok or large frying pan and cook the shallots and garlic for 2–3 minutes over a medium heat, until golden. Do not let the garlic burn or it will taste bitter.

3 Add the shredded cabbage, toss over the heat for 30 seconds, then add the corn cobs and repeat the process.

4 Add the red peppers, mangetouts and tofu in the same way, each time adding a single ingredient and tossing it over the heat for about 30 seconds before adding the next ingredient.

5 Pour in the stock and soy sauce. Mix together the sugar and vinegar in a small bowl, stirring until the sugar has dissolved, then add to the wok or pan. Sprinkle over the chilli flakes and coriander, toss to mix well and serve.

Energy 144kcal/604kJ; Protein 5.2g; Carbohydrate 23.7g, of which sugars 18.2g; Fat 3.7g, of which saturates 0.5g, of which polyunsaturates 2.2g; Cholesterol 0mg; Calcium 73mg; Fibre 4.7g; Sodium 611mg.

SPICY TOFU WITH BASIL AND PEANUTS ★★

AROMATIC PEPPER LEAVES ARE OFTEN USED AS THE HERB ELEMENT IN THAILAND BUT, BECAUSE THESE ARE QUITE DIFFICULT TO FIND OUTSIDE SOUTH-EAST ASIA, YOU CAN USE BASIL LEAVES INSTEAD.

SERVES FOUR

INGREDIENTS

3 lemon grass stalks, finely chopped
45ml/3 tbsp soy sauce
2 red Serrano chillies, seeded and
   finely chopped
2 garlic cloves, crushed
5ml/1 tsp ground turmeric
10ml/2 tsp sugar
300g/11oz tofu, rinsed, drained,
   patted dry and cut into
   bitesize cubes
15ml/1 tbsp sunflower oil
15ml/1 tbsp roasted peanuts,
   chopped
1 bunch fresh basil, stalks removed
salt

1 In a bowl, mix together the lemon grass, soy sauce, chillies, garlic, turmeric and sugar until the sugar has dissolved. Add a little salt to taste and add the tofu, making sure it is well coated. Leave to marinate for 1 hour.

VARIATION
Replace the fresh basil with kaffir lime leaves, coriander (cilantro) leaves or curry leaves, all of which would work well in this simple stir-fry.

2 Heat a wok or heavy pan. Pour in the oil, add the marinated tofu, and cook, stirring frequently, until it is golden brown on all sides. Add the peanuts and most of the basil leaves.

3 Divide the marinated tofu and peanut mixture among individual serving dishes. Then sprinkle the remaining basil leaves over the top and serve hot or at room temperature.

Energy 115kcal/480kJ; Protein 7.4g; Carbohydrate 4.5g, of which sugars 3.9g; Fat 7.6g, of which saturates 1g, of which polyunsaturates 3.7g; Cholesterol 0mg; Calcium 388mg; Fibre 0.2g; Sodium 804mg.

THAI VEGETABLE CURRY WITH LEMON GRASS RICE ★

FRAGRANT JASMINE RICE, SUBTLY FLAVOURED WITH LEMON GRASS AND CARDAMOM, IS THE PERFECT ACCOMPANIMENT FOR THIS RICHLY SPICED VEGETABLE CURRY.

SERVES FOUR

INGREDIENTS
10ml/2 tsp sunflower oil
200ml/7fl oz/scant 1 cup reduced-fat coconut milk
550ml/18fl oz/2½ cups vegetable stock
225g/8oz new potatoes, halved or quartered, if large
8 baby corn cobs
5ml/1 tsp golden caster (superfine) sugar
185g/6½oz/1¼ cups broccoli florets
1 red (bell) pepper, seeded and sliced lengthways
115g/4oz spinach, tough stalks removed, leaves shredded
30ml/2 tbsp chopped fresh coriander (cilantro)
salt and ground black pepper
For the spice paste
1 fresh red chilli, seeded and chopped
3 fresh green chillies, seeded and chopped
1 lemon grass stalk, outer leaves removed and lower 5cm/2in finely chopped
2 shallots, chopped
finely grated rind of 1 lime
2 garlic cloves, chopped
5ml/1 tsp ground coriander
2.5ml/½ tsp ground cumin
1cm/½in piece fresh galangal, finely chopped, or 2.5ml/½ tsp dried galangal (optional)
30ml/2 tbsp chopped fresh coriander (cilantro)
15ml/1 tbsp chopped fresh coriander (cilantro) roots and stems (optional)
For the rice
225g/8oz/1¼ cups jasmine rice, rinsed
6 cardamom pods, bruised
1 lemon grass stalk, outer leaves removed, cut into 3 pieces
475ml/16fl oz/2 cups water

1 Make the spice paste. Place all the ingredients in a food processor and process to a coarse paste. Heat the oil in a large, heavy pan. Add the paste and stir-fry over a medium heat for 1–2 minutes, until fragrant.

2 Pour in the coconut milk and stock and bring to the boil. Reduce the heat, add the potatoes and simmer gently for about 15 minutes, until almost tender.

3 Meanwhile, put the rice into a large pan with the cardamoms and lemon grass. Pour in the water. Bring to the boil, reduce the heat, cover, and cook for 10–15 minutes, until the water has been absorbed and the rice is tender.

4 When the rice is cooked and slightly sticky, season to taste with salt, then replace the lid and leave to stand for about 10 minutes.

5 Add the baby corn to the potatoes, season with salt and pepper to taste, then cook for 2 minutes. Stir in the sugar, broccoli and red pepper, and cook for 2 minutes more, or until the vegetables are tender.

6 Stir the shredded spinach and half the fresh coriander into the vegetable mixture. Cook for 2 minutes, then spoon the curry into a warmed serving dish.

7 Remove and discard the cardamom pods and lemon grass from the rice and fluff up the grains with a fork. Garnish the curry with the remaining fresh coriander and serve with the rice.

COOK'S TIP
Cardamom pods may be dark brown, cream, or pale green. The brown pods are usually larger, coarser and do not have such a good flavour as the others. Always remove them before serving.

Energy 313kcal/1313kJ; Protein 9.8g; Carbohydrate 61.4g, of which sugars 7.7g; Fat 3.2g, of which saturates 0.5g, of which polyunsaturates 1.5g; Cholesterol 0mg; Calcium 134mg; Fibre 4.1g; Sodium 439mg.

VEGETABLE FOREST CURRY ★

THIS IS A THIN, SOUPY CURRY WITH LOTS OF FRESH GREEN VEGETABLES AND ROBUST FLAVOURS. IN THE FORESTED REGIONS OF THAILAND, WHERE IT ORIGINATED, IT WOULD BE MADE USING EDIBLE WILD LEAVES AND ROOTS. SERVE IT WITH RICE OR NOODLES FOR A SIMPLE LUNCH OR SUPPER.

SERVES TWO

INGREDIENTS
  600ml/1 pint/2½ cups water
  5ml/1 tsp Thai vegetarian red
    curry paste
  5cm/2in piece fresh galangal or fresh
    root ginger
  90g/3½oz/scant 1 cup green beans
  2 kaffir lime leaves, torn
  8 baby corn cobs, halved widthways
  2 heads Chinese broccoli, chopped
  90g/3½oz/generous
    3 cups beansprouts
  15ml/1 tbsp drained bottled green
    peppercorns, crushed
  10ml/2 tsp granulated sugar
  5ml/1 tsp salt

1 Heat the water in a large pan. Add the red curry paste and stir until it has dissolved completely. Bring to the boil.

2 Meanwhile, using a sharp knife, peel and finely chop the fresh galangal or root ginger.

3 Add the galangal or ginger, green beans, lime leaves, baby corn cobs, broccoli and beansprouts to the pan. Stir in the crushed peppercorns, sugar and salt. Bring back to the boil, then reduce the heat to low and simmer for 2 minutes. Serve immediately.

Energy 154kcal/643kJ; Protein 14.9g; Carbohydrate 14.1g, of which sugars 11.8g; Fat 4.5g, of which saturates 0.8g, of which polyunsaturates 2.4g; Cholesterol 0mg; Calcium 173mg; Fibre 9.1g; Sodium 678mg.

JUNGLE CURRY ★

VARIATIONS OF THIS FIERY, FLAVOURSOME VEGETARIAN CURRY CAN BE FOUND ALL OVER SOUTHERN VIETNAM. A FAVOURITE WITH THE BUDDHIST MONKS AND OFTEN SOLD FROM COUNTRYSIDE STALLS, IT CAN BE SERVED WITH PLAIN RICE OR NOODLES, OR CHUNKS OF CRUSTY BREAD.

SERVES FOUR

INGREDIENTS
15ml/1 tbsp sunflower oil
2 onions, roughly chopped
2 lemon grass stalks, roughly chopped and bruised
4 green Thai chillies, seeded and finely sliced
4cm/1½in galangal or fresh root ginger, peeled and chopped
3 carrots, peeled, halved lengthways and sliced
115g/4oz long beans
grated rind of 1 lime
10ml/2 tsp soy sauce
15ml/1 tbsp rice vinegar
5ml/1 tsp black peppercorns, crushed
15ml/1 tbsp sugar
10ml/2 tsp ground turmeric
115g/4oz canned bamboo shoots
75g/3oz spinach, steamed and roughly chopped
150ml/¼ pint/⅔ cup reduced-fat coconut milk
salt
chopped fresh coriander (cilantro) and mint leaves, to garnish

COOK'S TIPS
• Also known as yard-long beans or asparagus beans, snake beans are eaten all over South-east Asia. They may grow up to 40cm/16in long and can be found in Asian stores. There are two common varieties, pale green and darker green, the latter have the better flavour. When buying, choose young, narrow specimens with under-developed seeds, as these will be the most tender. They do not have strings, and preparation is simply trimming and chopping them into short lengths. As they mature, snake beans can become quite tough. They should be used before they turn yellow.
• Jungle curry should be fiery, almost dominated by the chilli. In Vietnam it is often eaten for breakfast or a great pick-me-up at any time of day.

1 Heat a wok or heavy pan and add the oil. Once hot, stir in the onions, lemon grass, chillies and galangal or ginger. Add the carrots and beans with the lime rind and stir-fry for 1–2 minutes.

2 Add the soy sauce and rice vinegar to the wok and stir well. Add the crushed peppercorns, sugar and turmeric, then stir in the bamboo shoots and the chopped spinach.

3 Stir in the coconut milk and simmer for about 10 minutes, until the vegetables are tender. Season with salt, and serve hot, garnished with fresh coriander and mint.

Energy 119kcal/496kJ; Protein 3.8g; Carbohydrate 18.6g, of which sugars 15.3g; Fat 3.8g, of which saturates 0.5g, of which polyunsaturates 2.2g; Cholesterol 0mg; Calcium 125mg; Fibre 4.3g; Sodium 60mg.

AUBERGINE AND SWEET POTATO STEW WITH COCONUT MILK ★

SCENTED WITH FRAGRANT LEMON GRASS, GINGER AND LOTS OF GARLIC, THIS IS A PARTICULARLY GOOD COMBINATION OF FLAVOURS. AUBERGINES AND SWEET POTATOES GO WELL TOGETHER AND THE COCONUT MILK ADDS A MELLOW NOTE.

SERVES SIX

INGREDIENTS

 400g/14oz baby aubergines
  (eggplant) or 2 standard aubergines
 15ml/1 tbsp sunflower oil
 225g/8oz Thai red shallots or other
  small shallots or pickling onions
 5ml/1 tsp fennel seeds,
  lightly crushed
 4–5 garlic cloves, thinly sliced
 25ml/1½ tbsp finely chopped fresh
  root ginger
 475ml/16fl oz/2 cups vegetable stock
 2 lemon grass stalks, outer layers
  discarded, finely chopped
  or minced
 15g/½oz/⅔ cup fresh coriander
  (cilantro), stalks and leaves
  chopped separately
 3 kaffir lime leaves, lightly bruised
 2–3 small fresh red chillies
 45ml/3 tbsp Thai green curry paste
 675g/1½lb sweet potatoes, peeled
  and cut into thick chunks
 400ml/14fl oz/1⅔ cups reduced-fat
  coconut milk
 2.5–5ml/½–1 tsp palm sugar
 250g/9oz/3½ cups mushrooms,
  thickly sliced
 juice of 1 lime, to taste
 salt and ground black pepper
 boiled rice and 18 fresh Thai basil
  or ordinary basil leaves, to serve

1 Trim the aubergines. Slice baby aubergines in half lengthways. Cut standard aubergines into chunks.

2 Heat half the oil in a wide pan or deep, lidded frying pan. Add the aubergines and cook (uncovered) over a medium heat, stirring occasionally, until lightly browned on all sides. Remove from the pan and set aside.

3 Slice 4–5 of the shallots. Cook the whole shallots in the oil remaining in the pan, until lightly browned. Set aside with the aubergines. Add the remaining oil to the pan and cook the sliced shallots, fennel seeds, garlic and ginger over a low heat for 5 minutes.

4 Pour in the vegetable stock, then add the lemon grass, chopped coriander stalks and any roots, lime leaves and whole chillies. Cover and simmer over a low heat for 5 minutes.

5 Stir in 30ml/2 tbsp of the curry paste and the sweet potatoes. Simmer gently for about 10 minutes, then return the aubergines and browned shallots to the pan and cook for a further 5 minutes.

6 Stir in the coconut milk and the sugar. Season to taste with salt and pepper, then stir in the mushrooms and simmer gently for 5 minutes, or until all the vegetables are cooked and tender.

7 Stir in the remaining curry paste and lime juice to taste, followed by the chopped coriander leaves. Adjust the seasoning and ladle the vegetables into warmed bowls. Sprinkle basil leaves over the stew and serve with rice.

COOK'S TIP

Although this is called a stew, green curry paste is an important ingredient, as it is in most of these recipes. The quantity given is only a guide, however, so use less if you prefer.

Energy 147kcal/627kJ; Protein 3.2g; Carbohydrate 29.1g, of which sugars 11.3g; Fat 3g, of which saturates 0.6g, of which polyunsaturates 1.5g; Cholesterol 0mg; Calcium 72mg; Fibre 4.9g; Sodium 125mg.

FISH AND SHELLFISH

Fish is a main source of protein in the Thai diet, which is hardly surprising considering the vast lengths of coastline. Oily fish contains Omega-3 fatty acids that help lower cholesterol and reduce blood pressure. Fish is steamed, stir-fried, baked, grilled with local spices or herbs, and served in curries and sauces. Serving a fish whole, rather than cutting it into portions, has great appeal in Asia. Impress your guests with Stir-fried Baby Squid with Ginger, Hot and Fragrant Trout or Spicy Pan-seared Tuna.

SINIGANG ★

MANY FILIPINOS WOULD CONSIDER THIS SOURED HEALTHY SOUP-LIKE STEW TO BE THEIR NATIONAL DISH. IT IS ALWAYS SERVED WITH NOODLES OR RICE. IN ADDITION, FISH — IN THE FORM OF EITHER PRAWNS OR THIN SLIVERS OF FISH FILLET — IS OFTEN ADDED FOR GOOD MEASURE.

3 Pour the prepared fish stock into a large pan and add the diced mooli. Cook the mooli for 5 minutes, then add the beans and continue to cook for 3–5 minutes more.

SERVES SIX

INGREDIENTS
    15ml/1 tbsp tamarind pulp
    150ml/¼ pint/⅔ cup warm water
    2 tomatoes
    115g/4oz spinach or Chinese leaves
      (Chinese cabbage)
    115g/4oz peeled cooked large prawns
      (shrimp), thawed if frozen
    1.2 litres/2 pints/5 cups prepared
      fish stock (see Cook's Tip)
    ½ mooli (daikon), peeled and diced
    115g/4oz green beans, cut into
      1cm/½in lengths
    225g/8oz piece of cod or haddock
      fillet, skinned and cut into strips
    Thai fish sauce, to taste
    squeeze of lemon juice, to taste
    salt and ground black pepper
    boiled rice or noodles, to serve

1 Put the tamarind pulp in a bowl and pour over the warm water. Set aside while you peel and chop the tomatoes, discarding the seeds. Strip the spinach or Chinese leaves from the stems and tear into small pieces.

2 Remove the heads and shells from the prawns, leaving the tails intact.

4 Add the fish strips, tomato and spinach. Strain in the tamarind juice and cook for 2 minutes. Stir in the prawns and cook for 1–2 minutes to heat. Season with salt and pepper and add a little fish sauce and lemon juice to taste. Transfer to individual serving bowls and serve immediately, with rice or noodles.

COOK'S TIP
A good fish stock is essential for this dish. Ask your fishmonger for about 675g/1½lb fish bones. Wash them, then place in a large pan with 2 litres/ 3½ pints/8 cups water. Add half a peeled onion, a piece of bruised peeled ginger, and a little salt and pepper. Bring to the boil, skim, then simmer for 20 minutes. Cool slightly, then strain. Freeze unused fish stock.

Energy 52kcal/218kJ; Protein 10.6g; Carbohydrate 1.3g, of which sugars 1.3g; Fat 0.5g, of which saturates 0.1g, of which polyunsaturates 0.2g; Cholesterol 55mg; Calcium 31mg; Fibre 0.6g; Sodium 62mg.

STIR-FRIED PRAWNS WITH TAMARIND ★

THE SOUR, TANGY FLAVOUR THAT IS CHARACTERISTIC OF MANY THAI DISHES COMES FROM TAMARIND. FRESH TAMARIND PODS FROM THE TAMARIND TREE CAN SOMETIMES BE BOUGHT, BUT PREPARING THEM FOR COOKING IS A LABORIOUS PROCESS. IT IS MUCH EASIER TO USE A BLOCK OF TAMARIND PASTE.

SERVES FOUR TO SIX

INGREDIENTS
  6 dried red chillies
  15ml/1 tbsp sunflower oil
  30ml/2 tbsp chopped onion
  30ml/2 tbsp palm sugar or light
    muscovado (brown) sugar
  30ml/2 tbsp water
  15ml/1 tbsp Thai fish sauce
  90ml/6 tbsp tamarind juice, made
    by mixing tamarind paste with
    warm water
  450g/1lb raw prawns
    (shrimp), peeled
  15ml/1 tbsp fried chopped garlic
  30ml/2 tbsp fried sliced shallots
  2 spring onions (scallions), chopped,
    to garnish

1 Heat a wok or large frying pan, but do not add any oil at this stage. Add the dried chillies and dry-fry them by pressing them against the surface of the wok or pan with a spatula, turning them occasionally. Do not let them burn. Set them aside to cool slightly.

2 Add the oil to the wok or pan and reheat. Add the chopped onion and cook over a medium heat, stirring occasionally, for 2–3 minutes, until softened and golden brown.

3 Add the sugar, water, fish sauce, dry-fried red chillies and the tamarind juice, stirring constantly until the sugar has dissolved. Bring to the boil, then lower the heat slightly.

4 Add the prawns, garlic and shallots. Toss over the heat for 3–4 minutes, until the prawns are cooked. Garnish with the spring onions and serve.

COOK'S TIP
Leave a few prawns in their shells for a garnish, if you like.

Energy 100kcal/422kJ; Protein 13.6g; Carbohydrate 6.6g, of which sugars 6g; Fat 2.3g, of which saturates 0.3g, of which polyunsaturates 1.3g; Cholesterol 146mg; Calcium 65mg; Fibre 0.3g; Sodium 321mg.

SAMBAL GORENG WITH PRAWNS ★

THIS IS AN IMMENSELY USEFUL AND ADAPTABLE SAUCE. HERE IT IS COMBINED WITH PRAWNS AND GREEN PEPPER, BUT YOU COULD ADD FINE STRIPS OF FRESHLY COOKED CALF'S LIVER, CHICKEN LIVERS, TOMATOES, GREEN BEANS OR HARD-BOILED EGGS.

SERVES SIX

INGREDIENTS
350g/12oz peeled cooked
  prawns (shrimp)
1 green (bell) pepper, seeded
  and sliced
60ml/4 tbsp tamarind juice
pinch of sugar
45ml/3 tbsp reduced-fat
  coconut milk
boiled rice, to serve
lime rind and red onion, to garnish
For the sambal goreng
2.5cm/1in cube shrimp paste
2 onions, roughly chopped
2 garlic cloves, roughly chopped
2.5cm/1in piece fresh galangal,
  peeled and sliced
10ml/2 tsp chilli sambal
1.5ml/¼ tsp salt
15ml/1 tbsp sunflower oil
45ml/3 tbsp tomato purée (paste)
600ml/1 pint/2½ cups water

1 Make the sambal goreng. Grind the shrimp paste with the onions and garlic using a mortar and pestle. Alternatively put in a food processor and process to a paste. Add the galangal, chilli sambal and salt. Process or pound to a fine paste.

COOK'S TIP
Store the remaining sauce in the refrigerator for up to 3 days or freeze it for up to 3 months.

2 Heat the oil in a wok or frying pan and fry the paste for 1–2 minutes, without browning, until the mixture gives off a rich aroma. Stir in the tomato purée and the stock or water and cook for 10 minutes. Ladle half the sauce into a bowl and leave to cool. This leftover sauce can be used in another recipe (see Cook's Tip).

3 Add the prawns and green pepper to the remaining sauce. Cook over a medium heat for 3–4 minutes, then stir in the tamarind juice, sugar and coconut milk. Spoon into warmed serving bowls and garnish with strips of lime rind and sliced red onion. Serve immediately with boiled rice.

VARIATIONS
• To make tomato sambal goreng, add 450g/1lb peeled coarsely chopped tomatoes to the sauce mixture, before stirring in the stock or water.
• To make egg sambal goreng, add three or four chopped hard-boiled eggs, and two peeled chopped tomatoes to the sauce.

Energy 86kcal/359kJ; Protein 11.6g; Carbohydrate 4.6g, of which sugars 4.1g; Fat 2.4g, of which saturates 0.3g, of which polyunsaturates 1.3g; Cholesterol 118mg; Calcium 67mg; Fibre 0.9g; Sodium 175mg.

STIR-FRIED LONG BEANS WITH PRAWNS ★★

POPULAR THROUGHOUT SOUTH-EAST ASIA, LONG BEANS — LIKE MANY OTHER VEGETABLES — ARE OFTEN STIR-FRIED WITH GARLIC. THIS TRADITIONAL CAMBODIAN RECIPE WITH PRAWNS, GALANGAL AND LIMES WORKS WELL SERVED WITH RICE OR NOODLES.

SERVES FOUR

INGREDIENTS

30ml/2 tbsp sunflower oil
2 garlic cloves, finely chopped
25g/1oz galangal, finely shredded
450g/1lb fresh prawns (shrimp), shelled and deveined
1 onion, halved and finely sliced
450g/1lb long beans, trimmed and cut into 7.5cm/3in lengths
120ml/4fl oz/½ cup soy sauce

For the marinade

30ml/2 tbsp *tuk trey*
juice of 2 limes
10ml/2 tsp sugar
2 garlic cloves, crushed
1 lemon grass stalk, trimmed and finely sliced

1 To make the marinade, beat the *tuk trey* and lime juice in a bowl with the sugar, until it has dissolved. Stir in the garlic and lemon grass. Toss in the prawns, cover, and chill for 1–2 hours.

2 Heat half the oil in a wok or heavy pan. Stir in the chopped garlic and galangal. Just as they begin to colour, toss in the marinated prawns. Stir-fry for a minute or until the prawns turn pink. Lift the prawns out on to a plate, reserving as much of the oil, garlic and galangal as you can.

3 Add the remaining oil to the wok. Add the onion and stir-fry until slightly caramelized. Stir in the beans, then pour in the soy sauce. Cook for a further 2–3 minutes, until the beans are tender. Add the prawns and stir-fry for a minute until heated through. Serve immediately.

Energy 187kcal/782kJ; Protein 22.6g; Carbohydrate 9.3g, of which sugars 7.9g; Fat 6.9g, of which saturates 0.9g, of which polyunsaturates 4g; Cholesterol 219mg; Calcium 156mg; Fibre 3.2g; Sodium 485mg.

GREEN PRAWN CURRY ★

GREEN CURRY HAS BECOME A FIRM FAVOURITE IN THE WEST, AND THIS PRAWN DISH IS JUST ONE OF A RANGE OF DELICIOUS GREEN CURRY RECIPES. HOME-MADE GREEN CURRY PASTE HAS THE BEST FLAVOUR, BUT YOU CAN ALSO BUY IT FROM GOOD SUPERMARKETS.

2 Add the prawns, kaffir lime leaves and chopped lemon grass. Fry for 2 minutes, until the prawns are pink.

3 Stir in the coconut milk and bring to a gentle boil. Simmer, stirring for about 5 minutes or until the prawns are tender.

SERVES SIX

INGREDIENTS
15ml/1 tbsp sunflower oil
30ml/2 tbsp green curry paste
450g/1lb raw king prawns (jumbo shrimp), peeled and deveined
4 kaffir lime leaves, torn
1 lemon grass stalk, bruised and chopped
250ml/8fl oz/1 cup reduced-fat coconut milk
30ml/2 tbsp Thai fish sauce
½ cucumber, seeded and cut into thin batons
10–15 basil leaves
4 green chillies, sliced, to garnish

1 Heat the sunflower oil in a wok or large pan until sizzling hot. Add the green curry paste and fry over a gentle heat for several minutes until bubbling and fragrant, stirring the mixture continually with chopsticks.

4 Stir in the fish sauce, cucumber batons and whole basil leaves, then top with the green chillies and serve from the pan.

VARIATION
Strips of skinless chicken breast fillet can be used in place of the prawns if you prefer. Add them to the pan in step 2 and fry until browned on all sides.

Energy 92kcal/385kJ; Protein 13.7g; Carbohydrate 2.6g, of which sugars 2.5g; Fat 3g, of which saturates 0.5g, of which polyunsaturates 1.6g; Cholesterol 146mg; Calcium 92mg; Fibre 0.4g; Sodium 191mg.

PRAWNS <u>WITH</u> YELLOW CURRY PASTE ★

FISH AND SHELLFISH, SUCH AS PRAWNS, AND COCONUT MILK, WERE MADE FOR EACH OTHER. THIS IS A VERY QUICK RECIPE IF YOU MAKE THE YELLOW CURRY PASTE IN ADVANCE, OR BUY IT READY-MADE. IT KEEPS WELL IN A SCREW-TOP JAR IN THE REFRIGERATOR FOR UP TO FOUR WEEKS.

<u>SERVES SIX</u>

INGREDIENTS
600ml/1 pint/2½ cups reduced-fat
  coconut milk
30ml/2 tbsp yellow curry paste
15ml/1 tbsp Thai fish sauce
2.5ml/½ tsp salt
5ml/1 tsp granulated sugar
450g/1lb raw king prawns (jumbo
  shrimp), peeled and deveined
225g/8oz cherry tomatoes
juice of ½ lime
red (bell) peppers, seeded and
  cut into thin strips, and fresh
  coriander (cilantro) leaves,
  to garnish

1 Put half the coconut milk in a wok or large pan and bring to the boil. Add the yellow curry paste and stir until it disperses. Lower the heat and simmer gently for about 10 minutes.

2 Add the fish sauce, salt, sugar and remaining coconut milk to the sauce. Simmer for 5 minutes more.

3 Add the prawns and cherry tomatoes. Simmer very gently for about 5 minutes until the prawns are pink and tender.

4 Spoon into a serving dish, sprinkle with lime juice and garnish with strips of pepper and coriander.

COOK'S TIPS
• Unused coconut milk can be stored in the refrigerator for 1–2 days, or poured into a freezer container and frozen for up to a month.
• If making your own coconut milk, instead of discarding the spent coconut, it can be reused to make a second batch of coconut milk. However, this will be of a poorer quality and it should only be used to extend a good quality first quantity of milk.
• To make coconut cream, leave newly made coconut milk to stand for 10 minutes. The coconut cream will float to the top – skim it off with a spoon and use in the usual way.

Energy 94kcal/397kJ; Protein 13.8g; Carbohydrate 7g, of which sugars 6.9g; Fat 1.4g, of which saturates 0.4g, of which polyunsaturates 0.5g; Cholesterol 146mg; Calcium 92mg; Fibre 0.4g; Sodium 434mg.

CURRIED SEAFOOD WITH COCONUT MILK ★

THIS CURRY IS BASED ON A THAI CLASSIC. THE LOVELY GREEN COLOUR IS IMPARTED BY THE FINELY CHOPPED CHILLI AND FRESH HERBS ADDED DURING THE LAST FEW MOMENTS OF COOKING.

SERVES FOUR

INGREDIENTS
225g/8oz small ready-prepared squid
225g/8oz raw tiger prawns
   (jumbo shrimp)
400ml/14fl oz/1⅔ cups reduced-fat
   coconut milk
2 kaffir lime leaves, finely shredded
30ml/2 tbsp Thai fish sauce
450g/1lb firm white fish fillets,
   skinned, boned and cut into chunks
2 fresh green chillies, seeded and
   finely chopped
30ml/2 tbsp torn fresh basil or
   coriander (cilantro) leaves
squeeze of fresh lime juice
cooked Thai jasmine rice, to serve
For the curry paste
6 spring onions (scallions),
   coarsely chopped
4 fresh coriander (cilantro) stems,
   coarsely chopped, plus 45ml/3 tbsp
   chopped fresh coriander (cilantro)
4 kaffir lime leaves, shredded
8 fresh green chillies, seeded and
   coarsely chopped
1 lemon grass stalk,
   coarsely chopped
2.5cm/1in piece fresh root ginger,
   peeled and coarsely chopped
45ml/3 tbsp chopped fresh basil
5ml/1 tsp sunflower oil

1 Make the curry paste. Put all the ingredients, except the oil, in a food processor and process to a paste. Alternatively, pound together in a mortar with a pestle. Stir in the oil.

2 Rinse the squid and pat dry with kitchen paper. Cut the bodies into rings and halve the tentacles, if necessary.

3 Heat a wok until hot, add the prawns and stir-fry, without any oil, for about 4 minutes, until they turn pink.

4 Remove the prawns from the wok and leave to cool slightly, then peel off the shells, saving a few with shells on for the garnish. Make a slit along the back of each one and remove the black vein.

5 Pour the coconut milk into the wok, then bring to the boil over a medium heat, stirring constantly. Add 30ml/ 2 tbsp of curry paste, the shredded lime leaves and fish sauce and stir well to mix. Reduce the heat to low and simmer gently for about 10 minutes.

6 Add the squid, prawns and chunks of fish and cook for about 2 minutes, until the seafood is tender. Take care not to overcook the squid as it will become tough very quickly.

7 Just before serving, stir in the chillies and the torn basil or coriander leaves. Taste and adjust the flavour with a squeeze of lime juice. Garnish the curry with prawns in their shells, and serve with Thai jasmine rice.

VARIATIONS
• You can use any firm-fleshed white fish for this curry, such as monkfish, cod, haddock or John Dory.
• If you prefer, you could substitute shelled scallops for the squid. Slice them in half horizontally and add them with the prawns (shrimp). As with the squid, be careful not to overcook them.

Energy 211kcal/894kJ; Protein 39.8g; Carbohydrate 5.9g, of which sugars 5.2g; Fat 3.3g, of which saturates 0.7g, of which polyunsaturates 1.2g; Cholesterol 288mg; Calcium 116mg; Fibre 0.6g; Sodium 351mg.

STIR-FRIED SCALLOPS AND PRAWNS ★

SERVE THIS LIGHT, DELICATE DISH FOR LUNCH OR SUPPER ACCOMPANIED BY AROMATIC STEAMED RICE OR FINE RICE NOODLES AND STIR-FRIED PAK CHOI. THIS COMBINATION OF FRESH SEAFOOD AND LIGHTLY COOKED VEGETABLES PRODUCES A DISH THAT IS HIGH IN FLAVOUR AND LOW IN FAT.

SERVES FOUR

INGREDIENTS
  15ml/1 tbsp sunflower oil
  500g/1¼lb raw tiger prawns
    (shrimp), peeled
  1 star anise
  225g/8oz scallops, halved if large
  2.5cm/1in piece fresh root ginger,
    peeled and grated
  2 garlic cloves, thinly sliced
  1 red (bell) pepper, seeded and cut
    into thin strips
  115g/4oz/1¾ cups shiitake or button
    (white) mushrooms, thinly sliced
  juice of 1 lemon
  5ml/1 tsp cornflour (cornstarch)
  30ml/2 tbsp light soy sauce
  chopped fresh chives,
    to garnish
  salt and ground black pepper

1 Heat the oil in a wok until very hot. Put in the prawns and star anise and stir-fry over a high heat for 2 minutes. Add the scallops, ginger and garlic and stir-fry for 1 minute more, by which time the prawns should have turned pink and the scallops should be opaque. Season with a little salt and plenty of pepper and then remove from the wok using a slotted spoon. Discard the star anise.

2 Add the red pepper and mushrooms to the wok and stir-fry for 1–2 minutes.

3 Make a cornflour paste by combining the cornflour with 30ml/2 tbsp cold water. Stir until smooth.

4 Pour the lemon juice, cornflour paste and soy sauce into the wok, bring to the boil and bubble for 1–2 minutes, stirring all the time, until the sauce is smooth and slightly thickened.

VARIATIONS
Other types of shellfish can be used in this dish. Try it with thinly sliced rings of squid, or use mussels or clams. You could even substitute bitesize chunks of firm white fish, such as monkfish, cod or haddock, for the scallops. These can be added to the dish in step 1, as with the scallops.

Energy 212kcal/892kJ; Protein 36.2g; Carbohydrate 6.6g, of which sugars 3.3g; Fat 4.6g, of which saturates 0.8g, of which polyunsaturates 2.3g; Cholesterol 270mg; Calcium 122mg; Fibre 1g; Sodium 877mg.

STEAMED MUSSELS WITH CHILLI AND GINGER ★

THIS SIMPLE DISH IS VIETNAM'S VERSION OF THE FRENCH CLASSIC, MOULES MARINIÈRE. THE VIETNAMESE STEAM THE MUSSELS OPEN IN A HERB-INFUSED STOCK RATHER THAN IN WHITE WINE. LEMON GRASS AND CHILLI FLAVOUR THE DISH INSTEAD OF WINE AND PARSLEY.

SERVES FOUR

INGREDIENTS
600ml/1 pint/2½ cups chicken stock
1 Thai chilli, seeded and chopped
2 shallots, finely chopped
3 lemon grass stalks,
  finely chopped
1 bunch ginger or basil leaves
1kg/2¼lb fresh mussels, cleaned
  and bearded
salt and ground black pepper

COOK'S TIP
Aromatic ginger leaves are hard to find outside Asia. If you can't find them, basil or coriander (cilantro) will work well.

1 Pour the chicken stock into a deep pan. Add the chopped chilli, shallots, lemon grass and most of the ginger or basil leaves, retaining a few leaves for the garnish. Bring to the boil. Cover and simmer for 10–15 minutes, then season to taste.

2 Discard any mussels that remain open when tapped, then add the remaining mussels to the stock. Stir well, cover and cook for 2 minutes, or until the mussels have opened. Discard any that remain closed. Ladle the mussels and cooking liquid into individual bowls.

Energy 75kcal/318kJ; Protein 13.6g; Carbohydrate 1.5g, of which sugars 1.1g; Fat 1.7g, of which saturates 0.3g, of which polyunsaturates 0.5g; Cholesterol 30mg; Calcium 176mg; Fibre 0.8g; Sodium 162mg.

STIR-FRIED BABY SQUID WITH GINGER, GARLIC AND LEMON ★★

THE ABUNDANCE OF FISH AROUND THE GULF OF THAILAND SUSTAINS THRIVING MARKETS FOR THE RESTAURANT AND HOTEL TRADE, AND EVERY MARKET NATURALLY FEATURES STALLS WHERE DELICIOUS, FRESHLY CAUGHT SEAFOOD IS COOKED AND SERVED. THIS RECIPE IS POPULAR AMONG STREET TRADERS.

SERVES TWO

INGREDIENTS
  4 ready-prepared baby squid,
    total weight about 250g/9oz
  15ml/1 tbsp sunflower oil
  2 garlic cloves, finely chopped
  30ml/2 tbsp soy sauce
  2.5cm/1in piece fresh root ginger,
    peeled and finely chopped
  juice of ½ lemon
  5ml/1 tsp granulated sugar
  2 spring onions (scallions), chopped

VARIATIONS
This dish is often prepared with fresh galangal rather than ginger and works well with most kinds of seafood, including prawns (shrimp) and scallops.

1 Rinse the squid well and pat dry with kitchen paper. Cut the bodies into rings and halve the tentacles, if necessary.

2 Heat the oil in a wok or frying pan and cook the garlic until golden brown, but do not let it burn. Add the squid and stir-fry for 30 seconds over a high heat.

3 Add the soy sauce, ginger, lemon juice, sugar and spring onions. Stir-fry for a further 30 seconds, then serve.

COOK'S TIP
Squid has an undeserved reputation for being rubbery in texture. This is always a result of overcooking it.

Energy 169kcal/709kJ; Protein 20g; Carbohydrate 5.3g, of which sugars 3.6g; Fat 7.7g, of which saturates 1.2g, of which polyunsaturates 4.3g; Cholesterol 281mg; Calcium 26mg; Fibre 0.3g; Sodium 1207mg.

GRIDDLED SQUID AND TOMATOES IN A TAMARIND DRESSING ★

THIS IS A LOVELY FLAVOURSOME DISH — SWEET, CHARRED SQUID SERVED IN A TANGY DRESSING MADE WITH TAMARIND, LIME AND NUOC MAM. IT IS BEST MADE WITH BABY SQUID BECAUSE THEY ARE TENDER AND SWEET. THE TOMATOES AND HERBS ADD WONDERFUL FRESH FLAVOURS.

SERVES FOUR

INGREDIENTS
spray sunflower oil, for greasing
2 large tomatoes, skinned, halved
  and seeded
500g/1¼lb fresh baby squid
1 bunch each fresh basil, coriander
  (cilantro) and mint, stalks removed,
  leaves chopped
For the dressing
15ml/1 tbsp tamarind paste
juice of half a lime
30ml/2 tbsp *nuoc mam*
15ml/1 tbsp raw cane sugar
1 garlic clove, crushed
2 shallots, halved and finely sliced
2 Serrano chillies, seeded and sliced

1 Put the dressing ingredients in a bowl and stir until well mixed. Set aside.

2 Heat a ridged griddle, spray the pan with a little oil, and griddle the tomatoes until lightly charred on both sides. Transfer them to a board, chop into bitesize chunks, and place in a bowl.

3 Clean the griddle, then heat it up again and spray with a little more oil. Griddle the squid for 2–3 minutes each side, pressing them down with a spatula, until nicely browned. Transfer to the bowl with the tomatoes, add the herbs and the dressing and toss well. Serve immediately.

COOK'S TIPS
• To prepare squid yourself, get a firm hold of the head and pull it from the body. Reach down inside the body sac and then pull out and discard the transparent backbone, as well as any stringy parts. Rinse the body sac inside and out and pat dry. Cut the tentacles off above the eyes and add to the pile of squid you're going to cook. Discard everything else.
• Griddled scallops and prawns (shrimp) are also delicious in this tangy dressing.

VARIATION
Traditionally, the squid are steamed for this dish: you can steam them for a delicious low-fat meal. Steam the squid for 10–15 minutes.

Energy 153kcal/651kJ; Protein 20.4g; Carbohydrate 13.2g, of which sugars 11.3g; Fat 2.6g, of which saturates 0.6g, of which polyunsaturates 0.9g; Cholesterol 281mg; Calcium 54mg; Fibre 1.6g; Sodium 149mg.

PRAWN AND CAULIFLOWER CURRY ★

THIS IS A BASIC FISHERMAN'S CURRY FROM THE SOUTHERN COAST OF VIETNAM. SIMPLE TO MAKE, IT WOULD USUALLY BE EATEN FROM A COMMUNAL BOWL, OR FROM THE WOK ITSELF, AND SERVED WITH NOODLES, RICE OR CHUNKS OF BAGUETTE TO MOP UP THE DELICIOUSLY FRAGRANT SAUCE.

SERVES FOUR

INGREDIENTS

450g/1lb raw tiger prawns (jumbo shrimp), shelled and cleaned
juice of 1 lime
15ml/1 tbsp sunflower oil
1 red onion, roughly chopped
2 garlic cloves, roughly chopped
2 Thai chillies, seeded and chopped
1 cauliflower, broken into florets
5ml/1 tsp sugar
2 star anise, dry-fried and ground
10ml/2 tsp fenugreek, dry-fried and ground
450ml/¾ pint/2 cups reduced-fat coconut milk
chopped fresh coriander (cilantro) leaves, to garnish
salt and ground black pepper

1 In a bowl, toss the prawns in the lime juice and set aside. Heat a wok or heavy pan and add the oil. Stir in the onion, garlic and chillies. As they brown, add the cauliflower. Stir-fry for 2–3 minutes.

VARIATION
Other popular combinations include prawns with butternut squash or pumpkin.

2 Toss in the sugar and spices. Add the coconut milk, stirring to make sure it is thoroughly combined. Reduce the heat and simmer for 10–15 minutes, or until the liquid has reduced and thickened a little. Add the prawns and lime juice and cook for 1–2 minutes, or until the prawns turn opaque. Season to taste, and sprinkle with coriander. Serve hot.

Energy 157kcal/664kJ; Protein 24.7g; Carbohydrate 10.4g, of which sugars 9.4g; Fat 2.2g, of which saturates 0.6g, of which polyunsaturates 0.7g; Cholesterol 219mg; Calcium 169mg; Fibre 2.7g; Sodium 352mg.

LOBSTER AND CRAB STEAMED IN BEER ★

IN SPITE OF ITS APPEARANCE ON MENUS IN RESTAURANTS THAT SPECIALIZE IN THE COMPLEX AND REFINED IMPERIAL DISHES OF VIETNAM, THIS RECIPE IS VERY EASY TO MAKE. IT MAY BE EXPENSIVE, BUT IT'S A WONDERFUL DISH FOR A SPECIAL OCCASION.

SERVES FOUR TO SIX

INGREDIENTS

    4 uncooked lobsters, about
        450g/1lb each
    4 uncooked crabs, about
        225g/8oz each
    600ml/1 pint/2½ cups beer
    4 spring onions (scallions), trimmed
        and chopped into long pieces
    4cm/1½in fresh root ginger, peeled
        and finely sliced
    2 green or red Thai chillies, seeded
        and finely sliced
    3 lemon grass stalks, finely sliced
    1 bunch fresh dill, fronds chopped
    1 bunch each fresh basil and
        coriander (cilantro), stalks removed,
        leaves chopped
    about 30ml/2 tbsp *nuoc mam*, plus
        extra for serving
    juice of 1 lemon
    salt and ground black pepper

1 Clean the lobsters and crabs thoroughly and rub them with salt and pepper. Place them in a large steamer and pour the beer into the base.

2 Sprinkle half the spring onions, ginger, chillies, lemon grass and herbs over the lobsters and crabs, and steam for about 10 minutes, or until the lobsters turn red. Lift them on to a warmed serving dish.

VARIATIONS
Prawns (shrimp) and mussels are also delicious cooked this way. Replace the lemon with lime if you like.

3 Add the remaining flavouring ingredients to the beer with the *nuoc mam* and lemon juice. Pour into a dipping bowl and serve immediately with the hot lobsters and crabs, with extra splashes of *nuoc mam*, if you like.

COOK'S TIP
Whether you cook the lobsters and crabs at the same time depends on the number of people you are cooking for and the size of your steamer. However, they don't take long to cook so it is easy to steam them in batches. In the markets and restaurants of Vietnam, you can find crabs that are 60cm/24in in diameter, which may feed several people but require a huge steamer. Depending on the size and availability of the lobsters and crabs, you can make this recipe for as many people as you like, because the quantities are simple to adjust. For those who like their food fiery, splash a little chilli sauce into the beer broth.

Energy 190kcal/801kJ; Protein 35.2g; Carbohydrate 1.5g, of which sugars 1.4g; Fat 4.9g, of which saturates 0.7g, of which polyunsaturates 1.6g; Cholesterol 158mg; Calcium 86mg; Fibre 0.8g; Sodium 589mg.

NORTHERN FISH CURRY ★★

THIS IS A THIN, SOUPY CURRY WITH WONDERFULLY STRONG FLAVOURS. SERVE IT IN BOWLS WITH LOTS OF STICKY RICE TO SOAK UP THE DELICIOUS JUICES.

SERVES FOUR

INGREDIENTS

    350g/12oz salmon fillet
    500ml/17fl oz/2¼ cups
      vegetable stock
    4 shallots, finely chopped
    2 garlic cloves, finely chopped
    2.5cm/1in piece fresh galangal,
      finely chopped
    1 lemon grass stalk, finely chopped
    2.5ml/½ tsp dried chilli flakes
    15ml/1 tbsp Thai fish sauce
    5ml/1 tsp palm sugar or light
      muscovado (brown) sugar

1 Place the salmon in the freezer for 30–40 minutes to firm up the flesh slightly. Remove and discard the skin, then use a sharp knife to cut the fish into 2.5cm/1in cubes, removing any stray bones with your fingers or with tweezers as you do so.

2 Pour the stock into a large, heavy pan and bring it to the boil over a medium heat. Add the shallots, garlic, galangal, lemon grass, chilli flakes, fish sauce and sugar. Bring back to the boil, stir well, then reduce the heat and simmer gently for 15 minutes.

3 Add the fish, bring back to the boil, then turn off the heat. Leave the curry to stand for 10–15 minutes until the fish is cooked through, then serve.

Energy 172kcal/717kJ; Protein 18.2g; Carbohydrate 3.2g, of which sugars 2.5g; Fat 9.7g, of which saturates 1.7g, of which polyunsaturates 2.7g; Cholesterol 44mg; Calcium 24mg; Fibre 0.3g; Sodium 307mg.

ESCABECHE ★

THIS PICKLED FISH DISH IS EATEN WHEREVER THERE ARE — OR HAVE BEEN — SPANISH SETTLERS.
IT IS ESPECIALLY POPULAR IN THE PHILIPPINES WHERE IT IS SERVED WITH BOILED OR STEAMED RICE.

SERVES SIX

INGREDIENTS

675–900g/1½–2lb white fish fillets, such as sole or plaice
45–60ml/3–4 tbsp seasoned flour
sunflower oil, for shallow frying
For the sauce
2.5cm/1in piece fresh root ginger, peeled and thinly sliced
2–3 garlic cloves, crushed
1 onion, cut into thin rings
15ml/1 tbsp sunflower oil
½ large green (bell) pepper, seeded and cut in small neat squares
½ large red (bell) pepper, seeded and cut in small neat squares
1 carrot, cut into matchsticks
25ml/1½ tbsp cornflour (cornstarch)
450ml/¾ pint/scant 2 cups water
45–60ml/3–4 tbsp herb or cider vinegar
15ml/1 tbsp light soft brown sugar
5–10ml/1–2 tsp Thai fish sauce
salt and ground black pepper
1 small chilli, seeded and sliced and spring onions (scallions), finely shredded, to garnish (optional)
boiled rice, to serve

1 Wipe the fish fillets and leave them whole, or cut into serving portions, if you like. Pat dry on kitchen paper then dust lightly with seasoned flour.

2 Heat oil for shallow frying in a frying pan and fry the fish in batches until golden and almost cooked. Transfer to an ovenproof dish and keep warm.

3 Make the sauce in a wok or large frying pan. Fry the ginger, garlic and onion in the oil for 5 minutes or until the onion is softened but not browned.

4 Add the pepper squares and carrot strips and stir-fry for 1 minute.

5 Put the cornflour in a small bowl and add a little of the water to make a paste. Stir in the remaining water, the vinegar and the sugar. Pour the cornflour mixture over the vegetables in the wok and stir until the sauce boils and thickens a little. Season with fish sauce and salt and pepper if needed.

6 Add the fish to the sauce and reheat briefly without stirring. Transfer to a warmed serving platter and garnish with chilli and spring onions, if liked. Serve with boiled rice.

COOK'S TIP
Red snapper or small sea bass could be used for this recipe, in which case ask your fishmonger to cut them into fillets.

Energy 130kcal/550kJ; Protein 21.3g; Carbohydrate 9.3g, of which sugars 5.2g; Fat 1.1g, of which saturates 0.2g, of which polyunsaturates 0.4g; Cholesterol 52mg; Calcium 34mg; Fibre 1g; Sodium 74mg.

JUNGLE FISH COOKED IN BANANA LEAVES ★

STEAMING FRESHWATER FISH IN BANANA LEAVES OVER HOT CHARCOAL IS A TRADITIONAL METHOD OF COOKING IN THE JUNGLE. BANANA LEAVES ARE LARGE AND TOUGH, AND SERVE AS BASIC COOKING VESSELS AND WRAPPERS FOR ALL SORTS OF FISH AND MEAT.

SERVES FOUR

INGREDIENTS
   350g/12oz freshwater fish fillets,
     such as trout, cut into
     bitesize chunks
   6 banana leaves (see Cook's Tip)
   spray sunflower vegetable oil
   sticky rice, noodles or salad, to serve
For the marinade
   2 shallots
   5cm/2in turmeric root, peeled
     and grated
   2 spring onions (scallions),
     finely sliced
   2 garlic cloves, crushed
   1–2 green Thai chillies, seeded
     and finely chopped
   15ml/1 tbsp *nuoc mam*
   2.5ml/½ tsp raw cane sugar
   salt and ground black pepper

1 To make the marinade, grate the shallots into a bowl, then combine with the other marinade ingredients, Season with salt and pepper. Toss the chunks of fish in the marinade, then cover and chill for 6 hours, or overnight.

VARIATION
This dish can be made with any of the catfish or carp family, or even talapia.

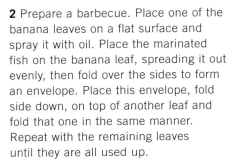

2 Prepare a barbecue. Place one of the banana leaves on a flat surface and spray it with oil. Place the marinated fish on the banana leaf, spreading it out evenly, then fold over the sides to form an envelope. Place this envelope, fold side down, on top of another leaf and fold that one in the same manner. Repeat with the remaining leaves until they are all used up.

3 Secure the last layer of banana leaf with a piece of bendy wire. Place the banana leaf packet on the barbecue. Cook for about 20 minutes, turning it over from time to time to make sure it is cooked on both sides – the outer leaves will burn. Carefully untie the wire (it will be hot) and unravel the packet. Check that the fish is cooked and serve with sticky rice, noodles or salad.

COOK'S TIP
Banana leaves are available in some African and Asian stores and markets. If you can't find them, wrap the fish in vine leaves that have been soaked in cold water, or large flexible cabbage leaves. You can also use foil.

Energy 84kcal/352kJ; Protein 16.3g; Carbohydrate 1.5g, of which sugars 1.1g; Fat 1.4g, of which saturates 0.2g, of which polyunsaturates 0.8g; Cholesterol 40mg; Calcium 12mg; Fibre 0.2g; Sodium 320mg.

STEAMED FISH WITH CHILLI SAUCE ★

STEAMING IS ONE OF THE HEALTHIEST METHODS OF COOKING FISH. BY LEAVING THE FISH WHOLE AND ON THE BONE, MAXIMUM FLAVOUR IS RETAINED AND THE FLESH REMAINS BEAUTIFULLY MOIST. THE BANANA LEAF IS BOTH AUTHENTIC AND ATTRACTIVE, BUT YOU CAN USE BAKING PARCHMENT.

SERVES FOUR

INGREDIENTS
  1 large or 2 medium firm fish such
    as sea bass or grouper, scaled
    and cleaned
  30ml/2 tbsp rice wine
  3 fresh red chillies, seeded and
    thinly sliced
  2 garlic cloves, finely chopped
  2cm/¾in piece fresh root ginger,
    peeled and finely shredded
  2 lemon grass stalks, crushed and
    finely chopped
  2 spring onions
    (scallions), chopped
  30ml/2 tbsp Thai fish sauce
  juice of 1 lime
  1 fresh banana leaf
For the chilli sauce
  10 fresh red chillies, seeded
    and chopped
  4 garlic cloves, chopped
  60ml/4 tbsp Thai fish sauce
  15ml/1 tbsp granulated sugar
  75ml/5 tbsp fresh lime juice

1 Thoroughly rinse the fish under cold running water. Pat it dry with kitchen paper. With a sharp knife, slash the skin of the fish a few times on both sides.

2 Mix together the rice wine, chillies, garlic, shredded ginger, lemon grass and spring onions in a non-metallic bowl. Add the fish sauce and lime juice and mix to a paste. Place the fish on the banana leaf and spread the spice paste evenly over it, rubbing it in well where the skin has been slashed.

3 Put a rack or a small upturned plate in the base of a wok. Pour in boiling water to a depth of 5cm/2in. Lift the banana leaf, together with the fish, and place it on the rack or plate. Cover with a lid and steam for 10–15 minutes, or until the fish is cooked.

4 Meanwhile, make the sauce. Place all the ingredients in a food processor and process until smooth. If the mixture seems to be too thick, add a little cold water. Scrape into a serving bowl.

5 Serve the fish hot, on the banana leaf if you like, with the sweet chilli sauce to spoon over the top.

Energy 147kcal/619kJ; Protein 28.4g; Carbohydrate 5.5g, of which sugars 5.3g; Fat 1.3g, of which saturates 0.2g, of which polyunsaturates 0.5g; Cholesterol 69mg; Calcium 56mg; Fibre 1g; Sodium 898mg.

FISH IN COCONUT CUSTARD ★★

This is a Khmer classic. Rich and sumptuous, amok trey crops up all over Cambodia. In Phnom Penh, there are restaurants that specialize in it. The fish is steamed in a custard, made with coconut milk and flavoured with the Cambodian herbal paste, kroeung.

SERVES FOUR

INGREDIENTS
   2 x 400ml/14oz cans reduced-fat
     coconut milk
   3 eggs
   80ml/3fl oz *kroeung*
   15ml/1 tbsp *tuk trey*
   10ml/2 tsp palm sugar or honey
   1 kg/2¼lb fresh, skinned white fish
     fillets, cut into 8 pieces
   1 small bunch chopped fresh
     coriander (cilantro), plus a few
     whole sprigs, to garnish
  jasmine rice or crusty bread and
     salad, to serve

VARIATION
This dish can also be cooked in the oven in a bain marie. Cook at 160°C/325°F/Gas 3 for about 50 minutes.

1 Half fill a wok or large pan with water. Set a bamboo or stainless-steel steamer over it and put the lid on. Bring the water to the boil.

2 In a bowl, beat the reduced-fat coconut milk with the eggs, *kroeung*, *tuk trey* and sugar or honey, until everything is well blended and the sugar has dissolved.

3 Place the fish fillets in a heatproof dish that will fit in the steamer. Pour the coconut mixture over the fish and place the dish in the steamer. Put the lid back on the steamer and reduce the heat so that the custard won't curdle. Steam over gently simmering water until the fish is cooked. Garnish with coriander and serve immediately with jasmine rice or crusty bread and salad.

Energy 314kcal/1324kJ; Protein 51.1g; Carbohydrate 13.6g, of which sugars 13.6g; Fat 6.5g, of which saturates 1.8g, of which polyunsaturates 1.2g; Cholesterol 258mg; Calcium 102mg; Fibre 0g; Sodium 423mg.

CATFISH COOKED <u>IN A</u> CLAY POT ★

WONDERFULLY EASY AND TASTY, THIS SOUTHERN~STYLE VIETNAMESE AND CAMBODIAN DISH IS A CLASSIC. IN THE SOUTH OF VIETNAM, CLAY POTS ARE REGULARLY USED FOR COOKING AND THEY ENHANCE BOTH THE LOOK AND TASTE OF THIS TRADITIONAL DISH.

SERVES FOUR

INGREDIENTS

- 30ml/2 tbsp sugar
- 15ml/1 tbsp sunflower oil
- 2 garlic cloves, crushed
- 45ml/3 tbsp *nuoc mam*
- 350g/12oz catfish fillets, cut diagonally into 2 or 3 pieces
- 4 spring onions (scallions), cut into bitesize pieces
- ground black pepper
- chopped fresh coriander (cilantro), to garnish
- fresh bread, to serve

1 Place the sugar in a clay pot or heavy pan, and add 15ml/1 tbsp water to wet it. Heat the sugar until it begins to turn golden brown, then add the oil and crushed garlic.

2 Stir the *nuoc mam* into the caramel mixture and add 120ml/4fl oz/½ cup boiling water, then toss in the catfish pieces, making sure they are well coated with the sauce. Cover the pot, reduce the heat and simmer for about 5 minutes.

3 Remove the lid, season with ground black pepper and gently stir in the spring onions. Simmer for a further 3–4 minutes to thicken the sauce, garnish with fresh coriander, and serve immediately straight from the pot with chunks of fresh bread.

Energy 128kcal/537kJ; Protein 16.4g; Carbohydrate 8.3g, of which sugars 8.3g; Fat 3.4g, of which saturates 0.4g, of which polyunsaturates 2g; Cholesterol 40mg; Calcium 18mg; Fibre 0.2g; Sodium 54mg.

SPICY PAN-SEARED TUNA <u>WITH</u> CUCUMBER, GARLIC <u>AND</u> GINGER ★★

THIS POPULAR DISH, WHICH CAN BE FOUND ALL OVER VIETNAM IN RESTAURANTS OR AT FOOD STALLS, IS MADE WITH MANY TYPES OF THICK-FLESHED FISH. TUNA IS PARTICULARLY SUITABLE BECAUSE IT IS DELICIOUS PAN-SEARED AND SERVED A LITTLE RARE.

SERVES FOUR

INGREDIENTS
   1 small cucumber
   10ml/2 tsp sesame oil
   2 garlic cloves, crushed
   4 tuna steaks
For the dressing
   4cm/1½in fresh root ginger, peeled
     and roughly chopped
   1 garlic clove, roughly chopped
   2 green Thai chillies, seeded and
     roughly chopped
   45ml/3 tbsp raw cane sugar
   45ml/3 tbsp *nuoc mam*
   juice of 1 lime
   60ml/4 tbsp water

1 To make the dressing, grind the ginger, garlic and chillies to a pulp with the sugar, using a mortar and pestle. Stir in the *nuoc mam*, lime juice and water, and mix well. Leave the dressing to stand for 15 minutes.

2 Cut the cucumber in half lengthways and remove the seeds. Cut the flesh into long, thin strips. Toss the cucumber in the dressing and leave to soak for at least 15 minutes.

3 Wipe a heavy pan with the oil and rub the garlic around it. Heat the pan and add the tuna steaks. Sear for a few minutes on both sides, so that the outside is slightly charred but the inside is still rare. Lift the steaks on to a warm serving dish. Using tongs or chopsticks, lift the cucumber strips out of the dressing and arrange them around the steaks. Drizzle the dressing over the tuna, and serve immediately.

Energy 228kcal/959kJ; Protein 36.2g; Carbohydrate 1.5g, of which sugars 1.4g; Fat 8.6g, of which saturates 2g, of which polyunsaturates 3.1g; Cholesterol 42mg; Calcium 55mg; Fibre 1g; Sodium 76mg.

CHARCOAL-GRILLED FISH WITH MUNG BEANSPROUTS AND HERBS ★

A WHOLE FISH GRILLED OVER CHARCOAL IS KNOWN IN CAMBODIA AS TREI AING *AND IT IS USUALLY SERVED WITH SALAD LEAVES, HERBS, CHOPPED PEANUTS, AND A STRONG-FLAVOURED SAUCE. CHUNKS OF THE COOKED FISH ARE WRAPPED IN THE LEAVES AND DIPPED IN THE SAUCE.*

SERVES FOUR

INGREDIENTS
 1 good-sized fish, such as trout,
  snakehead, barb or carp, gutted
  and rinsed, head removed,
  if you like
 225g/8oz mung beansprouts
 1 bunch each fresh basil, coriander
  (cilantro) and mint, stalks removed,
  leaves chopped
 1 lettuce, broken into leaves
 15ml/1 tbsp roasted unsalted
  peanuts, finely chopped
 steamed rice, to serve
For the sauce
 3 garlic cloves, chopped
 2 red Thai chillies, seeded
  and chopped
 25g/1oz fresh root ginger, peeled
  and chopped
 15ml/1 tbsp palm sugar
 45ml/3 tbsp *tuk trey*
 juice of 1 lime
 juice of 1 coconut

1 First prepare the sauce. Using a mortar and pestle, grind the garlic, chillies and ginger with the sugar to form a paste. Add the *tuk trey*, lime juice and coconut juice and bind well. Pour the sauce into a serving bowl.

2 Prepare the barbecue. Place the fish over the charcoal and grill it for 2–3 minutes each side, until cooked right through. Alternatively, use a conventional grill (broiler).

3 Lay out the beansprouts, herbs and lettuce leaves on a large plate and place the peanuts in a bowl. Put everything on the table, including the cooked fish, sauce and rice. Using chopsticks, if you like, lift up the charred skin and tear off pieces of fish. Place each piece on a lettuce leaf, sprinkle with beansprouts, herbs and peanuts, wrap it up and dip it into the sauce.

Energy 143kcal/604kJ; Protein 18.9g; Carbohydrate 9.1g, of which sugars 6.2g; Fat 3.7g, of which saturates 0.8g, of which polyunsaturates 1.2g; Cholesterol 64mg; Calcium 84mg; Fibre 2.5g; Sodium 69mg.

HOT AND FRAGRANT TROUT ★

THIS WICKEDLY HOT SPICE PASTE COULD BE USED AS A MARINADE FOR ANY FISH OR MEAT. IT ALSO MAKES A WONDERFUL SPICY DIP FOR GRILLED MEAT.

SERVES FOUR

INGREDIENTS
    2 large fresh green chillies, seeded
      and coarsely chopped
    5 shallots, peeled
    5 garlic cloves, peeled
    30ml/2 tbsp fresh lime juice
    30ml/2 tbsp Thai fish sauce
    15ml/1 tbsp palm sugar or light
      muscovado (brown) sugar
    4 kaffir lime leaves, rolled
      into cylinders and
      thinly sliced
    2 trout or similar firm-fleshed
      fish, about 350g/12oz
      each, cleaned
    fresh garlic chives, to garnish
    boiled rice, to serve

1 Wrap the chillies, shallots and garlic in a foil package. Place under a hot grill (broiler) for 10 minutes, until softened.

2 When the package is cool enough to handle, tip the contents into a mortar or food processor and pound with a pestle or process to a paste.

3 Add the lime juice, fish sauce, sugar and lime leaves and mix well. With a teaspoon, stuff this paste inside the fish. Smear a little on the skin too. Grill (broil) the fish for about 5 minutes on each side, until just cooked through. Lift the fish on to a platter, garnish with garlic chives and serve with rice.

Energy 117kcal/490kJ; Protein 14.8g; Carbohydrate 7.9g, of which sugars 6.7g; Fat 3.1g, of which saturates 0.7g, of which polyunsaturates 1g; Cholesterol 59mg; Calcium 36mg; Fibre 0.7g; Sodium 57mg.

TROUT WITH TAMARIND AND CHILLI SAUCE ★★

SOMETIMES TROUT CAN TASTE RATHER BLAND, BUT THIS SPICY SAUCE REALLY GIVES IT A ZING.
IF YOU LIKE YOUR FOOD VERY SPICY, ADD AN EXTRA CHILLI.

SERVES FOUR

INGREDIENTS

4 trout, cleaned
6 spring onions (scallions), sliced
60ml/4 tbsp soy sauce
spray sunflower oil, for frying
30ml/2 tbsp chopped fresh coriander
  (cilantro) and strips of fresh red
  chilli, to garnish
For the sauce
50g/2oz tamarind pulp
105ml/7 tbsp boiling water
2 shallots, coarsely chopped
1 fresh red chilli, seeded and chopped
1cm/½in piece fresh root ginger,
  peeled and chopped
5ml/1 tsp soft light brown sugar
45ml/3 tbsp Thai fish sauce

3 Make the sauce. Put the tamarind pulp in a small bowl and pour on the boiling water. Mash well with a fork until softened. Tip the tamarind mixture into a food processor or blender, and add the shallots, fresh chilli, ginger, sugar and fish sauce. Process to a coarse pulp. Scrape into a bowl.

4 Spray a large frying pan with oil. Heat and cook the trout, one at a time if necessary, for about 5 minutes on each side, until the skin is crisp and browned and the flesh cooked. Put on warmed plates and spoon over some of the sauce. Sprinkle with the coriander and chilli and serve with the remaining sauce.

1 Slash the trout diagonally four or five times on each side. Place them in a shallow dish that is large enough to hold them all in a single layer.

2 Fill the cavities with spring onions and douse each fish with soy sauce. Carefully turn the fish over to coat both sides with the sauce. Sprinkle any remaining spring onions over the top.

Energy 215kcal/904kJ; Protein 35.4g; Carbohydrate 3.2g, of which sugars 2.7g; Fat 6.8g, of which saturates 1.6g, of which polyunsaturates 2.3g; Cholesterol 144mg; Calcium 60mg; Fibre 0.2g; Sodium 932mg.

THAI-STYLE TROUT ★★

THE COMBINATION OF CLASSIC THAI AROMATIC INGREDIENTS — GINGER, LEMON GRASS, COCONUT MILK AND LIME — GIVES THIS SIMPLE DISH A FABULOUS FLAVOUR. SERVE WITH PLENTY OF STEAMED THAI FRAGRANT RICE TO SOAK UP THE DELICIOUS SAUCE.

SERVES FOUR

INGREDIENTS
    200g/7oz spinach leaves
    1 lemon grass stalk, finely chopped
    2.5cm/1in piece fresh root ginger,
      peeled and finely grated
    2 garlic cloves, crushed
    200ml/7fl oz/scant 1 cup reduced-fat
      coconut milk
    30ml/2 tbsp lime juice
    15ml/1 tbsp soft light brown sugar
    4 trout fillets, each about 200g/7oz
    salt and ground black pepper
    steamed Thai fragrant rice, to serve

COOK'S TIP
To steam Thai fragrant rice, cook it in a pan of salted boiling water for three-quarters of the time noted on the packet. Transfer it to a colander lined with muslin or cheesecloth and steam over simmering water for 5–10 minutes until just tender.

1 Preheat the oven to 200°C/400°F/Gas 6. Place the spinach in a pan, with just the water that adheres to the leaves after washing. Cover with a lid and cook gently for 3–4 minutes until the leaves have just wilted. Drain the spinach in a colander and press it with the back of a spoon to remove any excess moisture.

2 Transfer the spinach to a mixing bowl and stir in the chopped lemon grass, grated ginger and garlic.

3 Combine the coconut milk, lime juice, sugar and seasoning in a jug (pitcher). Place the trout fillets side by side in a shallow baking dish and pour the coconut milk mixture over.

4 Bake the trout for 20–25 minutes until cooked. Place on individual serving plates, on top of the steamed Thai fragrant rice. Toss the spinach mixture in the juices remaining in the dish, spoon on top of the fish and serve.

Energy 266kcal/1119kJ; Protein 40.5g; Carbohydrate 7.9g, of which sugars 7.7g; Fat 8.3g, of which saturates 0.2g, of which polyunsaturates 0.3g; Cholesterol 0mg; Calcium 140mg; Fibre 1.7g; Sodium 177mg.

THAI MARINATED SEA TROUT ★

SEA TROUT HAS A SUPERB TEXTURE AND A FLAVOUR LIKE THAT OF WILD SALMON. LIKE MANY OTHER FISH, IT IS BEST SERVED WITH STRONG BUT COMPLEMENTARY FLAVOURS, SUCH AS CHILLIES AND LIME, THAT CUT THROUGH THE RICHNESS OF ITS FLESH.

SERVES SIX

INGREDIENTS

6 sea trout cutlets, each about 115g/4oz
2 garlic cloves, chopped
1 fresh long red chilli, seeded and chopped
45ml/3 tbsp chopped Thai basil
15ml/1 tbsp granulated sugar
3 limes
400ml/14fl oz/1⅔ cups reduced-fat coconut milk
spray sunflower oil
15ml/1 tbsp Thai fish sauce

1 Place the sea trout cutlets side by side in a shallow dish. Using a pestle, pound the chopped garlic and chilli in a large mortar to break both up roughly. Add 30ml/2 tbsp of the chopped Thai basil with the sugar and continue to pound the mixture until it forms a rough paste.

2 Grate the rind from 1 lime and squeeze it. Mix the rind and juice into the chilli paste, with the reduced-fat coconut milk. Pour the mixture over the cutlets. Cover and chill for about 1 hour. Cut the remaining limes into wedges.

3 Spray a hinged wire fish basket or grill rack with oil. Remove the cutlets from the marinade and place them in the fish basket or directly on the grill rack. Cook the fish for 4 minutes on each side, trying not to move them. They may stick to the grill rack if not seared first.

4 Strain the remaining marinade into a pan, reserving the contents of the sieve. Bring the marinade to the boil, then simmer gently for 5 minutes, stirring. Stir in the contents of the sieve and continue to simmer for 1 minute more. Add the Thai fish sauce and the remaining Thai basil.

5 Lift each fish cutlet on to a plate, pour over the sauce and serve with the lime wedges.

COOK'S TIP
Sea trout is best cooked when the barbecue is cool to medium hot, and the coals have a medium to thick coating of ash. Take care when cooking any fish in a marinade, as the residue can cause flare-ups if it drips on to the coals.

VARIATION
If you prefer you could substitute wild or farmed salmon for the sea trout. Be careful not to overcook it.

Energy 158kcal/666kJ; Protein 23.1g; Carbohydrate 6.1g, of which sugars 6.1g; Fat 4.7g, of which saturates 0.1g, of which polyunsaturates 0g; Cholesterol 0mg; Calcium 48mg; Fibre 0.4g; Sodium 142mg.

CHICKEN
AND DUCK

Chicken is a low-fat meat and stars in an astonishing variety

of Asian recipes — stir-fried with ginger or chillies, roasted

with spices, or grilled, curried, or braised in coconut

milk. This chapter contains classic curries, traditional Chicken

Satay with Peanut Sauce, fruity Duck in a Spicy Orange

Sauce and also some more unusual recipes — including Spicy

Chicken with Young Ginger and Coriander — all specially

adapted for the low-fat, low-cholesterol diet.

CHICKEN SATAY <u>WITH</u> PEANUT SAUCE ★★

THESE MINIATURE KEBABS ARE POPULAR ALL OVER SOUTH-EAST ASIA. THE PEANUT DIPPING SAUCE IS A PERFECT PARTNER FOR THE MARINATED CHICKEN.

SERVES FOUR

INGREDIENTS
    4 skinless, chicken breast fillets
For the marinade
    2 garlic cloves, crushed
    2.5cm/1in piece fresh root ginger,
        finely grated
    10ml/2 tsp Thai fish sauce
    30ml/2 tbsp light soy sauce
    15ml/1 tbsp clear honey
For the satay sauce
    45ml/3 tbsp crunchy peanut butter
    ½ fresh red chilli, seeded and
        finely chopped
    juice of ½ lime
    30ml/2 tbsp reduced-fat
        coconut milk
    salt

1 First, make the satay sauce. Put all the ingredients in a food processor or blender. Process until smooth, then check the seasoning and add more salt or lime juice if necessary. Spoon the sauce into a bowl, cover with clear film (plastic wrap) and set aside.

2 Using a sharp knife, slice each chicken breast into four long strips. Put all the marinade ingredients in a large bowl and mix well, then add the chicken strips and toss together until thoroughly coated. Cover and leave for at least 30 minutes in the refrigerator to marinate. Meanwhile, soak 16 wooden satay sticks or kebab skewers in water, to prevent them from burning during cooking.

3 Preheat the grill (broiler) to high or prepare the barbecue. Drain the satay sticks or skewers. Drain the chicken strips. Thread one strip on to each satay stick or skewer. Grill (broil) for 3 minutes on each side, or until the chicken is golden brown and cooked through. Serve immediately with the satay sauce.

Energy 236kcal/992kJ; Protein 38.8g; Carbohydrate 3.4g, of which sugars 2.6g; Fat 7.5g, of which saturates 1.9g, of which polyunsaturates 2.2g; Cholesterol 105mg; Calcium 15mg; Fibre 0.6g; Sodium 672mg.

FRAGRANT GRILLED CHICKEN ★

IF YOU HAVE TIME, PREPARE THE CHICKEN IN ADVANCE AND LEAVE IT TO MARINATE IN THE REFRIGERATOR FOR SEVERAL HOURS — OR EVEN OVERNIGHT — UNTIL READY TO COOK.

SERVES FOUR

INGREDIENTS

450g/1lb chicken breast fillets,
  with the skin on
15ml/1 tbsp sesame oil
2 garlic cloves, crushed
2 coriander (cilantro) roots,
  finely chopped
2 small fresh red chillies, seeded
  and finely chopped
30ml/2 tbsp Thai fish sauce
5ml/1 tsp sugar
cooked rice, to serve
lime wedges, to garnish

For the sauce

90ml/6 tbsp rice vinegar
60ml/4 tbsp sugar
2.5ml/½ tsp salt
2 garlic cloves, crushed
1 small fresh red chilli, seeded and
  finely chopped
115g/4oz/4 cups fresh coriander
  (cilantro), finely chopped

1 Lay the chicken breast fillets between two sheets of clear film (plastic wrap), baking parchment or foil and beat with the side of a rolling pin or the flat side of a meat tenderizer until the meat is about half its original thickness. Place in a large, shallow dish or bowl.

2 Mix together the sesame oil, garlic, coriander roots, red chillies, fish sauce and sugar in a jug (pitcher), stirring until the sugar has dissolved. Pour the mixture over the chicken and turn to coat. Cover with clear film and set aside to marinate in a cool place for at least 20 minutes. Meanwhile, make the sauce.

3 Heat the vinegar in a small pan, add the sugar and stir until dissolved. Add the salt and stir until the mixture begins to thicken. Add the remaining sauce ingredients, stir well, then spoon the sauce into a serving bowl.

4 Preheat the grill (broiler) and cook the chicken for 5 minutes. Turn and baste with the marinade, then cook for 5 minutes more, or until cooked through and golden. Serve with rice and the sauce, garnished with lime wedges.

Energy 221kcal/934kJ; Protein 28.3g; Carbohydrate 17.8g, of which sugars 17.7g; Fat 4.5g, of which saturates 0.8g, of which polyunsaturates 1.4g; Cholesterol 79mg; Calcium 97mg; Fibre 2.1g; Sodium 82mg.

CHICKEN WITH LEMON SAUCE ★

SUCCULENT CHICKEN WITH A REFRESHING LEMONY SAUCE AND JUST A HINT OF LIME IS A SURE WINNER AS A FAMILY MEAL THAT IS QUICK AND EASY TO PREPARE.

2 Mix together the egg white and cornflour. Add the mixture to the chicken and turn the chicken with tongs until thoroughly coated. Heat the sunflower oil in a non-stick frying pan or wok and fry the chicken fillets for about 15 minutes until they are golden brown on both sides.

3 Meanwhile, make the sauce. Combine all the ingredients in a small pan. Add 1.5ml/¼ tsp salt. Bring to the boil over a low heat, stirring constantly until the sauce is smooth and has thickened.

SERVES FOUR

INGREDIENTS

4 small skinless chicken breast fillets
5ml/1 tsp sesame oil
15ml/1 tbsp dry sherry
1 egg white, lightly beaten
30ml/2 tbsp cornflour (cornstarch)
15ml/1 tbsp sunflower oil
salt and ground white pepper
chopped coriander (cilantro) leaves
  and spring onions (scallions) and
  lemon wedges, to garnish
For the sauce
45ml/3 tbsp fresh lemon juice
30ml/2 tbsp sweetened lime juice
45ml/3 tbsp caster (superfine) sugar
10ml/2 tsp cornflour (cornstarch)
90ml/6 tbsp cold water

1 Arrange the chicken in a single layer in a bowl. Mix the sesame oil with the sherry and add 2.5ml/½ tsp salt and 1.5ml/¼ tsp pepper. Pour over the chicken, cover and marinate for 15 minutes.

VARIATIONS
Turkey fillets can be substituted for chicken in this recipe. Any white fish can also be used in this dish.

4 Cut the chicken into pieces and place on a warm serving plate. Pour the sauce over, garnish with the coriander leaves, spring onions and lemon wedges.

Energy 235kcal/995kJ; Protein 30.9g; Carbohydrate 23.3g, of which sugars 14.1g; Fat 2.2g, of which saturates 0.5g, of which polyunsaturates 0.6g; Cholesterol 88mg; Calcium 15mg; Fibre 0g; Sodium 97mg.

BARBECUE CHICKEN ★

CHICKEN COOKED ON A BARBECUE IS SERVED ALMOST EVERYWHERE IN THAILAND, FROM ROADSIDE STALLS TO SPORTS STADIA. THIS IS THE PERFECT DISH FOR A SUMMER PARTY.

SERVES FOUR TO SIX

INGREDIENTS
  1 chicken, about 1.5kg/3–3½lb,
    cut into 8–10 pieces
  lime wedges and fresh red chillies,
    to garnish
For the marinade
  2 lemon grass stalks, roots trimmed
  2.5cm/1in piece fresh root ginger,
    peeled and thinly sliced
  6 garlic cloves, coarsely chopped
  4 shallots, coarsely chopped
  ½ bunch coriander (cilantro)
    roots, chopped
  15ml/1 tbsp palm sugar or light
    muscovado (brown) sugar
  120ml/4fl oz/½ cup reduced-fat
    coconut milk
  30ml/2 tbsp Thai fish sauce
  30ml/2 tbsp light soy sauce

1 Make the marinade. Cut off the lower 5cm/2in of the lemon grass stalks and chop them coarsely. Put into a food processor with the ginger, garlic, shallots, coriander, sugar, coconut milk and sauces and process until smooth.

2 Place the chicken pieces in a dish, pour over the marinade and stir to mix well. Cover the dish and leave in a cool place to marinate for at least 4 hours, or leave it in the refrigerator overnight.

3 Prepare the barbecue or preheat the oven to 200°C/400°F/Gas 6. Drain the chicken, reserving the marinade. If you are cooking in the oven, arrange the chicken pieces in a single layer on a rack set over a roasting pan.

4 Cook the chicken on the barbecue over moderately hot coals or on medium heat for a gas barbecue, or bake in the oven for 20–30 minutes. Turn the pieces and brush with the reserved marinade once or twice during cooking.

5 As soon as the chicken pieces are golden brown and cooked through, transfer them to a serving platter, garnish with the lime wedges and red chillies and serve immediately.

COOK'S TIPS
• Coriander roots are more intensely flavoured than the leaves, but the herb is not always available with the roots intact. One answer is to grow your own, but if this is impractical, use the bottom portion of the stem as a substitute.
• Coconut milk is available in cans or cartons from Asian food stores and most supermarkets. Reduced-fat versions contain less than half the fat.

Energy 145kcal/610kJ; Protein 28.5g; Carbohydrate 2.3g, of which sugars 2g; Fat 2.4g, of which saturates 0.7g, of which polyunsaturates 0.5g; Cholesterol 108mg; Calcium 14mg; Fibre 0.1g; Sodium 458mg.

STIR-FRIED CHICKEN WITH BASIL AND CHILLI ★

THIS QUICK AND EASY CHICKEN DISH IS AN EXCELLENT INTRODUCTION TO THAI CUISINE. THAI BASIL, WHICH IS SOMETIMES KNOWN AS HOLY BASIL, HAS A UNIQUE, PUNGENT FLAVOUR THAT IS BOTH SPICY AND SHARP. SKINLESS, BONELESS CHICKEN BREAST FILLETS ARE ESPECIALLY LOW IN FAT.

SERVES SIX

INGREDIENTS
15ml/1 tbsp sunflower oil
4 garlic cloves, thinly sliced
2–4 fresh red chillies, seeded and finely chopped
450g/1lb skinless chicken breast fillets, cut into bitesize pieces
45ml/3 tbsp Thai fish sauce
10ml/2 tsp dark soy sauce
5ml/1 tsp granulated sugar
10–12 fresh Thai basil leaves
2 fresh red chillies, seeded and finely chopped, and 18 deep-fried Thai basil leaves, to garnish (optional)

1 Heat the oil in a wok or large, heavy frying pan. Add the garlic and chillies and stir-fry over a medium heat for 1–2 minutes until the garlic is golden. Take care not to let the garlic burn, otherwise it will taste bitter.

2 Add the pieces of chicken to the wok or pan, in batches if necessary, and stir-fry until the chicken changes colour.

3 Stir in the fish sauce, soy sauce and sugar. Continue to stir-fry the mixture for 3–4 minutes, or until the chicken is fully cooked and golden brown.

4 Stir in the fresh Thai basil leaves. Spoon the mixture on to a warm platter, or into individual dishes. Garnish with the chopped chillies and deep-fried Thai basil and serve immediately.

COOK'S TIP
To deep-fry Thai basil leaves, first make sure that the leaves are completely dry or they will splutter when they are added to the oil. Heat vegetable or sunflower oil in a wok or deep-fryer to 190°C/375°F or until a cube of bread, added to the oil, browns in about 45 seconds. Add the leaves and deep-fry them briefly until they are crisp and translucent – this will take only about 30–40 seconds. Lift out the leaves using a slotted spoon or wire basket. Drain them well on kitchen paper before using.

Energy 113kcal/474kJ; Protein 19.1g; Carbohydrate 2.9g, of which sugars 1.6g; Fat 2.8g, of which saturates 0.5g, of which polyunsaturates 1.3g; Cholesterol 53mg; Calcium 22mg; Fibre 0.7g; Sodium 582mg.

CHICKEN WITH CHILLIES AND LEMON GRASS ★

THIS IS GOOD HOME COOKING. THERE ARE VARIATIONS OF THIS DISH, USING PORK OR SEAFOOD, THROUGHOUT SOUTH-EAST ASIA SO, FOR A SMOOTH INTRODUCTION TO THE COOKING OF THE REGION, THIS IS A GOOD PLACE TO START. SERVE WITH A SALAD, RICE WRAPPERS AND A DIPPING SAUCE.

SERVES FOUR

INGREDIENTS

15ml/1 tbsp sugar
15ml/1 tbsp sunflower oil
2 garlic cloves, finely chopped
2–3 green or red Thai chillies,
  seeded and finely chopped
2 lemon grass stalks, finely sliced
1 onion, finely sliced
350g/12oz skinless chicken breast
  fillets, cut into bitesize strips
30ml/2 tbsp soy sauce
15ml/1 tbsp *nuoc mam*
1 bunch fresh coriander (cilantro),
  stalks removed, leaves chopped
salt and ground black pepper
nuoc cham, to serve

1 To make a caramel sauce, put the sugar into a pan with 5ml/1 tsp water. Heat gently until the sugar has dissolved and turned golden. Set aside.

2 Heat a large wok or heavy pan and add the sunflower oil. Stir in the chopped garlic, chillies and lemon grass, and stir-fry until they become fragrant and golden. Add the onion and stir-fry for 1 minute, then add the chicken strips.

3 When the chicken is cooked through, add the soy sauce, *nuoc mam* and caramel sauce. Stir to mix and heat through, then season with a little salt and pepper. Toss the coriander into the chicken and serve with *nuoc cham* to drizzle over it.

Energy 142kcal/598kJ; Protein 21.6g; Carbohydrate 5.5g, of which sugars 5.1g; Fat 3.9g, of which saturates 0.6g, of which polyunsaturates 1.9g; Cholesterol 61mg; Calcium 35mg; Fibre 0.8g; Sodium 57mg.

FRAGRANT RICE WITH CHICKEN, MINT AND NUOC CHAM ★

THIS REFRESHING DISH CAN BE SERVED SIMPLY, DRIZZLED WITH NUOC CHAM, OR AS PART OF A CELEBRATORY MEAL THAT MIGHT INCLUDE FISH OR CHICKEN, EITHER GRILLED OR ROASTED WHOLE, AND ACCOMPANIED BY PICKLES AND A TABLE SALAD.

2 Put the rice in a heavy pan and stir in the stock. When the rice settles, check that the stock sits roughly 2.5cm/1in above the rice; if not, top it up. Bring the liquid to the boil, cover the pan and cook for about 25 minutes, or until all the water has been absorbed.

SERVES FOUR

INGREDIENTS
  350g/12oz/1¾ cups long grain rice,
    rinsed and drained
  2–3 shallots, halved and finely sliced
  1 bunch of fresh mint, stalks
    removed, leaves finely shredded
  2 spring onions (scallions), finely
    sliced, to garnish
  nuoc cham, to serve
For the stock
  2 meaty chicken legs
  1 onion, peeled and quartered
  4cm/1½in fresh root ginger, peeled
    and coarsely chopped
  15ml/1 tbsp *nuoc mam*
  3 black peppercorns
  1 bunch of fresh mint
  sea salt

1 To make the stock, put the chicken legs into a deep pan. Add all the other ingredients, except the salt, and pour in 1 litre/1¾ pints/4 cups water. Bring the water to the boil, skim off any foam, then reduce the heat and simmer gently with the lid on for 1 hour. Remove the lid, increase the heat and simmer for a further 30 minutes to reduce the stock. Skim off any fat, strain the stock and season with salt. Measure 750ml/1¼ pints/3 cups stock. Remove the chicken meat from the bone and shred.

VARIATIONS
Any meat or fish can be added to this basic recipe. Try strips of stir-fried pork, slices of Chinese sausage or a handful of prawns (shrimp). Simply toss into the rice along with the shredded chicken.

3 Remove the pan from the heat and, using a fork, add the shredded chicken, shallots and most of the mint. Cover the pan again and leave the flavours to mingle for 10 minutes. Tip the rice into bowls, or on to a serving dish, garnish with the remaining mint and the spring onions, and serve with *nuoc cham*.

Energy 426kcal/1784kJ; Protein 25.6g; Carbohydrate 72.9g, of which sugars 1.8g; Fat 3.1g, of which saturates 0.7g, of which polyunsaturates 0.6g; Cholesterol 92mg; Calcium 53mg; Fibre 0.5g; Sodium 82mg.

SPICY CHICKEN WITH YOUNG GINGER AND CORIANDER ★★

GINGER PLAYS A BIG ROLE IN CAMBODIAN COOKING, PARTICULARLY IN THE STIR-FRIED DISHES. WHENEVER POSSIBLE, THE JUICIER AND MORE PUNGENT YOUNG GINGER IS USED. THIS IS A SIMPLE AND DELICIOUS WAY TO COOK CHICKEN, PORK OR BEEF.

SERVES FOUR

INGREDIENTS

15ml/1 tbsp sunflower oil
3 garlic cloves, finely sliced
   in strips
50g/2oz fresh young root ginger,
   finely sliced in strips
2 Thai chillies, seeded and finely
   sliced in strips
4 skinless chicken fillets or 4 boned
   chicken legs, skinned and cut
   into bitesize chunks
30ml/2 tbsp *tuk prahoc*
10ml/2 tsp sugar
1 small bunch coriander (cilantro)
   stalks removed, roughly chopped
ground black pepper
jasmine rice and crunchy salad or
   baguette, to serve

1 Heat a wok or heavy pan and add the oil. Add the garlic, ginger and chillies, and stir-fry until fragrant and golden. Add the chicken and toss it around the wok for 1–2 minutes.

COOK'S TIP
Young ginger is available in Chinese and South-east Asian markets.

2 Stir in the *tuk prahoc* and sugar, and stir-fry for a further 4–5 minutes until cooked. Season with pepper and add some of the fresh coriander. Transfer the chicken to a serving dish and garnish with the remaining coriander. Serve hot with jasmine rice and a crunchy salad with fresh herbs, or with chunks of freshly baked baguette.

Energy 187kcal/786kJ; Protein 27.5g; Carbohydrate 4g, of which sugars 3.8g; Fat 6.9g, of which saturates 1g, of which polyunsaturates 3.7g; Cholesterol 79mg; Calcium 35mg; Fibre 0.9g; Sodium 75mg.

RED CHICKEN CURRY <u>WITH</u> BAMBOO SHOOTS ★

BAMBOO SHOOTS HAVE A LOVELY CRUNCHY TEXTURE. IT IS QUITE ACCEPTABLE TO USE CANNED ONES, AS FRESH BAMBOO IS NOT READILY AVAILABLE IN THE WEST. BUY CANNED WHOLE BAMBOO SHOOTS, WHICH ARE CRISPER AND OF BETTER QUALITY THAN SLICED SHOOTS. RINSE BEFORE USING.

SERVES SIX

INGREDIENTS
    475ml/16fl oz/2 cups reduced-fat
      coconut milk
    450g/1lb skinless chicken fillets, cut
      into bitesize pieces
    30ml/2 tbsp Thai fish sauce
    15ml/1 tbsp sugar
    475ml/16fl oz/2 cups
      chicken stock
    225g/8oz drained canned bamboo
      shoots, rinsed and sliced
    5 kaffir lime leaves, torn
    chopped fresh red chillies and
      kaffir lime leaves, to garnish
For the red curry paste
    5ml/1 tsp coriander seeds
    2.5ml/½ tsp cumin seeds
    12–15 fresh red chillies, seeded
      and roughly chopped
    4 shallots, thinly sliced
    2 garlic cloves, chopped
    15ml/1 tbsp chopped galangal
    2 lemon grass stalks, chopped
    3 kaffir lime leaves, chopped
    4 fresh coriander (cilantro) roots
    10 black peppercorns
    good pinch of ground cinnamon
    5ml/1 tsp ground turmeric
    2.5ml/½ tsp shrimp paste
    5ml/1 tsp salt
    15ml/1 tbsp sunflower oil

2 Add the oil, a little at a time, mixing or processing well after each addition. Transfer to a jar and keep in the refrigerator until ready to use.

3 Pour the coconut milk into a large heavy pan. Bring the milk to the boil, stirring constantly until it has separated.

1 Make the red curry paste. Dry-fry the coriander and cumin seeds for 1–2 minutes, then put in a mortar with the remaining ingredients except the oil and pound to a paste.

4 Stir in 30ml/2 tbsp of the red curry paste and cook the mixture for 2–3 minutes, stirring constantly. Remaining red curry paste can be kept in the refrigerator for up to 3 months.

5 Add the chicken fillets, Thai fish sauce and sugar to the pan. Stir well, then cook for 5–6 minutes until the chicken changes colour and is lightly golden and cooked through. Stir the chicken constantly to prevent the mixture from sticking to the bottom of the pan.

6 Pour the chicken stock into the pan, then add the sliced bamboo shoots and the torn kaffir lime leaves. Bring back to the boil over a medium heat, stirring constantly to prevent the chicken from sticking. Then remove the curry from the heat and season with salt and pepper to taste if necessary.

7 To serve, spoon the curry immediately into a warmed serving dish and garnish with chopped red chillies and kaffir lime leaves.

VARIATION
Instead of, or as well as, bamboo shoots, use straw mushrooms. These are available as dried mushrooms or in cans from Asian stores and supermarkets. Whether you are using dried or canned mushrooms, stir into the dish a few minutes before serving the curry.

COOK'S TIP
It is essential to use chicken breast fillets, rather than any other cut, for this curry, as it is cooked very quickly. Look out for diced chicken or strips of chicken (which are often labelled "stir-fry chicken") in the supermarket.

Energy 131kcal/552kJ; Protein 18.8g; Carbohydrate 7.5g, of which sugars 7.2g; Fat 3g, of which saturates 0.6g, of which polyunsaturates 1.3g; Cholesterol 55mg; Calcium 51mg; Fibre 0.5g; Sodium 153mg.

SOUTHERN CHICKEN CURRY ★★

*A MILD COCONUT CURRY FLAVOURED WITH TURMERIC, CORIANDER AND CUMIN SEEDS THAT
DEMONSTRATES THE INFLUENCE OF MALAYSIAN COOKING ON THAI CUISINE.*

SERVES SIX

INGREDIENTS
    30ml/2 tbsp sunflower oil
    1 large garlic clove, crushed
    1 chicken, weighing about 1.5kg/
        3–3½lb, chopped into
        12 large pieces
    400ml/14fl oz/1⅔ cups reduced-fat
        coconut milk
    250ml/8fl oz/1 cup chicken stock
    30ml/2 tbsp Thai fish sauce
    30ml/2 tbsp sugar
    juice of 2 limes
To garnish
    2 small fresh red chillies, seeded and
        finely chopped
    1 bunch spring onions (scallions),
        thinly sliced
For the curry paste
    5ml/1 tsp dried chilli flakes
    2.5ml/½ tsp salt
    5cm/2in piece fresh turmeric or
        5ml/1 tsp ground turmeric
    2.5ml/½ tsp coriander seeds
    2.5ml/½ tsp cumin seeds
    5ml/1 tsp dried shrimp paste

1 First make the curry paste. Put all the ingredients in a mortar, food processor or spice grinder and pound, process or grind to a smooth paste.

2 Heat the oil in a wok or frying pan and cook the garlic until golden. Add the chicken and cook until golden. Remove the chicken and set aside.

3 Reheat the oil and add the curry paste and then half the coconut milk. Cook for a few minutes until fragrant.

4 Return the chicken to the wok or pan, add the stock, mixing well, then add the remaining coconut milk, the fish sauce, sugar and lime juice. Stir well and bring to the boil, then lower the heat and simmer for 15 minutes.

5 Turn the curry into six warm serving bowls and sprinkle with the chopped fresh chillies and spring onions to garnish. Serve immediately.

VARIATION
For a delicious curry that is even lower in fat, remove the skin before cooking the chicken in step 2.

COOK'S TIP
Use a large sharp knife or a Chinese cleaver to chop the chicken into pieces. Wash the board, knife and your hands thoroughly afterwards in hot, soapy water as chicken is notorious for harbouring harmful micro-organisms and bacteria.

Energy 222kcal/935kJ; Protein 29g; Carbohydrate 9.8g, of which sugars 9.5g; Fat 7.7g, of which saturates 1.7g, of which polyunsaturates 3.2g; Cholesterol 144mg; Calcium 50mg; Fibre 0.4g; Sodium 231mg.

CHICKEN AND LEMON GRASS CURRY ★

THIS FRAGRANT AND TRULY DELICIOUS CURRY IS EXCEPTIONALLY EASY AND TAKES LESS THAN TWENTY MINUTES TO PREPARE AND COOK — A PERFECT MID-WEEK MEAL.

SERVES FOUR

INGREDIENTS
   10ml/2 tsp sunflower oil
   2 garlic cloves, crushed
   500g/1¼ lb skinless, boneless
      chicken thighs, chopped into
      small pieces
   45ml/3 tbsp Thai fish sauce
   120ml/4fl oz/½ cup
      chicken stock
   5ml/1 tsp granulated sugar
   1 lemon grass stalk, chopped into
      4 sticks and lightly crushed
   5 kaffir lime leaves, rolled into
      cylinders and thinly sliced across,
      plus extra to garnish
   chopped roasted peanuts
      and chopped fresh coriander
      (cilantro), to garnish
For the curry paste
   1 lemon grass stalk,
      coarsely chopped
   2.5cm/1in piece fresh galangal,
      peeled and coarsely chopped
   2 kaffir lime leaves, chopped
   3 shallots, coarsely chopped
   6 coriander (cilantro) roots,
      coarsely chopped
   2 garlic cloves
   2 fresh green chillies, seeded and
      coarsely chopped
   5ml/1 tsp shrimp paste
   5ml/1 tsp ground turmeric

1 Make the curry paste. Place all the ingredients in a large mortar, or food processor and pound with a pestle or process to a smooth paste.

2 Heat the sunflower oil in a wok or large, heavy frying pan, add the garlic and cook over a low heat, stirring frequently, until golden brown. Be careful not to let the garlic burn or it will taste bitter. Add the curry paste and stir-fry with the garlic for about 30 seconds more.

3 Add the chicken pieces to the pan and stir until thoroughly coated with the curry paste. Stir in the Thai fish sauce and chicken stock, with the sugar, and cook, stirring constantly, for 2 minutes more.

4 Add the lemon grass and lime leaves, reduce the heat and simmer for 10 minutes. If the mixture begins to dry out, add a little more stock or water.

5 Remove the lemon grass, if you like. Spoon the curry into four dishes, garnish with the lime leaves, peanuts and coriander and serve immediately.

Energy 122kcal/512kJ; Protein 17.4g; Carbohydrate 3.7g, of which sugars 3g; Fat 4.3g, of which saturates 0.8g, of which polyunsaturates 1.6g; Cholesterol 85mg; Calcium 77mg; Fibre 1.6g; Sodium 131mg.

GREEN CHICKEN CURRY ★★

USE ONE OR TWO FRESH GREEN CHILLIES IN THIS DISH, DEPENDING ON HOW HOT YOU LIKE YOUR CURRY. THE MILD AROMATIC FLAVOUR OF THE RICE IS A GOOD FOIL FOR THE SPICY CHICKEN.

SERVES FOUR

INGREDIENTS

    4 spring onions (scallions), trimmed
      and coarsely chopped
    1–2 fresh green chillies, seeded and
      coarsely chopped
    2cm/¾ in piece fresh root
      ginger, peeled
    2 garlic cloves
    5ml/1 tsp Thai fish sauce
    large bunch fresh coriander (cilantro)
    small handful of fresh parsley or
      1 lemon grass stalk, chopped into
      4 sticks and lightly crushed
    30–45ml/2–3 tbsp water
    15ml/1 tbsp sunflower oil
    4 skinless, chicken breast
      fillets, diced
    1 green (bell) pepper, seeded and
      thinly sliced
    600ml/1 pint/2½ cups reduced-fat
      coconut milk
    salt and ground black pepper
    hot coconut rice, to serve

1 Put the spring onions, chillies, ginger, garlic, fish sauce, coriander and parsley or lemon grass in a food processor or blender. Pour in 30ml/2 tbsp of the water and process to a smooth paste, adding a further 15ml/1 tbsp water if required.

COOK'S TIP

Virtually every Thai cook has their own recipe for curry pastes, which are traditionally made by pounding the ingredients in a mortar with a pestle. Using a food processor or blender simply makes the task less laborious.

2 Heat half the oil in a large frying pan. Cook the diced chicken until evenly browned. Transfer to a plate.

3 Heat the remaining oil in the frying pan. Add the thinly sliced green pepper and stir-fry for 3–4 minutes, then add the chilli and ginger paste. Stir-fry for 3–4 minutes, until the mixture becomes fairly thick.

4 Return the chicken to the pan and add the reduced-fat coconut milk. Season with salt and pepper to taste and bring to the boil, then reduce the heat, half cover the pan and simmer for 8–10 minutes.

5 When the chicken is cooked, transfer it, with the green pepper, to a plate. Boil the cooking liquid remaining in the pan for 10–12 minutes, until it is well reduced and fairly thick.

6 Return the chicken and green pepper to the green curry sauce, stir well and cook gently for 2–3 minutes to heat through thoroughly. Spoon the curry over the coconut rice, and serve immediately.

Energy 208kcal/877kJ; Protein 28g; Carbohydrate 8g, of which sugars 7.9g; Fat 7.4g, of which saturates 1.3g, of which polyunsaturates 3.7g; Cholesterol 79mg; Calcium 76mg; Fibre 0.7g; Sodium 237mg.

CHICKEN AND BASIL COCONUT RICE ★

FOR THIS DISH, THE RICE IS PARTIALLY BOILED BEFORE BEING SIMMERED WITH COCONUT SO THAT IT FULLY ABSORBS THE FLAVOUR OF THE CHILLIES, BASIL AND SPICES.

SERVES FOUR

INGREDIENTS

- 350g/12oz/1¾ cups Thai fragrant rice, rinsed
- 15ml/1 tbsp sunflower oil
- 1 large onion, finely sliced into rings
- 1 garlic clove, crushed
- 1 fresh red chilli, seeded and finely sliced
- 1 fresh green chilli, seeded and finely sliced
- generous handful of basil leaves
- 3 skinless chicken breast fillets, about 350g/12oz, finely sliced
- 5mm/¼in piece of lemon grass, pounded or finely chopped
- 600ml/1 pint/2½ cups reduced-fat coconut milk
- salt and ground black pepper

1 Bring a pan of lightly salted water to the boil. Add the rice to the pan and boil for about 6 minutes, until partially cooked. Drain and set aside.

2 Heat the oil in a frying pan and fry the onion rings for 5–10 minutes until golden and crisp. Lift out, drain on kitchen paper and set aside.

3 Fry the garlic and chillies in the oil remaining in the pan for 2–3 minutes, then add the basil leaves and fry briefly until they begin to wilt.

4 Remove a few basil leaves and set them aside for the garnish, then add the chicken slices with the lemon grass and fry for 2–3 minutes until golden.

5 Add the rice. Stir-fry for a few minutes to coat the grains, then pour in the coconut cream. Cook for 4–5 minutes or until the rice is tender, adding a little more water if necessary. Adjust the seasoning.

6 Pile the rice into a warmed serving dish, sprinkle with the fried onion rings and basil leaves, and serve immediately.

Energy 492kcal/2064kJ; Protein 28.8g; Carbohydrate 83.1g, of which sugars 11.6g; Fat 4.8g, of which saturates 0.9g, of which polyunsaturates 2g; Cholesterol 61mg; Calcium 83mg; Fibre 1.1g; Sodium 220mg.

JUNGLE CURRY OF GUINEA FOWL ★

A TRADITIONAL WILD FOOD COUNTRY CURRY FROM THE NORTH-CENTRAL REGION OF THAILAND,
THIS DISH CAN BE MADE USING ANY GAME, FISH OR CHICKEN.

SERVES FOUR

INGREDIENTS
    1 guinea fowl or similar game bird
    10ml/2 tsp sunflower oil
    10ml/2 tsp green curry paste
    15ml/1 tbsp Thai fish sauce
    2.5cm/1in piece fresh galangal,
      peeled and finely chopped
    15ml/1 tbsp fresh green
      peppercorns
    3 kaffir lime leaves, torn
    15ml/1 tbsp whisky,
      preferably Mekhong
    300ml/½ pint/1¼ cups
      chicken stock
    50g/2oz snake beans or yard-long
      beans, cut into 2.5cm/1in lengths
      (about ½ cup)
    225g/8oz/3¼ cups chestnut
      mushrooms, sliced
    1 piece drained canned bamboo
      shoot, about 50g/2oz, shredded
    5ml/1 tsp dried chilli flakes,
      to garnish (optional)

1 Cut up the guinea fowl, remove and discard the skin, then take all the meat off the bones. Chop the meat into bitesize pieces and set aside.

2 Heat the oil in a wok or frying pan and add the curry paste. Stir-fry over a medium heat for 30 seconds.

3 Add the fish sauce and the guinea fowl meat and stir-fry until the meat is browned all over. Add the galangal, peppercorns, lime leaves and whisky, then pour in the stock.

4 Bring to the boil. Add the vegetables, return to a simmer and cook gently for 2–3 minutes, until they are just cooked. Spoon into a dish, sprinkle with chilli flakes, if you like, and serve.

COOK'S TIPS
• Guinea fowl range from 675g/1½lb to 2kg/4½lb, but 1.2kg/2½lb is average. American readers could substitute two or three Cornish hens, depending on size.
• Bottled green peppercorns can be used as a substitute for fresh green peppercorns, but rinse well and drain them first.

Energy 200kcal/846kJ; Protein 38.5g; Carbohydrate 7.1g, of which sugars 4.9g; Fat 2.2g, of which saturates 0.5g, of which polyunsaturates 0.6g; Cholesterol 105mg; Calcium 37mg; Fibre 2.1g; Sodium 96mg.

YELLOW CHICKEN CURRY ★

THE PAIRING OF SLIGHTLY SWEET COCONUT MILK AND FRUIT WITH SAVOURY CHICKEN AND SPICES IS AT ONCE A COMFORTING, REFRESHING AND EXOTIC COMBINATION.

SERVES FOUR

INGREDIENTS

300ml/½ pint/1¼ cups
  chicken stock
30ml/2 tbsp thick tamarind juice,
  made by mixing tamarind paste with
  warm water
15ml/1 tbsp granulated sugar
200ml/7fl oz/scant 1 cup reduced-fat
  coconut milk
1 green papaya, peeled, seeded and
  thinly sliced
250g/9oz skinless chicken breast
  fillets, diced
juice of 1 lime
lime slices, to garnish
For the curry paste
  1 fresh red chilli, seeded and
    coarsely chopped
  4 garlic cloves, coarsely chopped
  3 shallots, coarsely chopped
  2 lemon grass stalks, sliced
  5cm/2in piece fresh turmeric,
    coarsely chopped, or 5ml/1 tsp
    ground turmeric
  5ml/1 tsp shrimp paste
  5ml/1 tsp salt

1 Make the yellow curry paste. Put the red chilli, garlic, shallots, lemon grass and turmeric in a mortar or food processor. Add the shrimp paste and salt. Pound or process to a paste, adding a little water if necessary.

COOK'S TIP
Fresh turmeric resembles root ginger in appearance and is a member of the same family. When preparing it, wear gloves to protect your hands from staining.

2 Pour the stock into a wok or medium pan and bring it to the boil. Stir in the curry paste. Bring back to the boil and add the tamarind juice, sugar and coconut milk. Add the papaya and chicken and cook over a medium to high heat for about 15 minutes, stirring frequently, until the chicken is cooked.

3 Stir in the lime juice, transfer to a warm dish and serve immediately, garnished with lime slices.

Energy 146kcal/619kJ; Protein 16.4g; Carbohydrate 18.6g, of which sugars 18g; Fat 1.2g, of which saturates 0.3g, of which polyunsaturates 0.2g; Cholesterol 44mg; Calcium 77mg; Fibre 3.5g; Sodium 103mg.

MARINATED DUCK CURRY ★★

A RICHLY SPICED CURRY THAT ILLUSTRATES THE POWERFUL CHINESE INFLUENCE ON THAI CUISINE. THE DUCK IS BEST MARINATED FOR AS LONG AS POSSIBLE, ALTHOUGH THE FLAVOUR WILL BE IMPROVED EVEN IF YOU ONLY HAVE TIME TO MARINATE IT BRIEFLY.

2 Meanwhile, bring a pan of water to the boil. Add the squash and cook for 10–15 minutes, until just tender. Drain well and set aside.

3 Pour the marinade from the duck into a wok and heat until boiling. Stir in the curry paste and cook for 2–3 minutes, until well blended and fragrant. Add the duck and cook for 3–4 minutes, stirring constantly, until browned on all sides.

4 Add the fish sauce and palm sugar and cook for 2 minutes more. Stir in the coconut milk until the mixture is smooth, then add the cooked squash, with the chillies and lime leaves.

5 Simmer gently, stirring frequently, for 5 minutes, then spoon into a dish, sprinkle with the coriander and serve.

VARIATION
This dish works just as well with skinless chicken breast fillets.

SERVES FOUR

INGREDIENTS
    4 duck breast portions, skin and
      bones removed
    30ml/2 tbsp five-spice powder
    15ml/1 tbsp sesame oil
    grated rind and juice of 1 orange
    1 medium butternut squash, peeled
      and cubed
    10ml/2 tsp Thai red curry paste
    30ml/2 tbsp Thai fish sauce
    15ml/1 tbsp palm sugar
    300ml/½ pint/1¼ cups reduced-fat
      coconut milk
    2 fresh red chillies, seeded
    4 kaffir lime leaves, torn
    small bunch coriander (cilantro),
      chopped, to garnish

1 Cut the duck meat into bitesize pieces and place in a bowl with the five-spice powder, sesame oil and orange rind and juice. Stir well to mix all the ingredients and coat the duck in the marinade. Cover the bowl with clear film (plastic wrap) and set aside in a cool place to marinate for at least 15 minutes.

Energy 182kcal/767kJ; Protein 20.3g; Carbohydrate 7.9g, of which sugars 7.9g; Fat 9.6g, of which saturates 1.9g, of which polyunsaturates 1.8g; Cholesterol 110mg; Calcium 61mg; Fibre 0.6g; Sodium 197mg.

DUCK IN A SPICY ORANGE SAUCE ★

DUCK HAS A DELICIOUSLY RICH FLAVOUR BUT THE SKIN CAN BE QUITE FATTY AND MAKE THIS MEAT DIFFICULT FOR THOSE FOLLOWING A LOW-FAT DIET. TO REDUCE THE FAT CONTENT OF THIS DISH SIMPLY REMOVE THE SKIN BEFORE SERVING. SERVE WITH STEAMED RICE AND BRIGHT VEGETABLES.

SERVES FOUR

INGREDIENTS

4 duck legs
4 garlic cloves, crushed
50g/2oz fresh root ginger, peeled and
  finely sliced
2 lemon grass stalks, trimmed,
  cut into 3 pieces and crushed
2 dried whole red Thai chillies
15ml/1 tbsp palm sugar
5ml/1 tsp five-spice powder
30ml/2 tbsp *nuoc cham* or *tuk trey*
900ml/1½ pints/3¾ cups fresh
  orange juice
sea salt and ground black pepper
1 lime, cut into quarters

3 Stir in the orange juice and place the duck legs back in the pan. Cover the pan and gently cook the duck for 1–2 hours, until the meat is tender and the sauce has reduced. Season and serve with lime wedges to squeeze over it.

1 Place the duck legs, skin side down, in a large heavy pan or flameproof clay pot. Cook them on both sides over a medium heat for about 10 minutes, until browned and crispy. Transfer them to a plate and set aside.

2 Stir the garlic, ginger, lemon grass and chillies into the fat left in the pan, and cook until golden. Add the sugar, five-spice powder and *nuoc cham* or *tuk trey*.

Energy 234kcal/986kJ; Protein 22.1g; Carbohydrate 26g, of which sugars 24.2g; Fat 6.9g, of which saturates 1.3g, of which polyunsaturates 0.6g; Cholesterol 110mg; Calcium 59mg; Fibre 1.2g; Sodium 137mg.

CRISPY ROAST DUCK ★★

This dish is Vietnam's answer to Peking duck, although here the succulent, crispy bird is enjoyed in one course. In a Vietnamese home, the duck is served with pickled vegetables or a salad, several dipping sauces, and a fragrant steamed rice.

2 Preheat the oven to 220°C/425°F/ Gas 7. Stuff the ginger, garlic, lemon grass and spring onions into the duck's cavity and tie the legs with string. Using a bamboo or metal skewer, poke holes in the skin, including the legs.

3 Place the duck, breast side down, on a rack over a roasting pan and cook it in the oven for 45 minutes, basting from time to time with the juices that have dripped into the pan. After 45 minutes, turn the duck over so that it is breast side up. Baste it generously and return it to the oven for a further 45 minutes, basting it every 15 minutes. The duck is ready once the juices run clear when the bird is pierced with a skewer.

4 Serve immediately, pulling at the skin and meat with your fingers, rather than neatly carving it. Serve with ginger dipping sauce, *nuoc mam gung*, pickled vegetables and salad leaves for wrapping up the morsels.

COOK'S TIP
Leaving the duck uncovered in the refrigerator for 24 hours will allow the skin to dry out thoroughly, ensuring that it becomes succulent and crispy when cooked.

SERVES SIX

INGREDIENTS
1 duck, about 2.25kg/5lb
90g/3½oz fresh root ginger, peeled, roughly chopped and lightly crushed
4 garlic cloves, peeled and crushed
1 lemon grass stalk, halved and bruised
4 spring onions (scallions), halved and crushed
ginger dipping sauce, *nuoc mam gung*, pickled vegetables and salad leaves, to serve
For the marinade
80ml/3fl oz *nuoc mam*
30ml/2 tbsp soy sauce
30ml/2 tbsp honey
15ml/1 tbsp five-spice powder
5ml/1 tsp ground ginger

1 In a bowl, beat the ingredients for the marinade together until well blended. Rub the skin of the duck lightly to loosen it, until you can get your fingers between the skin and the meat. Rub the marinade all over the duck, inside its skin and out, then place the duck on a rack over a tray and put it in the refrigerator for 24 hours.

Energy 210kcal/883kJ; Protein 27.4g; Carbohydrate 5.8g, of which sugars 4.5g; Fat 8.8g, of which saturates 2.7g, of which polyunsaturates 1.4g; Cholesterol 147mg; Calcium 35mg; Fibre 0.8g; Sodium 506mg.

DUCK WITH PINEAPPLE AND GINGER ★★

DUCK IS OFTEN THOUGHT OF AS A MEAT THAT IS HIGH IN FAT, BUT IN THIS RECIPE BONELESS DUCK BREAST FILLETS ARE SKINNED FOR A DISH THAT IS BURSTING WITH FLAVOUR AND LOW IN FAT. FRESH BABY SPINACH AND GREEN BEANS COMBINE PERFECTLY WITH THE PINEAPPLE AND GINGER.

SERVES THREE

INGREDIENTS
- 2 duck breast fillets
- 4 spring onions (scallions), chopped
- 15ml/1 tbsp light soy sauce
- 225g/8oz can pineapple rings
- 75ml/5 tbsp water
- 4 pieces drained stem ginger in syrup, plus 45ml/3 tbsp syrup from the jar
- 30ml/2 tbsp cornflour (cornstarch) mixed to a paste with a little water
- 1/4 each red and green (bell) pepper, seeded and cut into thin strips
- salt and ground black pepper
- cooked thin egg noodles, baby spinach and green beans, blanched, to serve

1 Strip the skin from the duck. Select a shallow bowl that will fit into your steamer and that will accommodate the duck fillets side by side. Spread out the chopped spring onions in the bowl, arrange the duck on top and cover with baking parchment. Set the steamer over boiling water and cook the duck for about 1 hour or until tender. Remove the duck from the steamer and leave to cool slightly.

2 Cut the duck fillets into thin slices. Place on a plate and moisten them with a little of the cooking juices from the steaming bowl. Strain the remaining juices into a small pan and set aside. Cover the duck slices with the baking parchment or foil and keep warm.

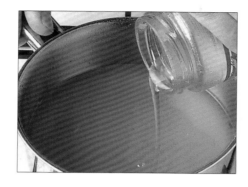

3 Drain the canned pineapple rings, reserving 75ml/5 tbsp of the juice. Add this to the reserved cooking juices in the pan, together with the measured water. Stir in the ginger syrup, then stir in the cornflour paste and cook, stirring until thickened. Season to taste.

4 Cut the pineapple and ginger into attractive shapes. Put the cooked noodles, baby spinach and green beans on a plate, add slices of duck and top with the pineapple, ginger and pepper strips. Pour over the sauce and serve.

Energy 253kcal/1071kJ; Protein 20.8g; Carbohydrate 33.1g, of which sugars 23.8g; Fat 6.8g, of which saturates 1.4g, of which polyunsaturates 0.7g; Cholesterol 110mg; Calcium 31mg; Fibre 1.1g; Sodium 515mg.

MEAT DISHES

Meat curries are traditional in many South-east Asian countries, but they contain relatively small amounts of meat and plenty of vegetables, rice and noodles, making them an excellent choice for anyone trying to cut down on red meat. Stir-frying is another popular way of cooking meat, a technique that has the advantage of combining speed with a minimum of fat. Try some of these delicious recipes for a quick and healthy supper, including Lemon Grass Pork and Thai Beef Salad.

PORK ON LEMON GRASS STICKS ★

THIS SIMPLE RECIPE MAKES A SUBSTANTIAL SNACK, AND THE LEMON GRASS STICKS NOT ONLY ADD A SUBTLE FLAVOUR BUT ALSO MAKE A GOOD TALKING POINT.

SERVES FOUR

INGREDIENTS
    300g/11oz minced (ground)
      lean pork
    4 garlic cloves, crushed
    4 fresh coriander (cilantro) roots,
      finely chopped
    2.5ml/½ tsp granulated sugar
    15ml/1 tbsp soy sauce
    salt and ground black pepper
    8 x 10cm/4in lengths of lemon
      grass stalk
    sweet chilli sauce, to serve

VARIATION
Slimmer versions of these pork sticks are perfect for parties. The mixture will be enough for 12 lemon grass sticks if you use it sparingly.

1 Place the minced pork, crushed garlic, chopped coriander root, sugar and soy sauce in a large bowl. Season with salt and pepper to taste and mix well.

2 Divide into eight portions and mould each one into a ball. It may help to dampen your hands before shaping the mixture to prevent it from sticking.

3 Stick a length of lemon grass halfway into each ball, then press the meat mixture around the lemon grass to make a shape like a chicken leg.

4 Cook the pork sticks under a hot grill (broiler) for 3–4 minutes on each side, until golden and cooked through. Serve with the chilli sauce for dipping.

Energy 111kcal/467kJ; Protein 17.5g; Carbohydrate 3.3g, of which sugars 1.4g; Fat 3.2g, of which saturates 1.1g, of which polyunsaturates 0.6g; Cholesterol 47mg; Calcium 29mg; Fibre 1g; Sodium 323mg.

LAMB SATÉ ★

THESE TASTY LAMB SKEWERS ARE TRADITIONALLY SERVED WITH DAINTY DIAMOND-SHAPED PIECES OF COMPRESSED RICE, WHICH ARE SURPRISINGLY SIMPLE TO MAKE. OFFER THE REMAINING SAUCE FOR DIPPING.

MAKES THIRTY SKEWERS

INGREDIENTS
  1kg/2¼lb leg of lamb, boned
  3 garlic cloves, crushed
  15–30ml/1–2 tbsp chilli sambal or
    5–10ml/1–2 tsp chilli powder
  90ml/6 tbsp dark soy sauce
  juice of 1 lemon
  salt and ground black pepper
  spray sunflower oil, for spraying
For the chilli sauce
  6 garlic cloves, crushed
  15ml/1 tbsp chilli sambal or
    2–3 fresh chillies, seeded and
    ground to a paste
  90ml/6 tbsp dark soy sauce
  25ml/1½ tbsp lemon juice
  30ml/2 tbsp boiling water
To serve
  thinly sliced onion
  cucumber wedges (optional)
  compressed-rice shapes (see
    Cook's Tip)

1 Cut the lamb into neat 1cm/½in cubes. Remove any pieces of gristle, and trim off any excess fat. Spread out the lamb cubes in a single layer in a shallow bowl.

2 Put the garlic, chilli sambal or chilli powder, soy sauce and lemon juice in a mortar. Add salt and pepper and grind to a paste. Alternatively, process the mixture using a food processor. Pour over the lamb and mix to coat. Cover and leave in a cool place for at least 1 hour. Soak wooden or bamboo skewers in water to prevent them from scorching during cooking.

3 Prepare the chilli sauce. Put the crushed garlic into a bowl. Add the chilli sambal or fresh chillies, soy sauce, lemon juice and boiling water. Stir well. Preheat the grill.

4 Thread the meat on to the skewers. Spray the skewered meat with oil and grill, turning often. Brush the saté with a little of the sauce and serve hot, with onion, cucumber wedges, if using, rice shapes and the sauce.

COOK'S TIP
Compressed rice shapes are easy to make. Cook two 115g/4oz packets of boil-in-the-bag rice in a large pan of salted, boiling water and simmer for 1¼ hours until the cooked rice fills each bag like a plump cushion. The bags must be covered with water throughout. When cool, cut each rice slab horizontally in half, then into diamond shapes using a sharp, wetted knife.

Energy 33kcal/139kJ; Protein 3.5g; Carbohydrate 0.6g, of which sugars 0.3g; Fat 1.9g, of which saturates 0.9g, of which polyunsaturates 0.1g; Cholesterol 13mg; Calcium 2mg; Fibre 0.1g; Sodium 86mg.

DRY-COOKED PORK STRIPS ★★

THIS TASTY DISH IS QUICK AND LIGHT ON A HOT DAY. PORK, CHICKEN, PRAWNS AND SQUID CAN ALL BE COOKED THIS WAY. WITH THE LETTUCE AND HERBS, IT'S A VERY FLAVOURSOME MEAL, BUT YOU CAN SERVE IT WITH JASMINE RICE AND A DIPPING SAUCE, IF YOU LIKE.

SERVES TWO

INGREDIENTS
    15ml/1 tbsp sunflower oil
    30ml/2 tbsp *tuk trey*
    30ml/2 tbsp soy sauce
    5ml/1 tsp sugar
    225g/8oz lean pork fillet, cut into
      thin, bitesize strips
    8 lettuce leaves
    chilli sauce, for drizzling
    fresh coriander (cilantro) leaves
    a handful of fresh mint leaves

VARIATION
Try basil, flat leaf parsley, spring onions
or sliced red onion in these parcels.

1 In a wok or heavy pan, heat the oil, *tuk trey* and soy sauce with the sugar. Add the pork and stir-fry over a medium heat, until all the liquid has evaporated. Cook the pork until it turns brown, almost caramelized, but not burnt.

2 Use a slotted spoon to lift the pork strips out of the wok. Drop spoonfuls of the cooked pork into lettuce leaves, drizzle a little chilli sauce over the top, add a few coriander and mint leaves, wrap them up and serve immediately.

Energy 104kcal/435kJ; Protein 12.5g; Carbohydrate 2.1g, of which sugars 2g; Fat 5.1g, of which saturates 1.2g, of which polyunsaturates 2.2g; Cholesterol 35mg; Calcium 13mg; Fibre 0.2g; Sodium 574mg.

CHA SHAO ★★

This dish is often known as barbecue pork and is very popular throughout South-east Asia. If you like, the marinade can be heated thoroughly, then served with the meat as a sauce. Serve it with steamed rice and a fresh green salad for a low-fat meal.

SERVES SIX

INGREDIENTS

900g/2lb lean pork fillet (tenderloin)
15ml/1 tbsp clear honey
45ml/3 tbsp rice wine or
   medium-dry sherry
spring onion (scallion) curls,
   to garnish
For the marinade
150ml/1/4 pint/2/3 cup dark
   soy sauce
90ml/6 tbsp rice wine or
   medium-dry sherry
150ml/1/4 pint/2/3 cup well-flavoured
   chicken stock
15ml/1 tbsp soft brown sugar
1cm/1/2in piece fresh root ginger,
   peeled and finely sliced
40ml/21/2 tbsp chopped onion

1 Mix all the marinade ingredients in a pan and stir over a medium heat until the mixture boils. Lower the heat and simmer gently for 15 minutes, stirring from time to time. Leave to cool.

2 Put the pork fillets in a shallow dish that is large enough to hold them side by side. Pour over 250ml/8fl oz/1 cup of the marinade, cover and chill for at least 8 hours, turning the meat over several times.

COOK'S TIP
You will have extra marinade when making this dish. Chill or freeze this and use to baste other grilled (broiled) dishes or meats, such as spare ribs.

3 Preheat the oven to 200°C/400°F/Gas 6. Drain the pork fillets, reserving the marinade in the dish. Place the meat on a rack over a roasting pan and pour water into the pan to a depth of 1cm/1/2in. Place the pan in the oven and roast for 20 minutes.

4 Stir the honey and rice wine or sherry into the marinade. Remove the meat from the oven and place in the marinade, turning to coat. Put back on the rack and roast for 20–30 minutes or until cooked. Serve hot or cold, in slices, garnished with spring onion curls.

Energy 211kcal/886kJ; Protein 32.5g; Carbohydrate 4.8g, of which sugars 4.7g; Fat 6g, of which saturates 2.1g, of which polyunsaturates 1.1g; Cholesterol 95mg; Calcium 14mg; Fibre 0g; Sodium 996mg.

SWEET-AND-SOUR PORK STIR-FRY ★

THIS IS A GREAT IDEA FOR A QUICK FAMILY SUPPER. REMEMBER TO CUT THE CARROTS INTO THIN MATCHSTICK STRIPS SO THAT THEY COOK IN TIME.

SERVES FOUR

INGREDIENTS
    450g/1lb lean pork fillet (tenderloin)
    30ml/2 tbsp plain (all-purpose) flour
    5ml/1 tsp sunflower oil
    1 onion, roughly chopped
    1 garlic clove, crushed
    1 green (bell) pepper, seeded
      and sliced
    350g/12oz carrots, cut into
      thin strips
    225g/8oz can bamboo shoots, drained
    15ml/1 tbsp white wine vinegar
    15ml/1 tbsp soft brown sugar
    10ml/2 tsp tomato purée (paste)
    30ml/2 tbsp light soy sauce
    salt and ground black pepper

1 Thinly slice the pork. Season the flour and toss the pork in it to coat.

2 Heat the oil and cook the pork for 5 minutes, until golden. Remove the pork and drain on kitchen paper. You may need to do this in several batches.

3 Add the onion and garlic to the pan and cook for 3 minutes. Stir in the pepper and carrots and stir-fry over a high heat for 6–8 minutes, or until beginning to soften slightly.

4 Return the meat to the pan with the bamboo shoots. Add the remaining ingredients with 120ml/4fl oz/½ cup water and bring to the boil. Simmer gently for 2–3 minutes, or until piping hot. Adjust the seasoning, if necessary, and serve immediately.

VARIATION
Finely sliced strips of skinless chicken breast fillet can be used in this recipe instead of the pork.

Energy 235kcal/988kJ; Protein 25.3g; Carbohydrate 23.9g, of which sugars 16.2g; Fat 4.9g, of which saturates 1.6g, of which polyunsaturates 1.1g; Cholesterol 63mg; Calcium 62mg; Fibre 4.2g; Sodium 637mg.

STIR-FRIED PORK <u>WITH</u> DRIED SHRIMP ★★

YOU MIGHT EXPECT THE DRIED SHRIMP TO GIVE THIS DISH A FISHY FLAVOUR, BUT INSTEAD IT SIMPLY IMPARTS A DELICIOUS SAVOURY TASTE.

<u>SERVES FOUR</u>

INGREDIENTS

    250g/9oz lean pork fillet
      (tenderloin), sliced
    15ml/1 tbsp sunflower oil
    2 garlic cloves, finely chopped
    45ml/3 tbsp dried shrimp
    10ml/2 tsp dried shrimp paste or
      5mm/¼ in piece from block of
      shrimp paste
    30ml/2 tbsp soy sauce
    juice of 1 lime
    15ml/1 tbsp palm sugar or light
      muscovado (brown) sugar
    1 small fresh red or green chilli,
      seeded and finely chopped
    4 pak choi (bok choy) or 450g/1lb
      spring greens (collards), shredded

1 Place the pork in the freezer for about 30 minutes, until firm. Using a sharp knife, cut it into thin slices.

2 Heat the oil in a wok or frying pan and cook the garlic until golden brown. Add the pork and stir-fry for about 4 minutes, until just cooked through.

3 Add the dried shrimp, then stir in the shrimp paste, with the soy sauce, lime juice and sugar. Add the chilli and pak choi or spring greens and toss over the heat until the vegetables are just wilted.

4 Transfer the stir-fry to warm individual bowls and serve immediately.

Energy 175kcal/731kJ; Protein 23.1g; Carbohydrate 6.3g, of which sugars 6.2g; Fat 6.4g, of which saturates 1.4g, of which polyunsaturates 2.8g; Cholesterol 96mg; Calcium 334mg; Fibre 2.4g; Sodium 1223mg.

RICE ROLLS STUFFED WITH PORK ★

IN THIS CLASSIC ASIAN DISH STEAMED RICE SHEETS ARE FILLED WITH MINCED PORK, ROLLED UP AND THEN DIPPED IN NUOC CHAM. SERVE WITH ANY OF THE VEGETARIAN SALADS IN THE VEGETABLES AND SALADS CHAPTER FOR A HEALTHY LOW-FAT MEAL.

SERVES SIX

INGREDIENTS

25g/1oz dried cloud ear (wood ear)
  mushrooms, soaked in warm water
  for 30 minutes
350g/12oz minced (ground) lean pork
30nl/2 tbsp *nuoc mam*
10ml/2 tsp sugar
15ml/1 tbsp sunflower oil
2 garlic cloves, finely chopped
2 shallots, finely chopped
2 spring onions (scallions), trimmed
  and finely chopped
24 fresh rice sheets, 7.5cm/3in square
ground black pepper
nuoc cham, for dipping

COOK'S TIP
To make life easy, prepared, fresh rice
sheets are available in Asian markets.

1 Drain the mushrooms and squeeze
out any excess water. Cut off and
discard the hard stems. Finely chop the
rest of the mushrooms and put them in
a bowl. Add the minced pork, *nuoc
mam*, and sugar and mix well.

2 Heat the oil in a wok or heavy pan.
Add the garlic, shallots and onions. Stir-
fry until golden. Add the pork mixture
and stir-fry for 5–6 minutes, until the
pork is cooked. Season with pepper.

3 Place the fresh rice sheets on a flat
surface. Spoon a tablespoon of the
pork mixture on to the middle of each
sheet. Fold one side over the filling,
tuck in the sides, and roll up to
enclose the filling, so that it resembles
a short spring roll.

4 Place the filled rice rolls on a serving
plate and serve with *nuoc cham* or any
other chilli or tangy sauce of your
choice, for dipping.

Energy 160kcal/670kJ; Protein 13.8g; Carbohydrate 16g, of which sugars 2.4g; Fat 4.4g, of which saturates 1.1g, of which polyunsaturates 1.6g; Cholesterol 37mg; Calcium 13mg; Fibre 0.6g; Sodium 43mg.

LEMON GRASS PORK ★★

CHILLIES AND LEMON GRASS FLAVOUR THIS SIMPLE STIR-FRY, WHILE PEANUTS ADD AN INTERESTING CONTRAST IN TEXTURE. LOOK FOR JARS OF CHOPPED LEMON GRASS, WHICH ARE HANDY WHEN THE FRESH VEGETABLE ISN'T AVAILABLE. THE PEANUTS ENRICH THE FLAVOUR WITHOUT SIGNIFICANTLY ADDING FAT.

SERVES FOUR

INGREDIENTS

500g/1¼lb boneless pork loin
2 lemon grass stalks,
  finely chopped
4 spring onions (scallions),
  thinly sliced
5ml/1 tsp salt
12 black peppercorns,
  coarsely crushed
15ml/1 tbsp sunflower oil
2 garlic cloves, chopped
2 fresh red chillies, seeded
  and chopped
5ml/1 tsp soft light brown sugar
30ml/2 tbsp Thai fish sauce
30ml/2 tbsp roasted unsalted
  peanuts, chopped
ground black pepper
cooked rice noodles, to serve
coarsely torn coriander (cilantro)
  leaves, to garnish

3 Add the garlic and red chillies and stir-fry for a further 5–8 minutes over a medium heat, until the pork is cooked through and tender.

4 Add the sugar, fish sauce and chopped peanuts and toss to mix, then season to taste with black pepper. Serve immediately on a bed of rice noodles, garnished with the coarsely torn coriander leaves.

COOK'S TIP
The heat in chillies is not in the seeds, but in the membranes surrounding them, which are removed along with the seeds.

1 Trim any excess fat from the pork. Cut the meat across into 5mm/¼in thick slices, then cut each slice into 5mm/¼in strips. Put the pork into a bowl with the finely chopped lemon grass, thinly sliced spring onions, salt and crushed peppercorns; mix well. Cover the bowl with clear film (plastic wrap) and leave to marinate in a cool place or the refrigerator for 30 minutes.

2 Preheat a wok, add the oil and swirl it around. Add the pork mixture and stir-fry over a medium heat for about 3 minutes, until browned all over.

Energy 205kcal/856kJ; Protein 27.9g; Carbohydrate 1.8g, of which sugars 1.6g; Fat 9.5g, of which saturates 2.4g, of which polyunsaturates 3.1g; Cholesterol 79mg; Calcium 16mg; Fibre 0.4g; Sodium 88mg.

SAENG WA OF GRILLED PORK ★

PORK FILLET IS CUT IN STRIPS BEFORE BEING GRILLED. SHREDDED AND THEN TOSSED WITH A DELICIOUS SWEET-SOUR SAUCE, IT MAKES A MARVELLOUS WARM SALAD.

3 Transfer the cooked pork strips to a board. Slice the meat across the grain, then shred it with a fork. Place in a large bowl and add the shallot slices, lemon grass, kaffir lime leaves, ginger, chilli and chopped coriander.

4 Make the dressing. Place the sugar, fish sauce, lime juice and tamarind juice in a bowl. Whisk until the sugar has completely dissolved. Pour the dressing over the pork mixture and toss well to mix, then serve.

VARIATION

If you want to extend this dish a little, add cooked rice or noodles. Thin strips of red or yellow (bell) pepper could also be added. For a colour contrast, add lightly cooked green beans, sugar snap peas or mangetouts (snow peas).

SERVES FOUR

INGREDIENTS
    30ml/2 tbsp dark soy sauce
    15ml/1 tbsp clear honey
    400g/14oz pork fillet (tenderloin)
    6 shallots, very thinly
        sliced lengthways
    1 lemon grass stalk, thinly sliced
    5 kaffir lime leaves, thinly sliced
    5cm/2in piece fresh root ginger,
        peeled and sliced into
        fine shreds
    ½ fresh long red chilli, seeded and
        sliced into fine shreds
    small bunch fresh coriander
        (cilantro), chopped
For the dressing
    30ml/2 tbsp palm sugar or light
        muscovado (brown) sugar
    30ml/2 tbsp Thai fish sauce
    juice of 2 limes
    20ml/4 tsp thick tamarind juice,
        made by mixing tamarind paste
        with warm water

1 Preheat the grill (broiler) to medium. Mix the soy sauce with the honey in a small bowl or jug (pitcher) and stir until the honey has completely dissolved.

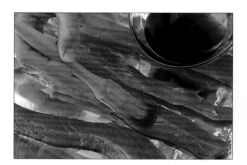

2 Using a sharp knife, cut the pork fillet lengthways into quarters to make four long, thick strips. Place the pork strips in a grill pan. Brush generously with the soy sauce and honey mixture, then grill (broil) for about 10–15 minutes, until cooked through and tender. Turn the strips over frequently and baste with the soy sauce and honey mixture.

Energy 182kcal/767kJ; Protein 22.6g; Carbohydrate 14.3g, of which sugars 13.5g; Fat 4.2g, of which saturates 1.4g, of which polyunsaturates 0.7g; Cholesterol 63mg; Calcium 45mg; Fibre 1g; Sodium 1144mg.

BRAISED BLACK PEPPER PORK ★

THIS CAMBODIAN DISH IS QUICK, TASTY AND BEAUTIFULLY WARMING THANKS TO THE GINGER AND BLACK PEPPER. IT IS SURE TO BE A POPULAR CHOICE FOR A FAMILY MEAL.

SERVES SIX

INGREDIENTS
- 1 litre/1¾ pints/4 cups water
- 45ml/3 tbsp *tuk trey*
- 30ml/2 tbsp soy sauce
- 15ml/1 tbsp sugar
- 4 garlic cloves, crushed
- 40g/1½oz fresh root ginger, peeled and finely shredded
- 15ml/1 tbsp freshly ground black pepper
- 675g/1½lb lean pork shoulder or rump, cut into bitesize cubes
- steamed jasmine rice, crunchy salad and pickles or stir-fried greens, such as water spinach or long beans, to serve

1 In a large heavy pan, bring the water, *tuk trey* and soy sauce to the boil. Reduce the heat and stir in the sugar, garlic, ginger, black pepper and pork. Cover the pan and simmer for about 1½ hours, until the pork is very tender and the liquid has reduced.

2 Serve the pork in individual bowls with steamed jasmine rice. Drizzle the braised juices over it, and accompany it with a fresh crunchy salad, pickles or stir-fried greens, such as the delicious stir-fried water spinach with *nuoc cham*, or long beans.

Energy 154kcal/647kJ; Protein 24.4g; Carbohydrate 4g, of which sugars 3.7g; Fat 4.5g, of which saturates 1.6g, of which polyunsaturates 0.8g; Cholesterol 71mg; Calcium 13mg; Fibre 0.1g; Sodium 613mg.

PORK AND PINEAPPLE COCONUT CURRY ★

THE HEAT OF THIS CURRY BALANCES OUT ITS SWEETNESS TO MAKE A SMOOTH AND FRAGRANT DISH. IT TAKES VERY LITTLE TIME TO COOK, SO IS IDEAL FOR A QUICK SUPPER BEFORE GOING OUT OR FOR A MID-WEEK FAMILY MEAL ON A BUSY EVENING.

SERVES FOUR

INGREDIENTS

- 400ml/14fl oz reduced-fat coconut milk
- 10ml/2 tsp Thai red curry paste
- 400g/14oz lean pork loin steaks, trimmed and thinly sliced
- 15ml/1 tbsp Thai fish sauce
- 5ml/1 tsp palm sugar or light muscovado (brown) sugar
- 15ml/1 tbsp tamarind juice, made by mixing tamarind paste with warm water
- 2 kaffir lime leaves, torn
- ½ medium pineapple, peeled and chopped
- 1 fresh red chilli, seeded and finely chopped

1 Pour the coconut milk into a bowl and let it settle, so that the cream rises to the surface. Scoop the cream into a measuring jug (cup). You should have about 250ml/8fl oz/1 cup. If necessary, add a little of the coconut milk.

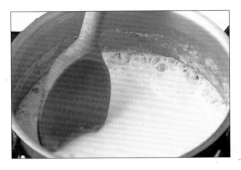

2 Pour the coconut cream into a large pan and bring it to the boil.

3 Cook the coconut cream for about 10 minutes, until the cream separates, stirring frequently to prevent it from sticking to the base of the pan and scorching. Add the red curry paste and stir until well mixed. Cook, stirring occasionally, for about 4 minutes, until the paste is fragrant.

4 Add the sliced pork and stir in the fish sauce, sugar and tamarind juice. Cook, stirring constantly, for 1–2 minutes, until the sugar has dissolved and the pork is no longer pink.

5 Add the remaining coconut milk and the lime leaves. Bring to the boil, then stir in the pineapple. Reduce the heat and simmer gently for 3 minutes, or until the pork is fully cooked. Sprinkle over the chilli and serve.

Energy 189kcal/800kJ; Protein 22.1g; Carbohydrate 16.1g, of which sugars 16.1g; Fat 4.5g, of which saturates 1.6g, of which polyunsaturates 0.8g; Cholesterol 63mg; Calcium 55mg; Fibre 1.2g; Sodium 182mg.

good.

SWEET AND SOUR PORK, THAI-STYLE ★

IT WAS THE CHINESE WHO ORIGINALLY CREATED SWEET AND SOUR COOKING, BUT THE THAIS ALSO DO IT VERY WELL. THIS VERSION HAS A FRESHER AND CLEANER FLAVOUR THAN THE ORIGINAL. IT MAKES A GOOD ONE-DISH MEAL WHEN SERVED OVER RICE.

SERVES FOUR

INGREDIENTS
    350g/12oz lean pork
    15ml/1 tbsp sunflower oil
    4 garlic cloves, thinly sliced
    1 small red onion, sliced
    30ml/2 tbsp Thai fish sauce
    15ml/1 tbsp granulated sugar
    1 red (bell) pepper, seeded and diced
    ½ cucumber, seeded and sliced
    2 plum tomatoes, cut into wedges
    115g/4oz piece of fresh pineapple,
      cut into small chunks
    2 spring onions (scallions), cut into
      short lengths
    ground black pepper
To garnish
    coriander (cilantro) leaves
    spring onions (scallions), shredded

1 Place the pork in the freezer for 30–40 minutes, until firm. Using a sharp knife, cut it into thin strips.

2 Heat the oil in a wok or large frying pan. Add the garlic. Cook over a medium heat until golden, then add the pork and stir-fry for 4–5 minutes. Add the onion slices and toss to mix.

3 Add the fish sauce, sugar and ground black pepper to taste. Toss the mixture over the heat for 3–4 minutes more.

4 Stir in the red pepper, cucumber, tomatoes, pineapple and spring onions. Stir-fry for 3–4 minutes more, then spoon into a bowl. Garnish with the coriander and spring onions and serve.

Energy 168kcal/708kJ; Protein 20.3g; Carbohydrate 13.5g, of which sugars 12.9g; Fat 4g, of which saturates 1.3g, of which polyunsaturates 0.9g; Cholesterol 55mg; Calcium 32mg; Fibre 2g; Sodium 604mg.

CURRIED PORK WITH PICKLED GARLIC ★★

THIS VERY RICH CURRY IS BEST ACCOMPANIED BY LOTS OF PLAIN RICE AND PERHAPS A LIGHT VEGETABLE DISH. IT COULD SERVE FOUR IF SERVED WITH A VEGETABLE CURRY. IT IS WELL WORTH INVESTING IN A JAR OF PICKLED GARLIC FROM ASIAN STORES, AS THE TASTE IS SWEET AND DELICIOUS.

SERVES TWO

INGREDIENTS
130g/4½oz lean pork steaks
15ml/1 tbsp sunflower oil
1 garlic clove, crushed
15ml/1 tbsp Thai red curry paste
130ml/4½fl oz/generous ½ cup
  reduced-fat coconut milk
2.5cm/1in piece fresh root ginger,
  finely chopped
30ml/2 tbsp vegetable or
  chicken stock
30ml/2 tbsp Thai fish sauce
5ml/1 tsp granulated sugar
2.5ml/½ tsp ground turmeric
10ml/2 tsp lemon juice
4 pickled garlic cloves,
  finely chopped
strips of lemon and lime rind,
  to garnish

1 Place the pork steaks in the freezer for 30–40 minutes, until firm, then, using a sharp knife, cut the meat into fine slivers, trimming off any excess fat.

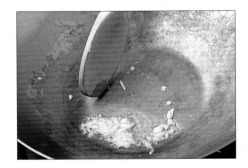

2 Heat the oil in a wok or large, heavy frying pan and cook the garlic over a low to medium heat until golden brown. Do not let it burn. Add the curry paste and stir it in well.

3 Add the coconut milk and stir until the liquid begins to reduce and thicken. Stir in the pork. Cook for 2 minutes more, until the pork is cooked through.

4 Add the ginger, stock, fish sauce, sugar and turmeric, stirring constantly, then add the lemon juice and pickled garlic. Spoon into bowls, garnish with strips of rind, and serve.

Energy 160kcal/667kJ; Protein 14.9g; Carbohydrate 6g, of which sugars 5.9g; Fat 8.6g, of which saturates 1.7g, of which polyunsaturates 4g; Cholesterol 41mg; Calcium 75mg; Fibre 1.3g; Sodium 126mg.

STIR-FRIED PORK AND BUTTERNUT CURRY ★

THIS CURRY CAN BE MADE WITH BUTTERNUT SQUASH, PUMPKIN OR WINTER MELON. FLAVOURED WITH GALANGAL AND TURMERIC, IT IS DELICIOUS SERVED WITH RICE AND A FRUIT-BASED SALAD, OR EVEN JUST WITH CHUNKS OF FRESH CRUSTY BREAD TO MOP UP THE TASTY SAUCE.

SERVES SIX

INGREDIENTS
- 10ml/2 tsp sunflower oil
- 25g/1oz galangal, finely sliced
- 2 red Thai chillies, peeled, seeded and finely sliced
- 3 shallots, halved and finely sliced
- 30ml/2 tbsp *kroeung*
- 10ml/2 tsp ground turmeric
- 5ml/1 tsp ground fenugreek
- 10ml/2 tsp palm sugar
- 450g/1lb lean pork loin, cut into bitesize chunks
- 30ml/2 tbsp *tuk prahoc*
- 900ml/1½ pints/3¾ cups reduced-fat coconut milk
- 1 butternut squash, peeled, seeded and cut into bitesize chunks
- 4 kaffir lime leaves
- sea salt and ground black pepper
- 1 small bunch fresh coriander (cilantro), coarsely chopped and
- 1 small bunch fresh mint, stalks removed, to garnish
- rice or noodles and salad, to serve

2 Stir in the chunks of pork loin and stir-fry until golden brown on all sides. Stir in the *tuk prahoc* and pour in the coconut milk.

COOK'S TIP
Increase the number of chillies if you want a really hot curry.

3 Bring to the boil, add the squash and the lime leaves, and reduce the heat. Cook gently, uncovered, for 15–20 minutes, until the squash and pork are tender and the sauce has reduced. Season to taste. Garnish the curry with the coriander and mint, and serve with rice or noodles and salad.

1 Heat the oil in a large wok or heavy pan. Stir in the galangal, chillies and shallots and stir-fry until fragrant. Add the *kroeung* and stir-fry until it begins to colour. Add the turmeric, fenugreek and sugar.

VARIATION
For a vegetarian option, omit the pork and use baby aubergines (eggplants) instead. The Cambodian flavourings and creamy coconut milk work well with many combinations.

Energy 149kcal/628kJ; Protein 17g; Carbohydrate 10.6g, of which sugars 10.2g; Fat 4.6g, of which saturates 1.5g, of which polyunsaturates 1.2g; Cholesterol 47mg; Calcium 71mg; Fibre 0.7g; Sodium 221mg.

BAKED CINNAMON MEAT LOAF ★

THIS TYPE OF MEAT LOAF IS USUALLY SERVED AS A SUPPER OR LIGHT LUNCH, WITH A CRUSTY BAGUETTE. ACCOMPANIED WITH EITHER TART PICKLES OR A CRUNCHY SALAD, AND SPLASHED WITH PIQUANT SAUCE, IT IS LIGHT AND TASTY.

SERVES FOUR TO SIX

INGREDIENTS

30ml/2 tbsp *nuoc mam*
25ml/1½ tbsp ground cinnamon
10ml/2 tsp sugar
5ml/1 tsp ground black pepper
15ml/1 tbsp potato starch
450g/1lb lean minced (ground) pork
30ml/2 tbsp sunflower oil
2–3 shallots, very finely chopped
spray sunflower oil, for greasing
nuoc cham, for drizzling
red chilli strips, to garnish
bread or noodles, to serve

COOK'S TIPS
• Serve the meat loaf as a nibble with drinks by cutting it into bitesize squares or fingers.
• Serve with a piquant sauce for dipping.
• Cut the meat loaf into wedges and take on a picnic to eat with bread and pickles or chutney.
• Fry slices of meat loaf until browned and serve with fried eggs.

VARIATION
For a delicious meat loaf that is even lower in fat, replace the lean minced (ground) pork with chicken breast fillets.

1 In a large bowl, mix together the *nuoc mam*, ground cinnamon, sugar and ground black pepper. Sprinkle over the potato starch and beat until the mixture is smooth.

2 Add the minced pork, the oil, and the very finely chopped shallots to the bowl and mix thoroughly. Cover with clear film (plastic wrap) and put in the refrigerator for 3–4 hours.

3 Preheat the oven to 180°C/350°F/ Gas 4. Lightly oil a baking tin (pan) and spread the pork and shallot mixture in the tin in an even layer – when pressed, the potato starch should mean it feels springy.

4 Cover with foil and bake in the oven for 35–40 minutes. If you want the top to turn brown and crunchy, remove the foil for the last 10 minutes.

5 Turn the meat loaf out on to a board and slice it into strips. Drizzle the strips with *nuoc cham*, and serve them hot with bread or noodles.

Energy 158kcal/661kJ; Protein 16.8g; Carbohydrate 7.7g, of which sugars 4.6g; Fat 6.8g, of which saturates 1.5g, of which polyunsaturates 2.9g; Cholesterol 47mg; Calcium 19mg; Fibre 0.8g; Sodium 54mg.

SEARED BEEF SALAD IN A LIME DRESSING ★★

THIS BEEF DISH IS AN INDO-CHINESE FAVOURITE AND VERSIONS OF IT ARE ENJOYED IN VIETNAM, THAILAND, CAMBODIA AND LAOS. IT IS ALSO ONE OF THE TRADITIONAL DISHES THAT APPEAR IN THE BEEF SEVEN WAYS FEAST IN WHICH SEVEN DIFFERENT BEEF DISHES ARE SERVED.

SERVES SIX

INGREDIENTS
about 7.5ml/1½ tsp sunflower oil
450g/1lb beef fillet, cut into steaks
  2.5cm/1in thick
115g/4oz/½ cup beansprouts
1 bunch each fresh basil and mint,
  stalks removed, leaves shredded
1 lime, cut into slices, to serve
For the dressing
  grated and juice (about 80ml/3fl oz)
    of 2 limes
  30ml/2 tbsp *nuoc mam*
  30ml/2 tbsp raw cane sugar
  2 garlic cloves, crushed
  2 lemon grass stalks, finely sliced
  2 red Serrano chillies, seeded and
    finely sliced

3 Drain the meat of any excess juice and transfer it to a wide serving bowl. Add the beansprouts and herbs and toss it all together. Serve with lime slices to squeeze over.

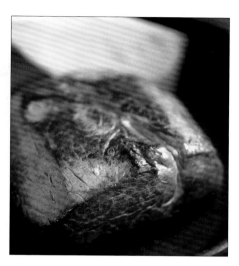

1 To make the dressing, beat the lime rind, juice and *nuoc mam* in a bowl with the sugar, until the sugar dissolves. Stir in the garlic, lemon grass and chillies and set aside.

2 Pour a little oil into a heavy pan and rub it over the base with a piece of kitchen paper. Heat the pan and sear the steaks for 1–2 minutes each side. Transfer them to a board and leave to cool a little. Using a sharp knife, cut the meat into thin slices. Toss the slices in the dressing, cover and leave to marinate for 1–2 hours.

COOK'S TIP
It is worth buying an excellent-quality piece of tender beef fillet for this recipe as the meat is only just seared.

Energy 174kcal/727kJ; Protein 18.4g; Carbohydrate 7.3g, of which sugars 6g; Fat 8.1g, of which saturates 3g, of which polyunsaturates 0.9g; Cholesterol 44mg; Calcium 28mg; Fibre 1g; Sodium 52mg.

LARP OF CHIANG MAI ★

CHIANG MAI IS A CITY IN THE NORTH-EAST OF THAILAND. THE CITY IS CULTURALLY VERY CLOSE TO LAOS AND FAMOUS FOR ITS CHICKEN SALAD, WHICH WAS ORIGINALLY CALLED "LAAP" OR "LARP". DUCK, BEEF OR PORK CAN BE USED INSTEAD OF CHICKEN.

SERVES FOUR

INGREDIENTS
450g/1lb minced (ground) chicken
    or pork
1 lemon grass stalk, root trimmed
3 kaffir lime leaves, finely chopped
4 fresh red chillies, seeded
    and chopped
60ml/4 tbsp lime juice
30ml/2 tbsp Thai fish sauce
15ml/1 tbsp roasted ground rice (see
    Cook's Tip)
2 spring onions (scallions), chopped
30ml/2 tbsp fresh coriander
    (cilantro) leaves
thinly sliced kaffir lime leaves, mixed
    salad leaves and fresh mint sprigs,
    to garnish

1 Heat a large non-stick frying pan. Add the minced chicken or pork and moisten with a little water. Stir constantly over a medium heat for 7–10 minutes until it is cooked. Meanwhile, cut off the lower 5cm/2in of the lemon grass stalk and chop finely.

2 Transfer the cooked chicken to a bowl and add the chopped lemon grass, lime leaves, chillies, lime juice, fish sauce, ground rice, spring onions and coriander. Mix thoroughly.

3 Spoon the chicken mixture into a salad bowl. Sprinkle sliced kaffir lime leaves over the top and garnish with salad leaves and sprigs of mint.

COOK'S TIP
Use glutinous rice for the roasted ground rice. Put the rice in a frying pan and dry-fry it until golden brown. Remove and grind to a powder, using a pestle and mortar or a food processor. When the rice is cold, store it in a glass jar in a cool and dry place.

THAI BEEF SALAD ★★

A HEARTY AND HEALTHY MAIN MEAL SALAD, PACKED WITH GREEN VEGETABLES, THIS COMBINES TENDER STRIPS OF STEAK WITH A WONDERFUL CHILLI AND LIME DRESSING.

SERVES FOUR

INGREDIENTS
2 sirloin steaks, each
    about 400g/14oz
1 lemon grass stalk, root trimmed
1 red onion or 4 Thai shallots,
    thinly sliced
1/2 cucumber, cut into strips
30ml/2 tbsp chopped spring
    onion (scallion)
juice of 2 limes
15–30ml/1–2 tbsp Thai
    fish sauce
Chinese mustard cress, salad cress, or
    fresh coriander (cilantro) to garnish

COOK'S TIP
Look out for gui chai leaves in Thai and Asian groceries. These look like very thin spring onions (scallions) and are often used as a substitute for the more familiar vegetable.

1 Pan-fry or grill (broil) the steaks in a large, heavy frying pan over a medium heat, for 6–8 minutes for medium-rare and about 10 minutes for well done. Remove from the pan and allow to rest for 10–15 minutes. Meanwhile, cut off the lower 5cm/2in from the lemon grass stalk and chop it finely.

2 When the meat is cool, slice it thinly and put the slices in a large bowl.

3 Add the sliced onion or shallots, cucumber, lemon grass and chopped spring onion to the meat slices.

4 Toss the salad and season with the lime juice and fish sauce to taste. Transfer the salad to a serving bowl or plate and serve at room temperature or chilled, garnished with the Chinese mustard cress, salad cress or coriander leaves.

Top: Energy 163kcal/682kJ; Protein 25.3g; Carbohydrate 4.4g, of which sugars 1.2g; Fat 4.8g, of which saturates 1.6g, of which polyunsaturates 0.8g; Cholesterol 71mg; Calcium 53mg; Fibre 1.1g; Sodium 620mg.
Bottom: Energy 186kcal/774kJ; Protein 23.3g; Carbohydrate 2g, of which sugars 1.6g; Fat 9.4g, of which saturates 3.8g, of which polyunsaturates 0.4g; Cholesterol 58mg; Calcium 16mg; Fibre 0.4g; Sodium 333mg.

BEEF STEW WITH STAR ANISE ★★★

Not a Western idea of a stew, but more of a fragrant soup with tender morsels of beef. The beansprouts, spring onion and coriander are added at the end of cooking for a delightful and healthy contrast in taste and texture.

SERVES FOUR

INGREDIENTS

1 litre/1¾ pints/4 cups vegetable or
  chicken stock
450g/1lb beef steak, cut into slivers
3 garlic cloves, finely chopped
3 coriander (cilantro) roots,
  finely chopped
2 cinnamon sticks
4 star anise
30ml/2 tbsp light soy sauce
30ml/2 tbsp Thai fish sauce
5ml/1 tsp granulated sugar
115g/4oz/1⅓ cups beansprouts
1 spring onion (scallion),
  finely chopped
small bunch fresh coriander
  (cilantro), coarsely chopped

1 Pour the stock into a large, heavy pan. Add the beef, garlic, chopped coriander roots, cinnamon sticks, star anise, soy sauce, fish sauce and sugar. Bring to the boil, then reduce the heat to low and simmer for 30 minutes. Skim off any foam that rises to the surface of the liquid with a slotted spoon.

2 Meanwhile, divide the beansprouts among four individual serving bowls. Remove and discard the cinnamon sticks and star anise from the stew with a slotted spoon. Ladle the stew over the beansprouts, garnish with the chopped spring onion and chopped fresh coriander and serve immediately.

Energy 221kcal/923kJ; Protein 27.3g; Carbohydrate 4.1g, of which sugars 2.4g; Fat 10.7g, of which saturates 4.3g, of which polyunsaturates 0.5g; Cholesterol 65mg; Calcium 16mg; Fibre 0.8g; Sodium 608mg.

STIR-FRIED BEEF IN OYSTER SAUCE ★★

ANOTHER SIMPLE BUT DELICIOUS RECIPE. IN THAILAND THIS IS OFTEN MADE WITH JUST STRAW MUSHROOMS, WHICH ARE READILY AVAILABLE FRESH, BUT OYSTER MUSHROOMS MAKE A GOOD SUBSTITUTE AND USING A MIXTURE MAKES THE DISH EXTRA INTERESTING.

SERVES SIX

INGREDIENTS
    450g/1lb rump (round) steak
    30ml/2 tbsp soy sauce
    15ml/1 tbsp cornflour (cornstarch)
    15ml/1 tbsp sunflower oil
    15ml/1 tbsp chopped garlic
    15ml/1 tbsp chopped fresh
      root ginger
    225g/8oz/3¼ cups mixed mushrooms
      such as shiitake, oyster and straw
    30ml/2 tbsp oyster sauce
    5ml/1 tsp granulated sugar
    4 spring onions (scallions), cut into
      short lengths
    ground black pepper
    2 fresh red chillies, seeded and cut
      into strips, to garnish

1 Place the steak in the freezer for 30–40 minutes, until firm, then, using a sharp knife, slice it on the diagonal into long thin strips.

2 Mix together the soy sauce and cornflour in a large bowl. Add the steak, turning to coat well, cover with clear film (plastic wrap) and leave to marinate at room temperature for 1–2 hours.

3 Heat half the oil in a wok or large, heavy frying pan. Add the garlic and ginger and cook for 1–2 minutes, until fragrant. Drain the steak, add it to the wok or pan and stir well to separate the strips. Cook, stirring frequently, for a further 1–2 minutes, until the steak is browned all over and tender. Remove from the wok or pan and set aside.

4 Heat the remaining oil in the wok or pan. Add the shiitake, oyster and straw mushrooms. Stir-fry over a medium heat until golden brown.

5 Return the steak to the wok and mix it with the mushrooms. Spoon in the oyster sauce and sugar, mix well, then add ground black pepper to taste. Toss over the heat until all the ingredients are thoroughly combined.

6 Stir in the spring onions. Tip the mixture on to a serving platter, garnish with the strips of red chilli and serve.

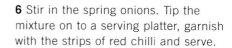

Energy 174kcal/725kJ; Protein 18.1g; Carbohydrate 5.2g, of which sugars 2.7g; Fat 9.1g, of which saturates 3.1g, of which polyunsaturates 1.6g; Cholesterol 44mg; Calcium 11mg; Fibre 0.6g; Sodium 489mg.

GREEN BEEF CURRY <u>WITH</u> THAI AUBERGINES ★★

THIS IS A VERY QUICK CURRY SO BE SURE TO USE GOOD QUALITY MEAT. SIRLOIN IS RECOMMENDED, BUT TENDER RUMP STEAK COULD BE USED INSTEAD.

SERVES SIX

INGREDIENTS

    450g/1lb lean beef sirloin
    15ml/1 tbsp sunflower oil
    45ml/3 tbsp Thai green curry paste
    600ml/1 pint/2½ cups reduced-fat
      coconut milk
    4 kaffir lime leaves, torn
    15–30ml/1–2 tbsp Thai fish sauce
    5ml/1 tsp palm sugar
    150g/5oz small Thai aubergines
      (eggplants), halved
    a small handful of fresh Thai basil
    2 fresh green chillies, to garnish

1 Trim off any excess fat from the beef. Using a sharp knife, cut it into long, thin strips. This is easiest to do if it is well chilled. Set it aside.

2 Heat the oil in a large, heavy pan or wok. Add the curry paste and cook for 1–2 minutes, until it is fragrant.

3 Stir in half the coconut milk, a little at a time. Cook, stirring frequently, for about 5–6 minutes, until an oily sheen appears on the surface of the liquid.

4 Add the beef to the pan with the kaffir lime leaves, Thai fish sauce, sugar and aubergine halves. Cook for 2–3 minutes, then stir in the remaining coconut milk.

5 Bring back to a simmer and cook until the meat and aubergines are tender. Stir in the Thai basil just before serving. Finely shred the green chillies and use to garnish the curry.

COOK'S TIP

To make the green curry paste, put 15 fresh green chillies, 2 chopped lemon grass stalks, 3 sliced shallots, 2 garlic cloves, 15ml/1 tbsp chopped galangal, 4 chopped kaffir lime leaves, 2.5ml/ ½ tsp grated kaffir lime rind, 5ml/1 tsp chopped coriander root, 6 black peppercorns, 5ml/1 tsp each roasted coriander and cumin seeds, 15ml/1 tbsp granulated sugar, 5ml/1 tsp salt and 5ml/1 tsp shrimp paste into a food processor and process until smooth. Gradually add 30ml/2 tbsp vegetable oil, processing after each addition.

Energy 174kcal/726kJ; Protein 17.6g; Carbohydrate 5.5g, of which sugars 5.4g; Fat 9.2g, of which saturates 3.3g, of which polyunsaturates 1.5g; Cholesterol 44mg; Calcium 35mg; Fibre 0.5g; Sodium 159mg.

FRIED RICE WITH BEEF ★★

ONE OF THE JOYS OF THAI COOKING IS THE EASE AND SPEED WITH WHICH A REALLY GOOD MEAL CAN BE PREPARED. THIS ONE CAN BE ON THE TABLE IN 15 MINUTES.

SERVES FOUR

INGREDIENTS
    200g/7oz lean beef steak
    5ml/1 tsp sunflower oil
    2 garlic cloves, finely chopped
    1 egg
    250g/9oz/2¼ cups cooked
      jasmine rice
    ½ medium head broccoli,
      coarsely chopped
    30ml/2 tbsp dark soy sauce
    15ml/1 tbsp light soy sauce
    5ml/1 tsp palm sugar or light
      muscovado (brown) sugar
    15ml/1 tbsp Thai fish sauce
    ground black pepper
    chilli sauce, to serve

1 Trim the steak and cut into very thin strips with a sharp knife.

2 Heat the oil in a wok or frying pan and cook the garlic over a low to medium heat until golden. Do not let it burn. Increase the heat to high, add the steak and stir-fry for 2 minutes.

3 Move the pieces of beef to the edges of the wok or pan and break the egg into the centre. When the egg starts to set, stir-fry it with the meat.

4 Add the rice and toss all the contents of the wok together, scraping up any residue on the base, then add the broccoli, soy sauces, sugar and fish sauce and stir-fry for 2 minutes more. Season to taste with pepper and serve immediately with chilli sauce.

COOK'S TIP
Soy sauce is made from fermented soya beans. The first extraction is sold as light soy sauce and has a delicate, "beany" fragrance. Dark soy sauce has been allowed to mature for longer.

Energy 232kcal/975kJ; Protein 16.9g; Carbohydrate 24.5g, of which sugars 5g; Fat 8.1g, of which saturates 2.7g, of which polyunsaturates 1.4g; Cholesterol 77mg; Calcium 52mg; Fibre 1.4g; Sodium 321mg.

RICE AND NOODLES

Low in fat and high in carbohydrate, rice and noodles form the
bulk of most meals in Thailand and South-east Asia, combined
with a healthy proportion of vegetables and just small amounts
of protein in the shape of meat, fish or tofu. Universally low
in saturated fat, many of these receipes contain all the delicious
flavours of classic Thai cooking and less than 1 gram per serving,
including Garlic and Ginger Rice with Coriander, Stir-fried
Noodles in Seafood Sauce and traditional Mixed Meat Noodles.

COCONUT RICE ★

THIS RICH DISH IS OFTEN SERVED WITH A TANGY PAPAYA SALAD TO BALANCE THE SWEETNESS OF THE COCONUT MILK AND SUGAR. IT IS ONE OF THOSE COMFORTING TREATS THAT EVERYONE ENJOYS.

SERVES SIX

INGREDIENTS
   250ml/8fl oz/1 cup water
   475ml/16fl oz/2 cups reduced-fat
     coconut milk
   2.5ml/½ tsp salt
   30ml/2 tbsp granulated sugar
   450g/1lb/2⅔ cups jasmine rice

COOK'S TIP
For a special occasion serve in a halved papaya and garnish with thin shreds of fresh coconut. Use a vegetable peeler to pare the coconut finely.

1 Place the measured water, coconut milk, salt and sugar in a heavy pan. Wash the rice in several changes of cold water until it runs clear.

2 Add the jasmine rice, cover tightly with a lid and bring to the boil over a medium heat. Reduce the heat to low and simmer gently, without lifting the lid unnecessarily, for 15–20 minutes, until the rice is tender and cooked through. Test it by biting a grain.

3 Turn off the heat and leave the rice to rest in the pan, still covered with the lid, for a further 5–10 minutes.

4 Gently fluff up the rice grains with chopsticks or a fork before transferring it to a warmed dish and serving.

Energy 306kcal/1286kJ; Protein 5.8g; Carbohydrate 69g, of which sugars 9.1g; Fat 0.6g, of which saturates 0.2g, of which polyunsaturates 0g; Cholesterol 0mg; Calcium 40mg; Fibre 0g; Sodium 218mg.

INDONESIAN COCONUT RICE ★

THIS WAY OF COOKING RICE IS VERY POPULAR THROUGHOUT THE WHOLE OF SOUTH-EAST ASIA.
COCONUT RICE GOES PARTICULARLY WELL WITH FISH, CHICKEN AND PORK.

SERVES SIX

INGREDIENTS

350g/12oz/1¾ cups Thai fragrant rice
400ml/14fl oz can reduced-fat
  coconut milk
300ml/½ pint/1¼ cups water
2.5ml/½ tsp ground coriander
5cm/2in cinnamon stick
1 lemon grass stalk, bruised
1 bay leaf
salt
crisp fried onions, to garnish

1 Put the rice in a strainer and rinse thoroughly under cold water. Drain well, then put in a pan. Pour in the coconut milk and water. Add the coriander, cinnamon stick, lemon grass and bay leaf. Season with salt. Bring to the boil, then lower the heat, cover and simmer for 8–10 minutes.

2 Lift the lid and check that all the liquid has been absorbed, then fork the rice through carefully, removing the cinnamon stick, lemon grass and bay leaf.

3 Cover the pan with a tight-fitting lid and continue to cook the rice over the lowest possible heat for 3–5 minutes more. Take care that the pan does not scorch.

4 Pile the rice on to a warm serving dish and serve garnished with the crisp fried onions.

VARIATION
For a quick and easy healthy supper, stir in strips of freshly cooked skinless chicken breast and peas 5-6 minutes before serving and heat through.

COOK'S TIP
When bringing the rice to the boil, stir it frequently to prevent it from settling on the bottom of the pan. Once the rice is nearly tender, continue to cook over a very low heat or just leave to stand for 5 minutes.

Energy 226kcal/945kJ; Protein 4.6g; Carbohydrate 49.9g, of which sugars 3.4g; Fat 0.6g, of which saturates 0.1g, of which polyunsaturates 0g; Cholesterol 0mg; Calcium 39mg; Fibre 0.2g; Sodium 75mg.

GARLIC AND GINGER RICE WITH CORIANDER ★

IN VIETNAM AND CAMBODIA, WHEN RICE IS SERVED ON THE SIDE, IT IS USUALLY STEAMED AND PLAIN, OR FRAGRANT WITH THE FLAVOURS OF GINGER AND HERBS. THE COMBINATION OF GARLIC AND GINGER IS POPULAR IN BOTH COUNTRIES AND COMPLEMENTS ALMOST ANY VEGETABLE, FISH OR MEAT DISH.

SERVES SIX

INGREDIENTS
    15ml/1 tbsp sunflower oil
    2–3 garlic cloves,
      finely chopped
    25g/1oz fresh root ginger,
      finely chopped
    225g/8oz/generous 1 cup
      long grain rice, rinsed in
      several bowls of cold water
      and drained
    900ml/1½ pints/3¾ cups
      chicken stock
    a bunch of fresh coriander (cilantro)
      leaves, finely chopped
    a bunch of fresh basil and mint,
      (optional), finely chopped

1 Heat the oil in a clay pot or heavy pan. Stir in the garlic and ginger and fry until golden. Stir in the rice and allow it to absorb the flavours for 1–2 minutes. Pour in the stock and stir to make sure the rice doesn't stick. Bring the stock to the boil, then reduce the heat.

2 Sprinkle the coriander over the surface of the stock, cover the pan, and leave to cook gently for 20–25 minutes, until the rice has absorbed all the liquid. Turn off the heat and gently fluff up the rice to mix in the coriander. Cover and leave to infuse for 10 minutes before serving.

Energy 162kcal/677kJ; Protein 3.7g; Carbohydrate 31.5g, of which sugars 0.3g; Fat 2.2g, of which saturates 0.2g, of which polyunsaturates 1.2g; Cholesterol 0mg; Calcium 25mg; Fibre 0.8g; Sodium 3mg.

SOUTHERN-SPICED CHILLI RICE ★

ALTHOUGH PLAIN STEAMED RICE IS SERVED AT ALMOST EVERY MEAL THROUGHOUT SOUTH-EAST ASIA, MANY FAMILIES LIKE TO SNEAK IN A LITTLE SPICE TOO. A BURST OF CHILLI FOR FIRE, TURMERIC FOR COLOUR, AND CORIANDER FOR ITS COOLING FLAVOUR, ARE ALL THAT'S NEEDED.

SERVES FOUR

INGREDIENTS
  15ml/1 tbsp sunflower oil
  2–3 green or red Thai chillies,
    seeded and finely chopped
  2 garlic cloves, finely chopped
  2.5cm/1in fresh root ginger, chopped
  5ml/1 tsp sugar
  10–15ml/2–3 tsp ground turmeric
  225g/8oz/generous 1 cup long
    grain rice
  30ml/2 tbsp *nuoc mam*
  600ml/1 pint/2½ cups water
  1 bunch of fresh coriander
    (cilantro), stalks removed, leaves
    finely chopped
  salt and ground black pepper

1 Heat the oil in a heavy pan. Stir in the chillies, garlic and ginger with the sugar. As they begin to colour, stir in the turmeric. Add the rice, coating it well, then pour in the *nuoc mam* and the water – the liquid should sit about 2.5cm/1in above the rice.

2 Tip the rice on to a serving dish. Add some of the coriander and lightly toss together using a fork. Garnish with the remaining coriander.

COOK'S TIP
This rice goes well with grilled and stir-fried fish and shellfish dishes, but you can serve it as an alternative to plain rice. Add extra chillies, if you like.

3 Season with salt and ground black pepper and bring the liquid to the boil. Reduce the heat, cover and simmer for about 25 minutes, or until the water has been absorbed. Remove from the heat and leave the rice to steam for a further 10 minutes.

Energy 247kcal/1032kJ; Protein 5.5g; Carbohydrate 48.3g, of which sugars 1.5g; Fat 3.3g, of which saturates 0.4g, of which polyunsaturates 1.8g; Cholesterol 0mg; Calcium 39mg; Fibre 1.1g; Sodium 5mg.

FESTIVE RICE ★

THIS PRETTY THAI DISH IS TRADITIONALLY SHAPED INTO A CONE AND SURROUNDED BY A VARIETY OF ACCOMPANIMENTS BEFORE BEING SERVED. SERVE AT A HEALTHY SUMMERTIME LUNCH.

2 Heat the oil in a frying pan with a lid. Cook the garlic, onions and turmeric over a low heat for 2–3 minutes, until the onions have softened. Add the rice and stir well to coat in oil.

3 Pour in the water and coconut milk and add the lemon grass. Bring to the boil, stirring. Cover the pan and cook gently for 12 minutes, or until all the liquid has been absorbed by the rice.

SERVES EIGHT

INGREDIENTS
450g/1lb/2⅔ cups jasmine rice
30ml/2 tbsp sunflower oil
2 garlic cloves, crushed
2 onions, thinly sliced
2.5ml/½ tsp ground turmeric
750ml/1¼ pints/3 cups water
400ml/14fl oz can reduced-fat
   coconut milk
1–2 lemon grass stalks, bruised
For the accompaniments
   omelette strips
   2 fresh red chillies, shredded
   cucumber chunks
   tomato wedges
   fried onions
   prawn (shrimp) crackers

1 Put the jasmine rice in a large strainer and rinse it thoroughly under cold water. Drain well.

COOK'S TIP
Jasmine rice is widely available in most supermarkets and Asian stores. It is also known as Thai fragrant rice.

4 Remove the pan from the heat and lift the lid. Cover with a clean dish towel, replace the lid and leave to stand in a warm place for 15 minutes. Remove the lemon grass, mound the rice mixture in a cone on a serving platter and garnish with the accompaniments, then serve.

Energy 224kcal/939kJ; Protein 4.8g; Carbohydrate 49.5g, of which sugars 4g; Fat 0.6g, of which saturates 0.1g, of which polyunsaturates 0g; Cholesterol 0mg; Calcium 44mg; Fibre 0.7g; Sodium 58mg.

BROWN RICE WITH LIME AND LEMON GRASS ★

IT IS UNUSUAL TO FIND BROWN RICE GIVEN THE THAI TREATMENT, BUT THE NUTTY FLAVOUR OF THE GRAINS IS ENHANCED BY THE FRAGRANCE OF LIMES AND LEMON GRASS IN THIS DELICIOUS DISH.

SERVES FOUR

INGREDIENTS

    2 limes
    1 lemon grass stalk
    225g/8oz/generous 1 cup brown
      long grain rice
    15ml/1 tbsp olive oil
    1 onion, chopped
    2.5cm/1in piece fresh root ginger,
      peeled and finely chopped
    7.5ml/1½ tsp coriander seeds
    7.5ml/1½ tsp cumin seeds
    750ml/1¼ pints/3 cups
      vegetable stock
    60ml/4 tbsp chopped fresh
      coriander (cilantro)
    spring onion (scallion) green and
      toasted coconut strips, to garnish
    lime wedges, to serve

1 Pare the limes, using a cannelle knife (zester) or fine grater, taking care to avoid cutting the bitter pith. Set the rind aside. Finely chop the lower portion of the lemon grass stalk and set it aside.

2 Rinse the rice in plenty of cold water until the water runs clear. Tip it into a sieve and drain thoroughly.

3 Heat the oil in a large pan. Add the onion, ginger, coriander and cumin seeds, lemon grass and lime rind and cook over a low heat for 2–3 minutes.

4 Add the rice to the pan and cook, stirring constantly, for 1 minute, then pour in the stock and bring to the boil. Reduce the heat to very low and cover the pan. Cook gently for 30 minutes, then check the rice. If it is still crunchy, cover the pan and cook for 3–5 minutes more. Remove from the heat.

5 Stir in the fresh coriander, fluff up the rice grains with a fork, cover the pan and leave to stand for 10 minutes. Transfer to a warmed dish, garnish with spring onion green and toasted coconut strips, and serve with lime wedges.

Energy 235kcal/996kJ; Protein 4.3g; Carbohydrate 47.3g, of which sugars 1.9g; Fat 4.5g, of which saturates 0.8g, of which polyunsaturates 0.8g; Cholesterol 0mg; Calcium 35mg; Fibre 1.9g; Sodium 6mg.

JASMINE RICE WITH PRAWNS AND THAI BASIL ★

THAI BASIL (BAI GRAPAO), ALSO KNOWN AS HOLY BASIL, HAS A UNIQUE, PUNGENT FLAVOUR THAT IS BOTH SPICY AND SHARP. IT CAN BE FOUND IN MOST ASIAN FOOD MARKETS.

SERVES SIX

INGREDIENTS
    15ml/1 tbsp sunflower oil
    1 egg, beaten
    1 onion, chopped
    15ml/1 tbsp chopped garlic
    15ml/1 tbsp shrimp paste
    1kg/2¼lb/4 cups cooked jasmine rice
    350g/12oz cooked shelled prawns
      (shrimp)
    50g/2oz thawed frozen peas
    oyster sauce, to taste
    2 spring onions (scallions), chopped
    15–20 Thai basil leaves, roughly
      snipped, plus an extra sprig,
      to garnish

1 Heat 15ml/1 tbsp of the oil in a wok or frying pan. Add the beaten egg and swirl it around to set like a thin omelette.

2 Cook the omelette (on one side only) over a gentle heat until golden. Slide the omelette on to a board, roll up and cut into thin strips. Set aside.

3 Heat the remaining oil in the wok or pan, add the onion and garlic and stir-fry for 2–3 minutes. Stir in the shrimp paste and mix well until thoroughly combined.

4 Add the rice, prawns and peas and toss and stir together, until everything is heated through.

5 Season with oyster sauce to taste, taking great care as the shrimp paste is salty. Mix in the spring onions and basil leaves. Transfer to a serving dish and top with the strips of omelette. Serve, garnished with a sprig of basil.

Energy 311kcal/1316kJ; Protein 16.3g; Carbohydrate 52.6g, of which sugars 0.3g; Fat 5.4g, of which saturates 1.1g, of which polyunsaturates 2.2g; Cholesterol 145mg; Calcium 84mg; Fibre 0.6g; Sodium 125mg.

THAI FRIED RICE ★★

THIS SUBSTANTIAL AND TASTY DISH IS BASED ON JASMINE RICE. DICED CHICKEN, RED PEPPER AND CORN KERNELS ADD COLOUR AND EXTRA FLAVOUR.

SERVES FOUR

INGREDIENTS
475ml/16fl oz/2 cups water
50g/2oz/½ cup coconut
 milk powder
350g/12oz/1¾ cups jasmine
 rice, rinsed
15ml/1 tbsp sunflower oil
2 garlic cloves, chopped
1 small onion, finely chopped
2.5cm/1in piece of fresh root ginger,
 peeled and grated
225g/8oz skinless, chicken breast
 fillets, cut into 1cm/½in dice
1 red (bell) pepper, seeded
 and sliced
115g/4oz/1 cup drained canned
 whole kernel corn
5ml/1 tsp chilli oil
5ml/1 tsp hot curry powder
2 eggs, beaten
salt
spring onion (scallion) shreds,
 to garnish

3 Push the onion mixture to the sides of the wok, add the chicken to the centre and stir-fry for 2 minutes. Add the rice and toss well. Stir-fry over a high heat for about 3 minutes more, until the chicken is cooked through.

4 Stir in the sliced red pepper, corn, chilli oil and curry powder, with salt to taste. Toss over the heat for 1 minute. Stir in the beaten eggs and cook for 1 minute more. Garnish with the spring onion shreds and serve.

1 Pour the water into a pan and whisk in the coconut milk powder. Add the rice and bring to the boil. Reduce the heat, cover and cook for 12 minutes, or until the rice is tender and the liquid has been absorbed. Spread the rice on a baking sheet and leave until cold.

2 Heat the oil in a wok, add the garlic, onion and ginger and stir-fry over a medium heat for 2 minutes.

COOK'S TIP
It is important that the rice is completely cold before being fried.

Energy 508kcal/2127kJ; Protein 24.7g; Carbohydrate 83.9g, of which sugars 8.7g; Fat 8g, of which saturates 1.6g, of which polyunsaturates 2.7g; Cholesterol 135mg; Calcium 57mg; Fibre 1.3g; Sodium 204mg.

PLAIN NOODLES WITH FOUR FLAVOURS ★

*A WONDERFULLY SIMPLE WAY OF SERVING NOODLES, THIS DISH ALLOWS EACH INDIVIDUAL DINER TO
SEASON THEIR OWN, SPRINKLING OVER THE FOUR FLAVOURS AS THEY LIKE. FLAVOURINGS ARE ALWAYS
PUT OUT IN LITTLE BOWLS WHENEVER NOODLES ARE SERVED.*

SERVES FOUR

INGREDIENTS
  4 small fresh red or green chillies
  60ml/4 tbsp Thai fish sauce
  60ml/4 tbsp rice vinegar
  granulated sugar
  mild or hot chilli powder
  350g/12oz rice noodles

1 Prepare the four flavours. For the first, finely chop 2 small red or green chillies, discarding the seeds or leaving them in, depending on how hot you like your flavouring. Place them in a small bowl and add the Thai fish sauce.

2 For the second flavour, chop the remaining chillies finely and mix them with the rice vinegar in a small bowl. Put the sugar and chilli powder in separate small bowls.

3 Cook the noodles until tender, following the instructions on the packet. Drain well, tip into a large bowl and serve immediately with the four flavours handed separately.

Energy 321kcal/1341kJ; Protein 4.5g; Carbohydrate 72.4g, of which sugars 1g; Fat 0.2g, of which saturates 0g, of which polyunsaturates 0g; Cholesterol 0mg; Calcium 12mg; Fibre 0.2g; Sodium 278mg.

THAI NOODLES <u>WITH</u> CHINESE CHIVES ★★

THIS RECIPE REQUIRES A LITTLE TIME FOR PREPARATION, BUT THE COOKING TIME IS VERY FAST. EVERYTHING IS COOKED IN A HOT WOK AND SHOULD BE EATEN IMMEDIATELY. THIS IS A FILLING AND TASTY VEGETARIAN DISH, IDEAL FOR A WEEKEND LUNCH.

SERVES FOUR

INGREDIENTS
    350g/12oz dried rice noodles
    1cm/½in piece fresh root ginger,
      peeled and grated
    30ml/2 tbsp light soy sauce
    225g/8oz Quorn (mycoprotein),
      cut into small cubes
    15ml/1 tbsp sunflower oil
    2 garlic cloves, crushed
    1 large onion, cut into
      thin wedges
    115g/4oz fried tofu, thinly sliced
    1 fresh green chilli, seeded and
      thinly sliced
    175g/6oz/2 cups beansprouts
    2 large bunches garlic chives, total
      weight about 115g/4oz, cut into
      5cm/2in lengths
    30ml/2 tbsp roasted peanuts, ground
    30ml/2 tbsp dark soy sauce
    30ml/2 tbsp chopped fresh coriander
      (cilantro), and 1 lemon, cut into
      wedges, to garnish

1 Place the noodles in a bowl, cover with warm water and leave to soak for 30 minutes. Drain and set aside.

2 Mix the ginger and light soy sauce in a bowl. Add the Quorn, then set aside for 10 minutes. Drain, reserving the marinade.

3 Heat half the oil in a frying pan and cook the garlic for a few seconds. Add the Quorn and stir-fry for 3–4 minutes. Using a slotted spoon, transfer to a plate and set aside.

4 Heat the remaining oil in the pan and stir-fry the onion for 3–4 minutes, until softened and tinged with brown. Add the tofu and chilli, stir-fry briefly and then add the noodles. Stir-fry over a medium heat for 4–5 minutes.

5 Stir in the beansprouts, garlic chives and most of the ground peanuts, reserving a little for the garnish. Stir well, then add the Quorn, the dark soy sauce and the reserved marinade.

6 When hot, spoon on to serving plates and garnish with the remaining ground peanuts, the coriander and lemon.

Energy 444kcal/1857kJ; Protein 16g; Carbohydrate 77.6g, of which sugars 4.3g; Fat 6.5g, of which saturates 0.9g, of which polyunsaturates 3.2g; Cholesterol 0mg; Calcium 230mg; Fibre 5g; Sodium 1227mg.

NOODLES AND VEGETABLES IN COCONUT SAUCE ★

WHEN EVERYDAY VEGETABLES ARE GIVEN THE THAI TREATMENT, THE RESULT IS A DELECTABLE DISH WHICH EVERYONE WILL ENJOY. NOODLES ADD BULK AND A WELCOME CONTRAST IN TEXTURE.

3 Increase the heat to medium, stir in the coconut milk and vegetable stock and bring to the boil. Add the broccoli florets and the noodles, lower the heat and simmer gently for 20 minutes.

4 Meanwhile, make the garnish. Split the lemon grass stalks lengthways through the root. Gather the coriander into a small bouquet and lay it on a platter, following the curve of the rim.

5 Tuck the lemon grass halves into the coriander bouquet and add the chillies to resemble flowers.

6 Stir the fish sauce, soy sauce and chopped coriander into the noodle mixture. Spoon on to the platter, taking care not to disturb the herb bouquet, and serve immediately.

SERVES SIX

INGREDIENTS
    10ml/2 tsp sunflower oil
    1 lemon grass stalk, finely chopped
    15ml/1 tbsp Thai red curry paste
    1 onion, thickly sliced
    3 courgettes (zucchini), thickly sliced
    115g/4oz Savoy cabbage,
      thickly sliced
    2 carrots, thickly sliced
    150g/5oz broccoli, stem sliced and
      head separated into florets
    2 × 400ml/14fl oz cans reduced-fat
      coconut milk
    475ml/16fl oz/2 cups vegetable stock
    150g/5oz dried egg noodles
    15ml/1 tbsp Thai fish sauce
    30ml/2 tbsp soy sauce
    60ml/4 tbsp chopped fresh
      coriander (cilantro)
For the garnish
    2 lemon grass stalks
    1 bunch fresh coriander (cilantro)
    8–10 small fresh red chillies

1 Heat the oil in a large pan or wok. Add the lemon grass and red curry paste and stir-fry for 2–3 seconds. Add the onion and cook over a medium heat, stirring occasionally, for about 5–10 minutes, until the onion has softened but not browned.

2 Add the courgettes, cabbage, carrots and slices of broccoli stem. Using two spoons, toss the vegetables with the onion mixture. Reduce the heat to low and cook gently, stirring occasionally, for a further 5 minutes.

Energy 181kcal/766kJ; Protein 7.2g; Carbohydrate 30.4g, of which sugars 12.3g; Fat 4.3g, of which saturates 1.1g, of which polyunsaturates 1.3g; Cholesterol 8mg; Calcium 115mg; Fibre 3.6g; Sodium 559mg.

SWEET AND HOT VEGETABLE NOODLES ★

THIS NOODLE DISH HAS THE COLOUR OF FIRE, BUT ONLY THE MILDEST SUGGESTION OF HEAT. GINGER AND PLUM SAUCE GIVE IT ITS FRUITY FLAVOUR, WHILE LIME ADDS A DELICIOUS TANG.

SERVES FOUR

INGREDIENTS

130g/4½oz dried rice noodles
15ml/1 tbsp sunflower oil
2.5cm/1in piece fresh root ginger,
  sliced into thin batons
1 garlic clove, crushed
130g/4½oz drained canned bamboo
  shoots, sliced into thin batons
2 medium carrots, sliced into batons
130g/4½oz/1½ cups beansprouts
1 small white cabbage, shredded
30ml/2 tbsp Thai fish sauce
30ml/2 tbsp soy sauce
30ml/2 tbsp plum sauce
5ml/1 tsp sesame oil
15ml/1 tbsp palm sugar or light
  muscovado (brown) sugar
juice of ½ lime
90g/3½oz mooli (daikon), sliced into
  thin batons
small bunch fresh coriander
  (cilantro), chopped
30ml/2 tbsp sesame seeds, toasted

1 Cook the noodles in a large pan of boiling water, following the instructions on the packet. Meanwhile, heat the oil in a wok or large frying pan and stir-fry the ginger and garlic for 2–3 minutes over a medium heat, until golden.

2 Drain the noodles and set them aside. Add the bamboo shoots to the wok, increase the heat to high and stir-fry for 5 minutes. Add the carrots, beansprouts and cabbage and stir-fry for a further 5 minutes, until they are beginning to char on the edges.

3 Stir in the sauces, sesame oil, sugar and lime juice. Add the mooli and coriander, toss to mix, then spoon into a warmed bowl, sprinkle with toasted sesame seeds and serve immediately.

COOK'S TIP
Use a large, sharp knife for shredding cabbage. Remove any tough outer leaves, if necessary, then cut the cabbage into quarters. Cut off and discard the hard core from each quarter, place flat side down, then slice the cabbage very thinly to make fine shreds.

Energy 207kcal/866kJ; Protein 5.6g; Carbohydrate 42.3g, of which sugars 14.2g; Fat 1.6g, of which saturates 0.2g, of which polyunsaturates 0.6g; Cholesterol 0mg; Calcium 94mg; Fibre 4.1g; Sodium 682mg.

RICE NOODLES WITH FRESH HERBS ★

BUN IS THE VIETNAMESE WORD USED TO DESCRIBE THE THIN, WIRY NOODLES KNOWN AS RICE STICKS OR RICE VERMICELLI. HOWEVER, WHEN THE VIETNAMESE TALK ABOUT A DISH CALLED BUN, THEY ARE USUALLY REFERRING TO THIS RECIPE, WHICH COULD BE DESCRIBED AS A NOODLE SALAD.

SERVES FOUR

INGREDIENTS
half a small cucumber
225g/8oz dried rice sticks (vermicelli)
4–6 lettuce leaves, shredded
115g/4oz/½ cup beansprouts
1 bunch mixed basil, coriander
(cilantro), mint and oregano, stalks
removed, leaves shredded
juice of half a lime
nuoc mam or *nuoc cham*, to drizzle

COOK'S TIP
In the street stalls and cafés of Hanoi,
different types of mint, ginger leaves,
oregano and thyme provide the herb
bedding for this dish, giving it a really
distinctive, fragrant flavour.

1 Peel the cucumber, cut it in half
lengthways, remove the seeds, and cut
into matchsticks.

2 Add the rice sticks to a pan of boiling
water, loosening them gently, and cook
for 3–4 minutes, or until *al dente*. Drain,
rinse under cold water, and drain again.

3 In a bowl, toss the shredded lettuce,
beansprouts, cucumber and herbs
together. Add the noodles and lime
juice and toss together. Drizzle with
a little *nuoc mam* or *nuoc cham* for
seasoning, and serve immediately on
its own, or with stir-fried seafood or
chicken as a complete meal.

Energy 225kcal/940kJ; Protein 6.9g; Carbohydrate 47.1g, of which sugars 2.5g; Fat 0.8g, of which saturates 0.1g, of which polyunsaturates 0.2g; Cholesterol 0mg; Calcium 66mg; Fibre 1.8g; Sodium 13mg.

STEAMBOAT ★★

THIS DISH IS NAMED AFTER THE UTENSIL IN WHICH IT IS COOKED — A TYPE OF FONDUE WITH A FUNNEL AND A MOAT. THE MOAT IS FILLED WITH STOCK, TRADITIONALLY KEPT HOT WITH CHARCOAL. ELECTRIC STEAMBOATS OR ANY TRADITIONAL FONDUE POTS CAN BE USED INSTEAD.

<u>SERVES EIGHT</u>

INGREDIENTS

    8 Chinese dried mushrooms, soaked
      for 30 minutes in warm water
    1.5 litres/2½ pints/6¼ cups well-
      flavoured chicken stock
    10ml/2 tsp rice wine or
      medium-dry sherry
    5ml/1 tsp sesame oil
    115g/4oz each lean pork and rump
      (round) steak, thinly sliced
    1 chicken breast fillet, thickly sliced
    225g/8oz raw prawns
      (shrimp), peeled
    450g/1lb white fish fillets, skinned
      and cubed
    200g/7oz fish balls (from Asian
      food stores)
    115g/4oz fried tofu, each
      piece halved
    leafy green vegetables, such as
      lettuce, Chinese leaves (Chinese
      cabbage), spinach and watercress,
      cut into 15cm/6in lengths
    225g/8oz rice vermicelli
    8 eggs
    selection of sauces, including soy
      sauce with sesame seeds; soy sauce
      with crushed ginger; chilli sauce;
      plum sauce and hot mustard
    ½ bunch spring onions
      (scallions), chopped
    salt and ground white pepper

1 Drain the mushrooms, reserving the soaking liquid. Cut off and discard the stems; slice the caps finely.

2 Pour the stock into a large pan, with the rice wine or sherry, sesame oil and reserved mushroom liquid. Bring the mixture to the boil, then season with salt and white pepper. Reduce the heat and simmer gently while you prepare the remaining ingredients.

VARIATION
Replace the egg in step 5 with long strips of finely cut omelette for an equally delicious result.

3 Put the meat, fish, tofu, green vegetables and mushrooms in bowls on the table. Soak the vermicelli in hot water for about 5 minutes, drain and place in eight soup bowls on a small table. Crack an egg for each diner in a small bowl; place on a side table. Put the sauces in bowls beside each diner.

4 Add the chopped spring onions to the pan of stock, bring it to a full boil and fuel the steamboat. Pour the stock into the moat and seat your guests at once. Each guest lowers a few chosen morsels into the boiling stock, using chopsticks or fondue forks, leaves them for a minute or two, then removes them with a small wire mesh ladle, a fondue fork or pair of chopsticks.

5 When all the meat, fish, tofu and vegetables have been cooked, the stock will be concentrated and wonderfully enriched. Add a little boiling water if necessary. Bring the soup bowls containing the soaked noodles to the table, pour in the hot soup and slide a whole egg into each, stirring until it cooks and forms threads.

Energy 243kcal/1020kJ; Protein 35g; Carbohydrate 4.1g, of which sugars 0.8g; Fat 9.7g, of which saturates 2.6g, of which polyunsaturates 1.6g; Cholesterol 299mg; Calcium 168mg; Fibre 0.4g; Sodium 304mg.

CURRIED RICE VERMICELLI ★

SIMPLE AND SPEEDILY PREPARED, THIS LIGHTLY FLAVOURED RICE NOODLE DISH WITH VEGETABLES AND PRAWNS IS ALMOST A COMPLETE MEAL IN A BOWL.

<u>SERVES FOUR</u>

INGREDIENTS
    225g/8oz/2 cups dried rice vermicelli
    10ml/2 tsp sunflower oil
    1 egg, lightly beaten
    2 garlic cloves, finely chopped
    1 large fresh red or green chilli,
      seeded and finely chopped
    15ml/1 tbsp medium curry powder
    1 red (bell) pepper, thinly sliced
    1 green (bell) pepper, thinly sliced
    1 carrot, cut into matchsticks
    1.5ml/¼ tsp salt
    60ml/4 tbsp vegetable stock
    115g/4oz cooked peeled prawns
      (shrimp), thawed if frozen
    75g/3oz lean ham, cut into cubes
    15ml/1 tbsp light soy sauce

1 Soak the rice vermicelli in a bowl of boiling water for 4 minutes, or according to the instructions on the packet, then drain thoroughly through a sieve or colander and set aside. Cover the bowl with a damp cloth or with clear film (plastic wrap) so that the vermicelli does not dry out.

2 Heat 5ml/1 tsp of the oil in a non-stick frying pan or wok. Add the egg and scramble until set, stirring with a pair of wooden chopsticks. Remove the egg with a slotted spoon and set aside.

3 Heat the remaining oil in the clean pan. Stir-fry the garlic and chilli for a few seconds, then stir in the curry powder. Cook for 1 minute, stirring, then stir in the peppers, carrot sticks, salt and stock.

4 Bring the mixture to the boil. Add the prawns, ham, scrambled egg, rice vermicelli and soy sauce. Mix well. Cook, stirring, until all the liquid has been absorbed and the mixture is hot. Serve immediately.

Energy 306kcal/1281kJ; Protein 16g; Carbohydrate 50.9g, of which sugars 6.5g; Fat 4.3g, of which saturates 0.9g, of which polyunsaturates 1.4g; Cholesterol 115mg; Calcium 56mg; Fibre 1.8g; Sodium 309mg.

STIR-FRIED NOODLES IN SEAFOOD SAUCE ★

THE ADDITION OF EXTRA SPECIAL INGREDIENTS SUCH AS CRAB AND ASPARAGUS IN THIS DISH CAN MAKE A SIMPLE STIR-FRY A REAL TREAT THAT IS STILL VIRTUALLY FAT FREE.

SERVES EIGHT

INGREDIENTS

225g/8oz fresh or dried Chinese
   egg noodles
8 spring onions (scallions), cleaned
   and trimmed
8 asparagus spears, plus extra
   steamed asparagus spears, to
   serve (optional)
15ml/1 tbsp sunflower oil
5cm/2in piece fresh root ginger,
   peeled and cut into very fine
   matchsticks
3 garlic cloves, chopped
60ml/4 tbsp oyster sauce
450g/1lb cooked crab meat (all
   white, or two-thirds white and
   one-third brown)
30ml/2 tbsp rice wine
   vinegar
15–30ml/1–2 tbsp light
   soy sauce

1 Put the noodles in a large pan or wok, cover with lightly salted boiling water, place a lid on top and simmer for 3–4 minutes, or for the time suggested on the packet. Drain and set aside.

2 Cut off the green spring onion tops and slice them thinly. Set aside. Cut the white parts into 2cm/¾in lengths and quarter them lengthways. Cut the asparagus spears on the diagonal into 2cm/¾in pieces.

3 Heat the oil in a pan or wok until very hot, then add the ginger, garlic and white spring onion batons. Stir-fry over a high heat for 1 minute. Add the oyster sauce, crab meat, rice wine vinegar and soy sauce to taste. Stir-fry for about 2 minutes, until the crab and sauce are hot. Add the noodles and toss until heated through. At the last moment, toss in the spring onion tops and serve with a few extra asparagus spears, if you like.

Energy 179kcal/756kJ; Protein 14.1g; Carbohydrate 22.9g, of which sugars 3.1g; Fat 4.1g, of which saturates 0.9g, of which polyunsaturates 1.2g; Cholesterol 49mg; Calcium 82mg; Fibre 1.1g; Sodium 617mg.

MIXED MEAT NOODLES ★

A CLASSIC SOUTH-EAST ASIAN DISH THAT ORIGINATED IN SINGAPORE AND HAS BEEN ADOPTED AND ADAPTED BY ITS NEIGHBOURING COUNTRIES. THE NOODLES ARE STANDARD STREET AND CAFÉ FOOD, AN IDEAL SNACK FOR ANYONE FEELING A LITTLE PECKISH.

SERVES FOUR

INGREDIENTS

    15ml/1 tbsp sesame oil
    1 onion, finely chopped
    3 garlic cloves, finely chopped
    3–4 green or red Thai chillies,
      seeded and finely chopped
    4cm/1½ in fresh root ginger,
      peeled and finely chopped
    6 spring onions (scallions), chopped
    1 skinless chicken breast fillet,
      cut into bitesize strips
    90g/3½ oz lean pork, cut into
      bitesize strips
    90g/3½ oz prawns (shrimp), shelled
    2 tomatoes, skinned, seeded
      and chopped
    30ml/2 tbsp tamarind paste
    15ml/1 tbsp *nuoc mam*
    grated rind and juice of 1 lime
    10ml/2 tsp sugar
    150ml/¼ pint/⅔ cup water or fish stock
    225g/8oz fresh rice sticks (vermicelli)
    salt and ground black pepper
    1 bunch each fresh basil and mint,
      and *nuoc cham*, to serve

1 Heat a wok or heavy pan and add the sesame oil. Stir in the finely chopped onion, garlic, chillies and ginger, and cook until they begin to colour. Add the spring onions and cook for 1 minute, add the chicken and pork, and cook for 1–2 minutes, then stir in the prawns.

2 Add the tomatoes, followed by the tamarind paste, *nuoc mam*, lime rind and juice, and sugar to the pan and stir well. Pour in the water or fish stock, and stir again before cooking gently for 2–3 minutes. Bubble up the liquid to reduce it.

VARIATIONS

• At noodle stalls in street markets in Thailand and South-east Asia, batches of cold, cooked noodles are kept ready to add to whatever delicious concoction is cooking in the wok.
• At home, you can make this dish with any kind of noodles – egg or rice, fresh or dried.
• Cured Chinese sausage and snails, or strips of squid, are sometimes added to the mixture to ring the changes.

3 Meanwhile, toss the noodles in a large pan of boiling water and cook for a few minutes until tender.

4 Drain the noodles and add to the chicken and prawn mixture. Season with salt and ground black pepper.

5 Serve immediately, with basil and mint leaves sprinkled over the top, and drizzled with spoonfuls of *nuoc cham*.

COOK'S TIP
It's important to serve this dish immediately once the noodles have been added, otherwise they will go soft.

Energy 314kcal/1316kJ; Protein 19.2g; Carbohydrate 50.3g, of which sugars 5.9g; Fat 4g, of which saturates 0.6g, of which polyunsaturates 1.5g; Cholesterol 70mg; Calcium 74mg; Fibre 1.6g; Sodium 81mg.

WHEAT NOODLES WITH STIR-FRIED PORK ★★

THIS DELICIOUS RECIPE IS SIMPLICITY ITSELF WITH A WONDERFUL CONTRAST OF TEXTURES AND TASTE. THE PORK IS MARINATED IN PEANUT OIL WHICH ADDS A MARVELLOUSLY NUTTY FLAVOUR.

SERVES FOUR

INGREDIENTS
225g/8oz pork loin, cut into thin strips
225g/8oz dried wheat noodles, soaked
 in lukewarm water for 20 minutes
15ml/1 tbsp sunflower oil
2 garlic cloves, finely chopped
2–3 spring onions (scallions),
 trimmed and cut into
 bitesize pieces
45ml/3 tbsp *kroeung*
15ml/1 tbsp *tuk trey*
30ml/2 tbsp unsalted roasted
 peanuts, finely chopped
chilli oil, for drizzling (optional)
For the marinade
30ml/2 tbsp *tuk trey*
30ml/2 tbsp soy sauce
15ml/1 tbsp peanut oil
10ml/2 tsp sugar

1 In a bowl, combine the *tuk trey,* soy sauce, peanut oil and sugar for the marinade, stirring constantly until all the sugar dissolves. Toss in the strips of pork, making sure they are well coated in the marinade. Put aside for 30 minutes.

2 Drain the wheat noodles. Bring a large pan of water to the boil. Drop in the noodles, untangling them with chopsticks, if necessary. Cook for 4–5 minutes, until tender. Allow the noodles to drain thoroughly, then divide them among individual serving bowls. Keep the noodles warm until the dish is ready to serve.

3 Meanwhile, heat a wok. Add the oil and stir-fry the garlic and spring onions, until fragrant. Add the pork, tossing it around the wok for 2 minutes. Stir in the *kroeung* and *tuk trey* for 2 minutes, adding a splash of water if the wok gets too dry, and tip the pork on top of the noodles. Sprinkle the peanuts over the top to serve.

VARIATION
Wheat noodles are especially popular in Cambodia. Sold dried, in straight bundles like sticks, they are versatile and robust. Noodles drying in the open air, hanging from bamboo poles, are common in the markets. This simple recipe comes from a noodle stall in Phnom Penh. It also tastes excellent when made with fresh egg noodles.

Energy 340kcal/1435kJ; Protein 19.6g; Carbohydrate 46g, of which sugars 4.4g; Fat 9.9g, of which saturates 1.4g, of which polyunsaturates 2.6g; Cholesterol 35mg; Calcium 23mg; Fibre 1.9g; Sodium 41mg.

RICE NOODLES WITH PORK ★★

ALTHOUGH RICE NOODLES HAVE LITTLE FLAVOUR THEMSELVES THEY HAVE THE MOST WONDERFUL ABILITY TO TAKE ON THE FLAVOUR OF OTHER INGREDIENTS.

SERVES SIX

INGREDIENTS
    450g/1lb lean pork fillet
    225g/8oz dried rice noodles
    115g/4oz/1 cup broccoli florets
    1 red (bell) pepper, quartered
      and seeded
    30ml/2 tbsp sunflower oil
    2 garlic cloves, crushed
    10 spring onions (scallions), trimmed
      and cut into 5cm/2in slices
    1 lemon grass stalk, finely chopped
    1–2 fresh red chillies, seeded and
      finely chopped
    300ml/½ pint/1¼ cups reduced-fat
      coconut milk
    15ml/1 tbsp tomato purée (paste)
    3 kaffir lime leaves (optional)
For the marinade
    45ml/3 tbsp light soy sauce
    15ml/1 tbsp rice wine
    15ml/1 tbsp oil
    2.5cm/1in piece of fresh root ginger

1 Cut the pork into strips about 2.5cm/1in long and 1cm/½in wide. Mix all ingredients for the marinade in a bowl, add the pork, stir to coat and marinate together for 1 hour.

2 Spread out the rice noodles in a shallow dish, pour over hot water to cover and soak for 20 minutes until soft. Drain.

3 Blanch the broccoli in a small pan of boiling water for 2 minutes, then drain and refresh under cold water. Set aside.

4 Place the pepper pieces under a hot grill (broiler) for a few minutes until the skin blackens and blisters. Put in a plastic bag for about 10 minutes and then, when cool enough to handle, peel away the skin and slice the flesh thinly.

5 Drain the pork, reserving the marinade. Heat half the oil in a large frying pan. Stir-fry the pork, in batches if necessary, for 3–4 minutes until the meat is tender. Transfer to a plate and keep warm.

6 Add a little more oil to the pan if necessary and fry the garlic, spring onions, lemon grass and chillies over a low to medium heat for 2–3 minutes. Add the broccoli and pepper and stir-fry for a few minutes more.

7 Stir in the reserved marinade, coconut milk and tomato purée, with the kaffir lime leaves, if using. Simmer gently until the broccoli is nearly tender, then add the pork and noodles. Toss over the heat, for 3–4 minutes until the noodles are completely heated through.

Energy 307kcal/1281kJ; Protein 19.5g; Carbohydrate 35.7g, of which sugars 5g; Fat 9.1g, of which saturates 2.1g, of which polyunsaturates 4g; Cholesterol 47mg; Calcium 44mg; Fibre 1.2g; Sodium 116mg.

VEGETABLES AND SALADS

These superb dishes are uniformly low in fat but raise any meal into another dimension with their fantastic colour, flavour and presentation. This selection of vegetable dishes stays well within sensible fat limits and goes particularly well with meat, poultry, fish and seafood dishes. Discover their classic combinations of crisp textures and sweet, sharp, spicy and aromatic flavours in Pak Choi with Lime Dressing, Fragrant Mushrooms in Lettuce Leaves and Thai Fruit and Vegetable Salad.

PAK CHOI WITH LIME DRESSING ★

THE COCONUT DRESSING FOR THIS THAI SPECIALITY IS TRADITIONALLY MADE USING FISH SAUCE, BUT VEGETARIANS COULD USE MUSHROOM SAUCE INSTEAD. BEWARE, THIS IS A FIERY DISH!

SERVES FOUR

INGREDIENTS
15ml/1 tbsp sunflower oil
3 fresh red chillies, thinly sliced
4 garlic cloves, thinly sliced
6 spring onions (scallions),
  sliced diagonally
2 pak choi (bok choy), shredded
15ml/1 tbsp crushed peanuts
For the dressing
30ml/2 tbsp fresh lime juice
15–30ml/1–2 tbsp Thai fish sauce
250ml/8fl oz/1 cup reduced-fat
  coconut milk

1 Make the dressing. Put the lime juice and fish sauce in a bowl and mix well together, then gradually whisk in the coconut milk until combined.

2 Heat the oil in a wok and stir-fry the chillies for 2–3 minutes, until crisp. Transfer to a plate using a slotted spoon. Add the garlic to the wok and stir-fry for 30–60 seconds, until golden brown. Transfer to the plate.

3 Stir-fry the white parts of the spring onions for about 2–3 minutes, then add the green parts and stir-fry for 1 minute more. Transfer to the plate.

4 Bring a large pan of lightly salted water to the boil and add the pak choi. Stir twice, then drain immediately.

5 Place the pak choi in a large bowl, add the dressing and toss to mix. Spoon into a large serving bowl and sprinkle with the crushed peanuts and the stir-fried chilli mixture. Serve warm or cold.

VARIATION
If you don't like particularly spicy food, substitute red (bell) pepper strips for some or all of the chillies.

Energy 58kcal/244kJ; Protein 2.2g; Carbohydrate 5g, of which sugars 4.8g; Fat 3.5g, of which saturates 0.5g, of which polyunsaturates 2g; Cholesterol 0mg; Calcium 113mg; Fibre 1.4g; Sodium 408mg.

THAI ASPARAGUS ★

THIS IS AN EXCITINGLY DIFFERENT WAY OF COOKING ASPARAGUS. THE CRUNCHY TEXTURE IS RETAINED AND THE FLAVOUR IS COMPLEMENTED BY THE ADDITION OF GALANGAL AND CHILLI.

SERVES FOUR

INGREDIENTS

  350g/12oz asparagus stalks
  15ml/1 tbsp sunflower oil
  1 garlic clove, crushed
  15ml/1 tbsp sesame seeds, toasted
  2.5cm/1in piece fresh galangal,
    finely shredded
  1 fresh red chilli, seeded and
    finely chopped
  15ml/1 tbsp Thai fish sauce
  15ml/1 tbsp light soy sauce
  45ml/3 tbsp water
  5ml/1 tsp palm sugar or light
    muscovado (brown) sugar

VARIATIONS

Try this with broccoli or pak choi (bok choy). The sauce also works very well with green beans.

1 Snap the asparagus stalks. They will break naturally at the junction between the woody base and the more tender portion of the stalk. Discard the woody parts of the stems.

2 Heat the oil in a wok and stir-fry the garlic, sesame seeds and galangal for 3–4 seconds, until the garlic is just beginning to turn golden.

3 Add the asparagus stalks and chilli, toss to mix, then add the fish sauce, soy sauce, water and sugar. Using two spoons, toss over the heat for a further 2 minutes, or until the asparagus just begins to soften and the liquid is reduced by half.

4 Carefully transfer to a warmed platter and serve immediately.

Energy 50kcal/207kJ; Protein 3.4g; Carbohydrate 3.1g, of which sugars 3g; Fat 2.7g, of which saturates 0.4g, of which polyunsaturates 1.1g; Cholesterol 0mg; Calcium 50mg; Fibre 1.8g; Sodium 269mg.

STIR-FRIED ASPARAGUS WITH CHILLI, GALANGAL AND LEMON GRASS ★

ONE OF THE CULINARY LEGACIES OF FRENCH COLONIZATION IN VIETNAM AND CAMBODIA IS ASPARAGUS. TODAY IT IS GROWN IN VIETNAM AND FINDS ITS WAY INTO STIR-FRIES IN BOTH COUNTRIES. CAMBODIAN IN STYLE, THIS IS A LOVELY WAY TO EAT ASPARAGUS.

SERVES FOUR

INGREDIENTS

    15ml/1 tbsp sunfllower oil
    2 garlic cloves, finely chopped
    2 Thai chillies, seeded and finely chopped
    25g/1oz galangal, finely shredded
    1 lemon grass stalk, trimmed and finely sliced
    350g/12oz fresh asparagus stalks, trimmed
    30ml/2 tbsp *tuk trey*
    30ml/2 tbsp soy sauce
    5ml/1 tsp sugar
    15ml/1 tbsp unsalted roasted peanuts, finely chopped
    1 small bunch fresh coriander (cilantro), finely chopped

1 Heat a large wok and add the oil. Stir in the garlic, chillies, galangal and lemon grass and stir-fry until they become fragrant and begin to turn golden.

2 Add the asparagus and stir-fry for a further 1–2 minutes, until it is just tender but not too soft.

3 Stir in the *tuk trey*, soy sauce and sugar. Stir in the peanuts and coriander and serve immediately.

VARIATION
This recipe also works well with broccoli, green beans and courgettes (zucchini), cut into strips.

Energy 79kcal/327kJ; Protein 4g; Carbohydrate 4.9g, of which sugars 4.5g; Fat 4.9g, of which saturates 0.7g, of which polyunsaturates 2.3g; Cholesterol 0mg; Calcium 53mg; Fibre 2.5g; Sodium 540mg.

STEAMED VEGETABLES WITH CHIANG MAI SPICY DIP ★

IN THAILAND, STEAMED VEGETABLES ARE OFTEN PARTNERED WITH RAW ONES TO CREATE THE CONTRASTING TEXTURES THAT ARE SUCH A FEATURE OF THE NATIONAL CUISINE. BY HAPPY COINCIDENCE, IT IS AN EXTREMELY HEALTHY WAY TO SERVE THEM.

SERVES FOUR

INGREDIENTS
  1 head broccoli, divided
    into florets
  130g/4½oz 1 cup green
    beans, trimmed
  130g/4½oz asparagus, trimmed
  ½ head cauliflower, divided
    into florets
  8 baby corn cobs
  130g/4½oz mangetouts (snow peas)
    or sugar snap peas
  salt
For the dip
  1 fresh green chilli, seeded
  4 garlic cloves, peeled
  4 shallots, peeled
  2 tomatoes, halved
  5 pea aubergines (eggplants)
  30ml/2 tbsp lemon juice
  30ml/2 tbsp soy sauce
  2.5ml/½ tsp salt
  5ml/1 tsp granulated sugar

COOK'S TIP
Cauliflower varieties with pale green florets have a more delicate flavour than those with white florets.

1 Place the broccoli, green beans, asparagus and cauliflower in a steamer and steam over boiling water for about 4 minutes, until just tender but still with a "bite". Transfer them to a bowl and add the corn cobs and mangetouts or sugar snap peas. Season to taste with a little salt. Toss to mix, then set aside.

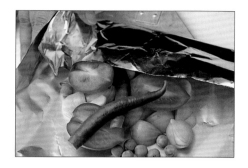

2 Make the dip. Preheat the grill (broiler). Wrap the chilli, garlic cloves, shallots, tomatoes and aubergines in a foil package. Grill (broil) for 10 minutes, until the vegetables have softened, turning the package over once or twice.

3 Unwrap the foil and tip its contents into a mortar or food processor. Add the lemon juice, soy sauce, salt and sugar. Pound with a pestle or process to a fairly liquid paste.

4 Scrape the dip into a serving bowl or four individual bowls. Serve, surrounded by the steamed and raw vegetables.

VARIATIONS
You can use a combination of other vegetables if you like. Use pak choi (bok choy) instead of the cauliflower or substitute raw baby carrots for the corn cobs and mushrooms in place of the mangetouts (snow peas).

Energy 101kcal/422kJ; Protein 9.5g; Carbohydrate 11.9g, of which sugars 10.2g; Fat 2g, of which saturates 0.4g, of which polyunsaturates 1g; Cholesterol 0mg; Calcium 98mg; Fibre 6.7g; Sodium 1082mg.

MORNING GLORY WITH GARLIC AND SHALLOTS ★

MORNING GLORY GOES BY VARIOUS NAMES, INCLUDING WATER SPINACH, WATER CONVOLVULUS AND SWAMP CABBAGE. IT IS A GREEN LEAFY VEGETABLE WITH LONG JOINTED STEMS AND ARROW-SHAPED LEAVES. THE STEMS REMAIN CRUNCHY WHILE THE LEAVES WILT LIKE SPINACH WHEN COOKED.

SERVES FOUR

INGREDIENTS

2 bunches morning glory, total weight
about 250g/9oz, trimmed and
coarsely chopped into 2.5cm/
1in lengths
15ml/1 tbsp sunflower oil
4 shallots, thinly sliced
6 large garlic cloves, thinly sliced
sea salt
1.5ml/¼ tsp dried chilli flakes

VARIATIONS
Use spinach instead of morning glory, or
substitute young spring greens (collards),
sprouting broccoli or Swiss chard.

1 Place the morning glory in a steamer
and steam over a pan of boiling water
for 30 seconds, until just wilted. If
necessary, cook it in batches. Place the
leaves in a bowl or spread them out on
a large serving plate.

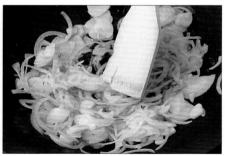

2 Heat the oil in a wok and stir-fry the
shallots and garlic over a medium to
high heat until golden. Spoon the
mixture over the morning glory, sprinkle
with a little sea salt and the chilli flakes
and serve immediately.

Energy 58kcal/240kJ; Protein 2.9g; Carbohydrate 4.2g, of which sugars 2g; Fat 3.4g, of which saturates 0.4g, of which polyunsaturates 2.1g; Cholesterol 0mg; Calcium 113mg; Fibre 2g; Sodium 89mg.

STIR-FRIED PINEAPPLE WITH GINGER ★

THIS DISH MAKES AN INTERESTING ACCOMPANIMENT TO GRILLED MEAT OR STRONGLY FLAVOURED FISH SUCH AS TUNA OR SWORDFISH. IF THE IDEA SEEMS STRANGE, THINK OF IT AS RESEMBLING A FRESH MANGO CHUTNEY, BUT WITH PINEAPPLE AS THE PRINCIPAL INGREDIENT.

SERVES FOUR

INGREDIENTS

1 pineapple
15ml/1 tbsp sunflower oil
2 garlic cloves, finely chopped
2 shallots, finely chopped
5cm/2in piece fresh root ginger,
  peeled and finely shredded
30ml/2 tbsp light soy sauce
juice of ½ lime
1 large fresh red chilli, seeded and
  finely shredded

VARIATION
This also tastes excellent if peaches or nectarines are substituted for the diced pineapple. Use three or four, depending on their size.

1 Trim and peel the pineapple. Cut out the core and dice the flesh.

2 Heat the oil in a wok or frying pan. Stir-fry the garlic and shallots over a medium heat for 2–3 minutes, until golden. Do not let the garlic burn or the dish will taste bitter.

3 Add the pineapple. Stir-fry for about 2 minutes, or until the pineapple cubes start to turn golden on the edges.

4 Add the ginger, soy sauce, lime juice and chopped chilli. Toss together until well mixed. Cook over a low heat for a further 2 minutes, then serve.

Energy 119kcal/507kJ; Protein 1.3g; Carbohydrate 22.8g, of which sugars 22.4g; Fat 3.2g, of which saturates 0.4g, of which polyunsaturates 2g; Cholesterol 0mg; Calcium 42mg; Fibre 2.8g; Sodium 539mg.

PINEAPPLE WITH GINGER AND CHILLI ★

THROUGHOUT SOUTH-EAST ASIA, FRUIT IS OFTEN TREATED LIKE A VEGETABLE AND TOSSED IN A SALAD, OR STIR-FRIED, TO ACCOMPANY SPICY DISHES. IN THIS CAMBODIAN DISH, THE PINEAPPLE IS COMBINED WITH THE TANGY FLAVOURS OF GINGER AND CHILLI AND SERVED AS A SIDE DISH.

SERVES FOUR

INGREDIENTS

- 15ml/1 tbsp sunflower oil
- 2 garlic cloves, finely shredded
- 40g/1½oz fresh root ginger, peeled and finely shredded
- 2 red Thai chillies, seeded and finely shredded
- 1 pineapple, trimmed, peeled, cored and cut into bitesize chunks
- 15ml/1 tbsp *tuk trey*
- 30ml/2 tbsp soy sauce
- 15ml–30ml/1–2 tbsp sugar
- 15ml/1 tbsp roasted unsalted peanuts, finely chopped
- 1 lime, cut into quarters, to serve

1 Heat a large wok or heavy pan and add the sunflower oil. Stir in the finely shredded garlic, ginger and chilli. Stir-fry until they begin to colour, then add the pineapple chunks and stir-fry for a further 1–2 minutes, until the edges turn golden.

2 Add the *tuk trey*, soy sauce and sugar to taste and continue to stir-fry until the pineapple begins to caramelize.

3 Transfer to a serving dish, sprinkle with the roasted peanuts and serve with lime wedges.

Energy 136kcal/577kJ; Protein 2.1g; Carbohydrate 22.8g, of which sugars 22.5g; Fat 4.8g, of which saturates 0.6g, of which polyunsaturates 2.4g; Cholesterol 0mg; Calcium 41mg; Fibre 3g; Sodium 539mg.

SOUTHERN-STYLE YAM ★

THE FOOD OF SOUTHERN THAILAND IS NOTORIOUSLY HOT AND BECAUSE OF THE PROXIMITY TO THE BORDERS WITH MALAYSIA, THAILAND'S MUSLIM MINORITY ARE MOSTLY TO BE FOUND IN THIS AREA. THEY HAVE INTRODUCED RICHER CURRY FLAVOURS REMINISCENT OF INDIAN FOOD.

SERVES FOUR

INGREDIENTS

90g/3½oz Chinese leaves (Chinese cabbage), shredded

90g/3½oz/generous 1 cup beansprouts

90g/3½oz/scant 1 cup green beans, trimmed

90g/3½oz broccoli, preferably the purple sprouting variety, divided into florets

15ml/1 tbsp sesame seeds, toasted

For the yam

120ml/4fl oz/½ cup reduced-fat coconut milk

5ml/1 tsp Thai red curry paste

90g/3½oz/1¼ cups oyster mushrooms or field (portabello) mushrooms, sliced

5ml/1 tsp ground turmeric

5ml/1 tsp thick tamarind juice, made by mixing tamarind paste with warm water

juice of ½ lemon

60ml/4 tbsp light soy sauce

5ml/1 tsp palm sugar or light muscovado (brown) sugar

1 Steam the shredded Chinese leaves, beansprouts, green beans and broccoli separately or blanch them in boiling water for 1 minute per batch. Drain, place in a serving bowl and leave to cool.

2 Make the yam. Pour half the coconut milk into a wok and heat gently for 2–3 minutes, until it separates. Stir in the red curry paste. Cook over a low heat for 30 seconds, until the mixture is fragrant.

3 Increase the heat to high and add the mushrooms to the wok or pan. Cook for a further 2–3 minutes.

4 Pour in the remaining coconut milk and add the ground turmeric, tamarind juice, lemon juice, soy sauce and sugar to the wok or pan. Mix thoroughly.

5 Pour the mixture over the prepared vegetables and toss well to combine. Sprinkle with the toasted sesame seeds and serve immediately.

COOK'S TIP

Oyster mushrooms need gentle handling. Tear large specimens apart and don't overcook them or they will be rubbery.

Energy 68kcal/286kJ; Protein 4g; Carbohydrate 7g, of which sugars 6.1g; Fat 2.9g, of which saturates 0.5g, of which polyunsaturates 1.3g; Cholesterol 0mg; Calcium 75mg; Fibre 2.4g; Sodium 1108mg.

Fragrant Mushrooms in Lettuce Leaves ★

THIS QUICK AND EASY VEGETABLE DISH IS SERVED ON LETTUCE LEAF "SAUCERS" SO CAN BE EATEN WITH THE FINGERS — A GREAT TREAT FOR CHILDREN.

SERVES FOUR

INGREDIENTS
    15ml/1 tbsp sunflower oil
    2 garlic cloves, finely chopped
    2 baby cos or romaine lettuces,
        or 2 Little Gem (Bibb) lettuces
    1 lemon grass stalk, finely chopped
    2 kaffir lime leaves, rolled in
        cylinders and thinly sliced
    200g/7oz/3 cups oyster or chestnut
        mushrooms, sliced
    1 small fresh red chilli, seeded
        and finely chopped
    juice of ½ lemon
    30ml/2 tbsp light soy sauce
    5ml/1 tsp palm sugar or light
        muscovado (brown) sugar
    small bunch fresh mint, leaves
        removed from the stalks

1 Heat a wok or large, heavy frying pan and add the sunflower oil. Add the finely chopped garlic and cook over a medium heat, stirring occasionally, until golden. Do not let it burn or it will taste bitter.

2 Meanwhile, separate the individual lettuce leaves and set aside.

3 Increase the heat under the wok or pan and add the lemon grass, lime leaves and sliced mushrooms. Stir-fry for about 2 minutes.

4 Add the chilli, lemon juice, soy sauce and sugar to the wok or pan. Toss the mixture over the heat to combine the ingredients together, then stir-fry for a further 2 minutes.

5 Arrange the lettuce leaves on a large plate. Spoon a small amount of the mushroom mixture on to each leaf, top with a mint leaf and serve.

Energy 52kcal/217kJ; Protein 2g; Carbohydrate 3.5g, of which sugars 3.3g; Fat 3.5g, of which saturates 0.5g, of which polyunsaturates 2.1g; Cholesterol 0mg; Calcium 45mg; Fibre 1.8g; Sodium 543mg.

FRIED VEGETABLES <u>WITH</u> NAM PRIK ★★

*THIS DISH PROVIDES AN EASY WAY TO ACHIEVING FIVE FRUIT AND VEGETABLE PORTIONS A DAY AND IS
SERVED WITH A PIQUANT DIP FOR MAXIMUM FLAVOUR.*

SERVES SIX

INGREDIENTS

- 3 large (US extra large) eggs
- 1 aubergine (eggplant), halved lengthways and cut into long, thin slices
- ½ small butternut squash, peeled, seeded and cut into long, thin slices
- 2 courgettes (zucchini), trimmed and cut into long, thin slices
- 75ml/5 tbsp sunflower oil
- salt and ground black pepper
- *nam prik* or sweet chilli sauce, to serve (see Cook's Tip)

1 Beat the eggs in a large bowl. Add the aubergine, butternut squash and courgette slices. Toss the vegetables until coated all over in the egg, then season with salt and pepper.

2 Heat the oil in a wok. When it is hot, add the vegetables, one strip at a time, making sure that each strip has plenty of egg clinging to it. Do not cook more than eight strips at a time or the oil will cool down too much.

COOK'S TIP
Nam prik is quite a complex sauce, numbering dried shrimp, tiny aubergines (eggplant), shrimp paste and lime or lemon juice among its ingredients.

3 As each strip turns golden and is cooked, lift it out, using a wire basket or slotted spoon, and drain on kitchen paper. Keep hot while cooking the remaining vegetables. Transfer to a warmed dish and serve with the *nam prik* or sweet chilli sauce as a dip.

Energy 113kcal/468kJ; Protein 5.2g; Carbohydrate 3.6g, of which sugars 3.1g; Fat 8.8g, of which saturates 1.6g, of which polyunsaturates 4g; Cholesterol 95mg; Calcium 56mg; Fibre 2g; Sodium 36mg.

PICKLED VEGETABLE SALAD ★

*EVERYDAY VIETNAMESE AND CAMBODIAN PICKLES GENERALLY CONSIST OF CUCUMBER, MOOLI AND
CARROT — GREEN, WHITE AND ORANGE IN COLOUR — AND ARE SERVED FOR NIBBLING ON, AS PART
OF THE TABLE SALAD, OR AS AN ACCOMPANIMENT TO GRILLED MEATS AND SHELLFISH.*

SERVES SIX

INGREDIENTS
    300ml/½ pint/1¼ cups white
      rice vinegar
    90g/3½oz/½ cup sugar
    450g/1lb carrots, cut into 5cm/2in
      matchsticks
    450g/1lb mooli (daikon), halved,
      and cut into thin crescents
    600g/1lb 6oz cucumber, partially
      peeled in strips and cut into
      5cm/2in matchsticks
    15ml/1 tbsp salt

1 In a large bowl, whisk the vinegar with
the sugar, until it dissolves.

2 Add the carrots and mooli to the
vinegar mixture and toss well to coat.
Cover them and place in the refrigerator
for 24 hours, turning them occasionally.

3 Put the cucumber on a plate and
sprinkle with the salt. Leave for 30
minutes, then rinse under cold water
and drain well. Add to the carrot and
mooli and toss well in the pickling
liquid. Cover and refrigerate as before.

4 Lift the vegetables out of the pickling
liquid to serve, or spoon them into a jar
and store in the refrigerator.

Energy 104kcal/438kJ; Protein 1.8g; Carbohydrate 24.5g, of which sugars 24.1g; Fat 0.5g, of which saturates 0.2g, of which polyunsaturates 0.2g; Cholesterol 0mg; Calcium 59mg; Fibre 3.1g; Sodium 31mg.

HOT THAI PICKLED SHALLOTS ★

PICKLING THAI SHALLOTS IN THIS WAY DEMANDS SOME PATIENCE, WHILE THE VINEGAR AND SPICES WORK THEIR MAGIC, BUT THE RESULTS ARE DEFINITELY WORTH THE WAIT. THINLY SLICED, THE SHALLOTS ARE OFTEN USED AS A CONDIMENT WITH SOUTH-EAST ASIAN MEALS.

MAKES TWO TO THREE JARS

INGREDIENTS
   5–6 small red or green bird's
   eye chillies
   500g/1¼lb Thai pink
   shallots, peeled
   2 large garlic cloves, peeled, halved
   and green shoots removed
For the vinegar
   40g/1½oz/3 tbsp granulated sugar
   10ml/2 tsp salt
   5cm/2in piece fresh root ginger,
   peeled and sliced
   15ml/1 tbsp coriander seeds
   2 lemon grass stalks, cut in
   half lengthways
   4 kaffir lime leaves or pared strips of
   lime rind
   600ml/1 pint/2½ cups cider vinegar
   15ml/1 tbsp chopped fresh
   coriander (cilantro)

1 The chillies can be left whole or halved and seeded. The pickle will be hotter if you leave the seeds in. If leaving the chillies whole, prick them several times with a cocktail stick (toothpick). Bring a large pan of water to the boil. Add the chillies, shallots and garlic. Blanch for 1–2 minutes, then drain. Rinse all the vegetables under cold water, then drain again.

2 Prepare the vinegar. Put the sugar, salt, ginger, coriander seeds, lemon grass and lime leaves or lime rind in a pan, pour in the vinegar and bring to the boil. Reduce the heat to low and simmer for 3–4 minutes. Leave to cool.

3 Remove and discard the ginger, then bring the vinegar back to the boil. Add the fresh coriander, garlic and chillies and cook for 1 minute.

4 Pack the shallots into sterilized jars, distributing the lemon grass, lime leaves, chillies and garlic among them. Pour over the hot vinegar. Cool, then seal and store in a cool, dark place for 2 months before eating.

COOK'S TIPS
• Always be careful when making pickles to be sure that bowls and pans used for vinegar are non-reactive, that is, they are not chemically affected by the acid of the vinegar. China and glass bowls and stainless steel pans are suitable. Kilner and Mason jars are ideal containers.
• When packing pickles, make sure that metal lids will not come in contact with the pickle. The acid in the vinegar will corrode the metal. Use plastic-coated or glass lids with rubber rings. Alternatively, cover the top of the jar with a circle of cellophane or waxed paper to prevent direct contact when using metal lids.
• Take care when handling hot jars. Let them cool slightly after sterilizing and before filling to avoid burning yourself. However, do not let them cool down completely, or they may crack when the hot vinegar is poured in.

Energy 135kcal/566kJ; Protein 3.9g; Carbohydrate 30.3g, of which sugars 23.9g; Fat 0.7g, of which saturates 0g, of which polyunsaturates 0.2g; Cholesterol 0mg; Calcium 85mg; Fibre 3.9g; Sodium 12mg.

GREEN PAPAYA SALAD ★

THIS SALAD APPEARS IN MANY GUISES IN SOUTH-EAST ASIA. AS GREEN PAPAYA IS NOT EASY TO GET HOLD OF, FINELY GRATED CARROTS, CUCUMBER OR EVEN CRISP GREEN APPLE CAN BE USED INSTEAD. ALTERNATIVELY, USE VERY THINLY SLICED WHITE CABBAGE.

SERVES FOUR

INGREDIENTS
 1 green papaya
 4 garlic cloves, coarsely chopped
 15ml/1 tbsp chopped shallots
 3–4 fresh red chillies, seeded
  and sliced
 2.5ml/½ tsp salt
 2–3 snake beans or 6 green beans,
  cut into 2cm/¾ in lengths
 2 tomatoes, cut into thin wedges
 45ml/3 tbsp Thai fish sauce
 15ml/1 tbsp caster (superfine) sugar
 juice of 1 lime
 15ml/1 tbsp crushed roasted peanuts
 sliced fresh red chillies, to garnish

1 Cut the papaya in half lengthways. Scrape out the seeds with a spoon and discard, then peel, using a swivel vegetable peeler or a small sharp knife. Shred the flesh finely in a food processor or using a grater.

2 Put the garlic, shallots, red chillies and salt in a large mortar and grind to a paste with a pestle. Add the shredded papaya, a small amount at a time, pounding with the pestle until it becomes slightly limp and soft.

3 Add the sliced snake or green beans and wedges of tomato to the mortar and crush them lightly with the pestle until they are incorporated.

4 Season the mixture with the fish sauce, sugar and lime juice. Transfer the salad to a serving dish and sprinkle with the crushed roasted peanuts. Garnish with the sliced red chillies and serve the salad immediately.

Energy 68kcal/286kJ; Protein 1.3g; Carbohydrate 15.9g, of which sugars 15.6g; Fat 0.3g, of which saturates 0.1g, of which polyunsaturates 0.1g; Cholesterol 0mg; Calcium 37mg; Fibre 3.1g; Sodium 543mg.

GREEN MANGO SALAD ★

ALTHOUGH THE ORANGE AND YELLOW MANGOES AND PAPAYAS ARE DEVOURED IN VAST QUANTITIES WHEN RIPE AND JUICY, THEY ARE ALSO POPULAR WHEN GREEN. THEIR TART FLAVOUR AND CRUNCHY TEXTURE MAKE THEM IDEAL FOR SALADS AND STEWS.

SERVES FOUR

INGREDIENTS
  450g/1lb green mangoes
  grated rind and juice of 2 limes
  30ml/2 tbsp sugar
  30ml/2 tbsp *nuoc mam*
  2 green Thai chillies, seeded and
    finely sliced
  1 small bunch fresh coriander
    (cilantro), stalks removed,
    finely chopped
  salt

1 Peel, halve and stone (pit) the green mangoes, and slice them into thin strips.

2 In a bowl, mix together the lime rind and juice, sugar and *nuoc mam*. Add the mango strips with the chillies and coriander. Add salt to taste and leave to stand for 20 minutes to allow the flavours to mingle before serving.

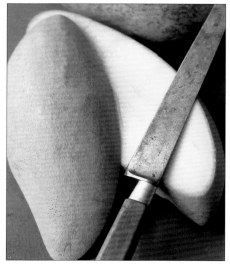

Energy 69kcal/293kJ; Protein 1.2g; Carbohydrate 16.2g, of which sugars 15.8g; Fat 0.4g, of which saturates 0.1g, of which polyunsaturates 0g; Cholesterol 0mg; Calcium 39mg; Fibre 3.6g; Sodium 7mg.

SWEET AND SOUR SALAD ★

INDONESIAN ACAR BENING MAKES A PERFECT ACCOMPANIMENT TO A VARIETY OF SPICY DISHES AND CURRIES, WITH ITS CLEAN TASTE AND BRIGHT, JEWEL-LIKE COLOURS, AND POMEGRANATE SEEDS, THOUGH NOT TRADITIONAL, MAKE A BEAUTIFUL GARNISH. THIS IS AN ESSENTIAL DISH FOR A BUFFET PARTY.

SERVES EIGHT

INGREDIENTS
    1 small cucumber
    1 onion, thinly sliced
    1 small, ripe pineapple or 425g/
        15oz can pineapple rings
    1 green (bell) pepper, seeded and
        thinly sliced
    3 firm tomatoes, chopped
    30ml/2 tbsp golden granulated sugar
    45–60ml/3–4 tbsp white wine vinegar
    120ml/4fl oz/¹⁄₂ cup water
    salt
    seeds of 1–2 pomegranates,
        to garnish

1 Halve the cucumber lengthways, remove the seeds, slice and spread on a plate with the onion. Sprinkle with salt. After 10 minutes, rinse and dry.

2 If using a fresh pineapple, peel and core it, removing all the eyes, then cut it into bitesize pieces. If using canned pineapple, drain the rings and cut them into small wedges. Place the pineapple in a bowl with the cucumber, onion, green pepper and tomatoes.

3 Heat the sugar, white wine vinegar and measured water in a pan, stirring until the sugar has dissolved. Remove the pan from the heat and leave to cool. When cold, add a little salt to taste and pour over the fruit and vegetables. Cover and chill until required. Serve in small bowls, garnished with pomegranate seeds.

VARIATION
To make an Indonesian-style cucumber salad, salt a salad cucumber as described in the recipe. Make a half quantity of the sugar, vinegar and salt dressing and pour it over the cucumber. Add a few chopped spring onions (scallions). Cover and chill. Serve sprinkled with toasted sesame seeds.

Energy 53kcal/224kJ; Protein 0.9g; Carbohydrate 12.3g, of which sugars 12.1g; Fat 0.3g, of which saturates 0.1g, of which polyunsaturates 0.2g; Cholesterol 0mg; Calcium 20mg; Fibre 1.5g; Sodium 6mg.

THAI FRUIT AND VEGETABLE SALAD ★

THIS FRUIT SALAD IS TRADITIONALLY PRESENTED WITH THE MAIN COURSE AND SERVES AS A COOLER TO COUNTERACT THE HEAT OF THE CHILLIES THAT WILL INEVITABLY BE PRESENT IN THE OTHER DISHES. IT IS A TYPICALLY HARMONIOUS BALANCE OF FLAVOURS.

SERVES SIX

INGREDIENTS

    1 small pineapple
    1 small mango, peeled and sliced
    1 green apple, cored and sliced
    6 rambutans or lychees, peeled and
      stoned (pitted)
    115g/4oz/1 cup green beans,
      trimmed and halved
    1 red onion, sliced
    1 small cucumber, cut into
      short sticks
    115g/4oz/1⅓ cups beansprouts
    2 spring onions (scallions), sliced
    1 ripe tomato, quartered
    225g/8oz cos, romaine or iceberg
      lettuce leaves
For the coconut dipping sauce
    30ml/2 tbsp reduced-fat coconut milk
    30ml/2 tbsp granulated sugar
    75ml/5 tbsp boiling water
    1.5ml/¼ tsp chilli sauce
    15ml/1 tbsp Thai fish sauce
    juice of 1 lime

1 Make the coconut dipping sauce. Spoon the coconut milk, sugar and boiling water into a screw-top jar. Add the chilli and fish sauces and lime juice, close tightly and shake to mix.

2 Trim both ends of the pineapple with a serrated knife, then cut away the outer skin. Remove the central core with an apple corer. Alternatively, quarter the pineapple lengthways and remove the portion of core from each wedge with a knife. Chop the pineapple and set aside with the other fruits.

3 Bring a small pan of lightly salted water to the boil over a medium heat. Add the green beans and cook for 3–4 minutes, until just tender but still retaining some "bite". Drain, refresh under cold running water, drain well again and set aside.

4 To serve, arrange all the fruits and vegetables in small heaps on a platter or in a shallow bowl. Pour the coconut sauce into a small serving bowl and serve separately as a dip.

Energy 100kcal/425kJ; Protein 2.3g; Carbohydrate 22.6g, of which sugars 21.7g; Fat 0.7g, of which saturates 0.1g, of which polyunsaturates 0.3g; Cholesterol 0mg; Calcium 50mg; Fibre 3.2g; Sodium 190mg.

SOYA BEANSPROUT HERB SALAD ★

HIGH IN PROTEIN AND FAT, SOYA BEANSPROUTS ARE PARTICULARLY FAVOURED IN CAMBODIA. UNLIKE MUNG BEANSPROUTS, THEY ARE SLIGHTLY POISONOUS WHEN RAW AND NEED TO BE PARBOILED BEFORE USING. TOSSED IN A SALAD, THEY ARE OFTEN EATEN WITH NOODLES AND RICE.

2 Bring a pan of salted water to the boil. Drop in the beansprouts and blanch for a minute only. Drain and refresh under cold water until cool. Drain again and put them into a clean dish towel. Shake out the excess water.

3 Put the beansprouts into a bowl with the spring onions. Pour over the dressing and toss well. Garnish with coriander leaves and serve.

SERVES FOUR

INGREDIENTS
    450g/1lb fresh soya beansprouts
    2 spring onions (scallions), finely
       sliced
    1 small bunch fresh coriander
       (cilantro), stalks removed
For the dressing
    5ml/1 tsp sesame oil
    30ml/2 tbsp *tuk trey*
    15ml/1 tbsp white rice vinegar
    10ml/2 tsp palm sugar
    1 red chilli, seeded and
       finely sliced
    15g/½oz fresh young root ginger,
       finely shredded

1 First make the dressing. In a bowl, beat the oil, *tuk trey* and rice vinegar with the sugar, until it dissolves. Stir in the chilli and ginger and leave to stand for 30 minutes to allow the flavours to develop.

Energy 58kcal/245kJ; Protein 3.8g; Carbohydrate 7.9g, of which sugars 5.8g; Fat 1.5g, of which saturates 0.2g, of which polyunsaturates 0.6g; Cholesterol 0mg; Calcium 52mg; Fibre 2.5g; Sodium 11mg.

VIETNAMESE TABLE SALAD ★

WHEN THIS VIETNAMESE TABLE SALAD IS SERVED ON ITS OWN, THE VEGETABLES AND FRUIT ARE USUALLY FOLDED INTO LITTLE PACKETS USING LETTUCE LEAVES OR RICE WRAPPERS, AND THEN DIPPED IN A SAUCE, OR ADDED BIT BY BIT TO BOWLS OF RICE OR NOODLES.

SERVES SIX

INGREDIENTS

half a cucumber, peeled and sliced
200g/7oz/scant 1 cup beansprouts
2 carrots, peeled and finely sliced
2 unripe star fruit (carambola),
 finely sliced
2 green bananas, finely sliced
1 firm papaya, cut in half, seeds
 removed, peeled and finely sliced
1 bunch each fresh mint and basil,
 stalks removed
1 crunchy lettuce, leaves separated
juice of 1 lime
dipping sauce, to serve

1 Arrange the cucumber, beansprouts, carrots, star fruit, green bananas, papaya, mint and basil attractively on a large plate. Place the lettuce leaves on one side so that they can be used as wrappers.

2 Squeeze the lime juice over the sliced fruits, particularly the bananas to help them retain their colour, and place the salad in the middle of the table. Serve with a dipping sauce.

Energy 94kcal/397kJ; Protein 2.5g; Carbohydrate 20.6g, of which sugars 11.6g; Fat 0.7g, of which saturates 0.1g, of which polyunsaturates 0.3g; Cholesterol 0mg; Calcium 61mg; Fibre 3.4g; Sodium 14mg.

SWEET-AND-SOUR CUCUMBER <u>WITH</u> CHILLIES, CORIANDER <u>AND</u> MINT ★

SHORT, FAT CUCUMBERS ARE A COMMON SIGHT IN THE MARKETS THROUGHOUT SOUTH-EAST ASIA. THIS SALAD IS A GREAT ADDITION TO A SUMMER BARBECUE OR THE SALAD TABLE, AND IS A DELIGHTFUL ACCOMPANIMENT TO ANY MEAT, POULTRY AND SEAFOOD DISHES.

SERVES SIX

INGREDIENTS

2 cucumbers
30ml/2 tbsp sugar
100ml/3½fl oz/½ cup rice vinegar
juice of half a lime
2 green Thai chillies, seeded and
  finely sliced
2 shallots, halved and finely sliced
1 small bunch each fresh coriander
  (cilantro) and mint, stalks removed,
  leaves finely chopped
salt
fresh coriander leaves, to garnish

COOK'S TIP
Decorate the dish with edible flowers,
such as nasturtiums, to add colour.

1 Use a vegetable peeler to remove strips of the cucumber peel. Halve the cucumbers lengthways and cut into slices. Place the slices on a plate and sprinkle with a little salt. Leave them to stand for 15 minutes. Rinse well, drain the slices and pat them dry with kitchen paper.

2 In a bowl, mix the sugar with the vinegar until it has dissolved, then stir in the lime juice and a little salt to taste.

3 Add the chillies, shallots, herbs and cucumber to the dressing and leave to stand for 15–20 minutes. Garnish with coriander leaves and a flower, if you like.

Energy 33kcal/138kJ; Protein 0.9g; Carbohydrate 7.2g, of which sugars 6.9g; Fat 0.2g, of which saturates 0g, of which polyunsaturates 0g; Cholesterol 0mg; Calcium 34mg; Fibre 1g; Sodium 5mg.

LOTUS STEM SALAD WITH SHALLOTS AND SHREDDED FRESH BASIL ★

YOU MAY BE LUCKY ENOUGH TO FIND FRESH LOTUS STEMS IN AN ASIAN MARKET, OR, AS HERE, YOU CAN USE THE ONES PRESERVED IN BRINE. ALTERNATIVELY, TRY THIS RECIPE WITH FRESHLY STEAMED, CRUNCHY ASPARAGUS TIPS FOR A LOW-FAT RECIPE THAT TASTES DELICIOUS.

SERVES FOUR

INGREDIENTS
    half a cucumber
    225g/8oz jar preserved lotus
      stems, drained and cut into
      5cm/2in strips
    2 shallots, finely sliced
    25g/1oz/½ cup fresh basil
      leaves, shredded
    salt
    fresh coriander (cilantro) leaves,
      to garnish
For the dressing
    juice of 1 lime
    30ml/2 tbsp *nuoc mam*
    1 red Thai chilli, seeded
      and chopped
    1 garlic clove, crushed
    15ml/1 tbsp sugar

1 To make the dressing, mix together the dressing ingredients in a bowl and set aside.

2 Peel the cucumber and cut it into 5cm/2in batons. Soak the batons in cold salted water for 20 minutes. Put the lotus stems into a bowl of water. Using a pair of chopsticks, stir the water so that the loose fibres of the stems wrap around the sticks.

VARIATION
Try this recipe with freshly steamed, crunchy asparagus tips instead of lotus stems for a healthy and delicious, low-fat, low-cholesterol recipe.

3 Drain the stems and put them in a bowl. Drain the cucumber batons and add to the bowl, then add the shallots, shredded basil leaves and the prepared dressing. Leave the salad to marinate for 20 minutes before serving. Garnish with fresh coriander leaves.

COOK'S TIP
If you cannot find the stems, fresh lotus roots make a good substitute and are readily available in Asian markets. They grow in sausage-like links, each one about 18–23cm/7–9in long. Once the mud that coats them has been washed off, a pale beige-pink skin is revealed. When buying fresh lotus roots, choose ones that feel heavy for their size, as this is an indication that they are full of liquid. This means that the roots will absorb the flavours of the dressing while retaining a crunchy texture. They should be peeled and soaked in water with a little lemon juice before being added to the salad, to retain their pale colour.

Energy 40kcal/168kJ; Protein 1.4g; Carbohydrate 8.3g, of which sugars 7.5g; Fat 0.3g, of which saturates 0g, of which polyunsaturates 0.1g; Cholesterol 0mg; Calcium 55mg; Fibre 1.7g; Sodium 573mg.

AUBERGINE SALAD ★

AN APPETIZING AND UNUSUAL SALAD THAT YOU WILL FIND YOURSELF MAKING OVER AND OVER AGAIN.
ROASTING THE AUBERGINES REALLY BRINGS OUT THEIR FLAVOUR.

SERVES SIX

INGREDIENTS
  2 aubergines (eggplant)
  15ml/1 tbsp sunflower oil
  30ml/2 tbsp dried shrimp, soaked in
    warm water for 10 minutes
  15ml/1 tbsp coarsely chopped garlic
  1 hard-boiled egg, chopped
  4 shallots, thinly sliced
    into rings
  fresh coriander (cilantro) leaves and
    2 fresh red chillies, seeded and
    sliced, to garnish
For the dressing
  30ml/2 tbsp fresh lime juice
  5ml/1 tsp palm sugar or light
    muscovado (brown) sugar
  30ml/2 tbsp Thai fish sauce

1 Preheat the grill (broiler) to medium or preheat the oven to 180°C/350°F/ Gas 4. Prick the aubergines several times with a skewer, then arrange on a baking sheet. Cook them under the grill for 30–40 minutes, or until they are charred and tender. Alternatively, roast them by placing them directly on the shelf of the oven for about 1 hour, turning them at least twice. Remove the aubergines and set aside until they are cool enough to handle.

2 Meanwhile, make the dressing. Put the lime juice, palm or muscovado sugar and fish sauce into a small bowl. Whisk well with a fork or balloon whisk. Cover with clear film (plastic wrap) and set aside until required.

3 When the aubergines are cool enough to handle, peel off the skin and cut the flesh into medium slices.

4 Heat the oil in a small frying pan. Drain the dried shrimp thoroughly and add them to the pan with the garlic. Cook over a medium heat for about 3 minutes, until golden. Remove from the pan and set aside.

5 Arrange the aubergine slices on a serving dish. Top with the hard-boiled egg, shallots and dried shrimp mixture. Drizzle over the dressing and garnish with the coriander and red chillies.

VARIATION
For a special occasion, use salted duck's or quail's eggs, cut in half, instead of chopped hen's eggs.

Energy 61kcal/254kJ; Protein 4.8g; Carbohydrate 3.6g, of which sugars 2.8g; Fat 3.2g, of which saturates 0.6g, of which polyunsaturates 1.5g; Cholesterol 57mg; Calcium 75mg; Fibre 1.6g; Sodium 408mg.

CABBAGE SALAD ★

THIS IS A SIMPLE AND DELICIOUS WAY OF SERVING A SOMEWHAT MUNDANE VEGETABLE. CLASSIC THAI FLAVOURS OF CHILLI AND PEANUTS PERMEATE THIS COLOURFUL WARM SALAD.

SERVES SIX

INGREDIENTS
15ml/1 tbsp sunflower oil
2 large fresh red chillies, seeded and cut into thin strips
6 garlic cloves, thinly sliced
6 shallots, thinly sliced
1 small cabbage, shredded
15ml/1 tbsp coarsely chopped roasted peanuts, to garnish
For the dressing
30ml/2 tbsp Thai fish sauce
grated rind of 1 lime
30ml/2 tbsp fresh lime juice
120ml/4fl oz/½ cup reduced-fat coconut milk

VARIATION
Cauliflower and broccoli can also be cooked in this way.

1 Make the dressing by mixing the fish sauce, lime rind and juice and coconut milk in a bowl. Whisk until thoroughly combined, then set aside.

2 Heat the oil in a wok. Stir-fry the chillies, garlic and shallots over a medium heat for 3–4 minutes, until the shallots are brown and crisp. Remove with a slotted spoon and set aside.

3 Bring a large pan of lightly salted water to the boil. Add the cabbage and blanch for 2–3 minutes. Tip it into a colander, drain well and put into a bowl.

4 Whisk the dressing again, add it to the warm cabbage and toss to mix. Transfer the salad to a serving dish. Sprinkle with the fried shallot mixture and the peanuts. Serve immediately.

Energy 70kcal/290kJ; Protein 2.2g; Carbohydrate 8.3g, of which sugars 7g; Fat 3.3g, of which saturates 0.5g, of which polyunsaturates 1.6g; Cholesterol 0mg; Calcium 51mg; Fibre 2.2g; Sodium 206mg.

POMELO AND CRAB SALAD ★

TYPICALLY, A THAI MEAL INCLUDES A SELECTION OF ABOUT FIVE DISHES, ONE OF WHICH IS OFTEN A REFRESHING AND PALATE-CLEANSING SALAD THAT FEATURES TROPICAL FRUIT.

SERVES SIX

INGREDIENTS
  15ml/1 tbsp sunflower oil
  4 shallots, finely sliced
  2 garlic cloves, finely sliced
  1 large pomelo
  15ml/1 tbsp roasted peanuts
  115g/4oz cooked peeled
    prawns (shrimp)
  115g/4oz cooked crab meat
  10–12 small fresh mint leaves
For the dressing
  30ml/2 tbsp Thai fish sauce
  15ml/1 tbsp palm sugar or light
    muscovado (brown) sugar
  30ml/2 tbsp fresh lime juice
For the garnish
  2 spring onions (scallions),
    thinly sliced
  2 fresh red chillies, seeded and
    thinly sliced
  fresh coriander (cilantro) leaves
  shredded fresh coconut (optional)

1 Make the dressing. Mix the fish sauce, sugar and lime juice in a bowl. Whisk well, then cover with clear film (plastic wrap) and set aside.

2 Heat the oil in a small frying pan, add the shallots and garlic and cook over a medium heat until they are golden. Remove from the pan and set aside.

3 Peel the pomelo and break the flesh into small pieces, taking care to remove any membranes.

4 Grind the peanuts coarsely and put them in a salad bowl. Add the pomelo flesh, prawns, crab meat, mint leaves and the shallot mixture. Pour over the dressing, toss lightly and sprinkle with the spring onions, chillies and coriander leaves. Add the shredded coconut, if using. Serve immediately.

COOK'S TIP
The pomelo is a large citrus fruit that looks rather like a grapefruit, although it is not, as is sometimes thought, a hybrid. It is slightly pear-shaped with thick, yellow, dimpled skin and pinkish-yellow flesh that is both sturdier and drier than that of a grapefruit. It also has a sharper taste. Pomelos are sometimes known as "shaddocks" after the sea captain who brought them from their native Polynesia to the Caribbean.

Energy 71kcal/300kJ; Protein 8g; Carbohydrate 5.8g, of which sugars 5.4g; Fat 2g, of which saturates 0.3g, of which polyunsaturates 0.7g; Cholesterol 51mg; Calcium 53mg; Fibre 0.8g; Sodium 144mg.

SEAFOOD SALAD <u>WITH</u> FRAGRANT HERBS ★★

THIS IS A SPECTACULAR SALAD. THE LUSCIOUS COMBINATION OF PRAWNS, SCALLOPS AND SQUID, MAKES IT THE IDEAL CHOICE FOR A SPECIAL CELEBRATION.

SERVES FOUR TO SIX

INGREDIENTS

- 250ml/8fl oz/1 cup fish stock or water
- 350g/12oz squid, cleaned and cut into rings
- 12 raw king prawns (jumbo shrimp), peeled, with tails intact
- 12 scallops
- 50g/2oz cellophane noodles, soaked in warm water for 30 minutes
- ½ cucumber, cut into thin batons
- 1 lemon grass stalk, finely chopped
- 2 kaffir lime leaves, finely shredded
- 2 shallots, thinly sliced
- 30ml/2 tbsp chopped spring onions (scallions)
- 30ml/2 tbsp fresh coriander (cilantro) leaves
- 12–15 fresh mint leaves, coarsely torn
- 4 fresh red chillies, seeded and cut into slivers
- juice of 1–2 limes
- 30ml/2 tbsp Thai fish sauce
- fresh coriander sprigs, to garnish

1 Pour the fish stock or water into a medium pan, set over a high heat and bring to the boil. Cook each type of seafood separately in the stock for 3–4 minutes. Remove with a slotted spoon and set aside to cool.

2 Drain the noodles. Using scissors, cut them into short lengths, about 5cm/2in long. Place them in a serving bowl and add the cucumber, lemon grass, kaffir lime leaves, shallots, spring onions, coriander, mint and chillies.

3 Pour over the lime juice and fish sauce. Mix well, then add the seafood. Toss lightly. Garnish with the fresh coriander sprigs and serve.

Energy 339kcal/1420kJ; Protein 27.3g; Carbohydrate 42g, of which sugars 2.3g; Fat 6.8g, of which saturates 0.9g, of which polyunsaturates 3.2g; Cholesterol 219mg; Calcium 148mg; Fibre 1.7g; Sodium 861mg.

THAI PRAWN SALAD <u>WITH</u> GARLIC DRESSING AND FRIZZLED SHALLOTS ★

IN THIS INTENSELY FLAVOURED SALAD, SWEET PRAWNS AND MANGO ARE PARTNERED WITH A SWEET-SOUR GARLIC DRESSING HEIGHTENED WITH THE HOT TASTE OF CHILLI. THE CRISP FRIZZLED SHALLOTS ARE A TRADITIONAL ADDITION TO THAI SALADS.

SERVES SIX

INGREDIENTS
675g/1½lb medium raw prawns
　(shrimp), peeled and deveined,
　with tails intact
finely shredded rind of 1 lime
½ fresh red chilli, seeded and
　finely chopped
15ml/1 tbsp olive oil, plus extra
　for spraying
1 ripe but firm mango
2 carrots, cut into long thin shreds
10cm/4in piece cucumber, sliced
1 small red onion, halved and
　thinly sliced
a few fresh mint sprigs
a few fresh coriander (cilantro) sprigs
15ml/1 tbsp roasted peanuts,
　coarsely chopped
4 large shallots, thinly sliced and
　fried until crisp in 5ml/1 tsp
　sunflower oil
salt and ground black pepper
For the dressing
1 large garlic clove, chopped
10–15ml/2–3 tsp caster
　(superfine) sugar
juice of 2 limes
15–30ml/1–2 tbsp Thai fish sauce
1 fresh red chilli, seeded and
　finely chopped
5–10ml/1–2 tsp light rice vinegar

1 Place the prawns in a glass dish with the lime rind, chilli, oil and seasoning. Toss to mix and leave to marinate at room temperature for 30–40 minutes.

2 Make the dressing. Place the garlic in a mortar with 10ml/2 tsp of the caster sugar. Pound with a pestle until smooth, then work in about three-quarters of the lime juice, followed by 15ml/1 tbsp of the Thai fish sauce.

3 Transfer the dressing to a jug (pitcher). Stir in half the chopped red chilli. Taste the dressing and add more sugar, lime juice and/or fish sauce, if you think they are necessary, and stir in light rice vinegar to taste.

4 Peel and stone (pit) the mango. The best way to do this is to cut either side of the large central stone (pit), as close to it as possible, with a sharp knife. Cut the flesh into very fine strips and cut off any flesh still adhering to the stone.

5 Place the strips of mango in a bowl and add the carrots, cucumber slices and red onion. Pour over about half the dressing and toss thoroughly. Arrange the salad on four to six individual serving plates or in bowls.

6 Heat a ridged, cast-iron griddle pan or heavy frying pan until very hot. Spray with a little oil, then sear the marinated prawns for 2–3 minutes on each side, until they turn pink and are patched with brown on the outside. Arrange the prawns on the salads.

7 Sprinkle the remaining dressing over the salads and garnish with the mint and coriander sprigs. Sprinkle over the remaining chilli with the peanuts and crisp-fried shallots. Serve immediately.

COOK'S TIP
To devein the prawns (shrimp), make a shallow cut down the back of each prawn, using a small, sharp knife. Using the tip of the knife, lift out the thin, black vein, then rinse the prawn thoroughly under cold, running water, drain it and pat it dry with kitchen paper.

Energy 156kcal/656kJ; Protein 20.9g; Carbohydrate 8.9g, of which sugars 8.4g; Fat 4.3g, of which saturates 0.7g, of which polyunsaturates 1g; Cholesterol 219mg; Calcium 102mg; Fibre 1.4g; Sodium 397mg.

SAMBAL NANAS ★

SAMBALS ARE THE LITTLE SIDE DISHES SERVED AT ALMOST EVERY MALAY MEAL. IN POORER SOCIETIES, A MAIN MEAL MAY SIMPLY BE A BOWL OF RICE AND A SAMBAL MADE FROM POUNDED SHRIMP PASTE, CHILLIES AND LIME JUICE. THIS SAMBAL INCLUDES CUCUMBER AND PINEAPPLE.

SERVES TEN

INGREDIENTS

   1 small or ½ large fresh
     ripe pineapple
   ½ cucumber, halved lengthways
   50g/2oz dried shrimps
   1 large fresh red chilli, seeded
   1cm/½in cube shrimp paste,
     prepared (see Cook's Tip)
   juice of 1 large lemon or lime
   light brown sugar, to taste (optional)

1 Cut off both ends of the pineapple. Stand it upright on a board, then slice off the skin from top to bottom, cutting out the spines. Slice the pineapple, removing the central core. Cut into thin slices and set aside.

2 Trim the ends from the cucumber and slice thinly. Sprinkle with salt and set aside. Place the dried shrimps in a food processor and chop fairly finely. Add the chilli, prepared shrimp paste and lemon or lime juice and process again to a paste.

3 Rinse the cucumber, drain and dry on kitchen paper.

4 Mix the cucumber with the pineapple and chill. Just before serving, spoon in the spice mixture with sugar to taste. Mix well and serve.

COOK'S TIP

The pungent shrimp paste, also called *balachan*, is popular in many South-east Asian countries, and is available in Asian supermarkets. Since it can taste a bit raw in a sambal, dry fry it by wrapping in foil and heating in a frying pan over a low heat for 5 minutes, turning from time to time. If the shrimp paste is to be fried with other spices, this preliminary cooking can be eliminated.

Energy 48kcal/203kJ; Protein 3.2g; Carbohydrate 8.6g, of which sugars 8.5g; Fat 0.3g, of which saturates 0g, of which polyunsaturates 0.1g; Cholesterol 25mg; Calcium 77mg; Fibre 1.1g; Sodium 219mg.

CHICKEN AND SHREDDED CABBAGE SALAD ★

IN SOME VIETNAMESE AND CAMBODIAN HOUSEHOLDS, A WHOLE CHICKEN IS COOKED IN WATER WITH HERBS AND FLAVOURINGS TO MAKE A BROTH. THE CHICKEN IS THEN SHREDDED. SOME OF THE MEAT GOES BACK INTO THE BROTH, THE REST IS TOSSED IN A SALAD.

SERVES SIX

INGREDIENTS
  450g/1lb chicken, cooked and torn
    into thin strips
  1 white Chinese cabbage, trimmed
    and finely shredded
  2 carrots, finely shredded
    or grated
  a small bunch fresh mint, stalks
    removed, finely shredded
  1 small bunch fresh coriander
    (cilantro) leaves, to garnish
For the dressing
  15ml/1 tbsp sunflower oil
  30ml/2 tbsp white rice vinegar

  45ml/3 tbsp *nuoc mam* or *tuk trey*
  juice of 2 limes
  30ml/2 tbsp palm sugar
  2 red Thai chillies, seeded and
    finely chopped
  25g/1oz fresh young root
    ginger, sliced
  3 garlic cloves, crushed
  2 shallots, finely chopped

1 First make the dressing. In a bowl, beat the oil, vinegar, *nuoc mam* or *tuk trey*, and lime juice with the sugar, until it has dissolved. Stir in the other ingredients and leave to stand for about 30 minutes to let the flavours mingle.

2 Put the cooked chicken strips, cabbage, carrots and mint in a large bowl. Pour over the dressing and toss well. Garnish with coriander leaves and serve.

Energy 170kcal/715kJ; Protein 20.4g; Carbohydrate 15.8g, of which sugars 13.7g; Fat 3.1g, of which saturates 0.5g, of which polyunsaturates 1.5g; Cholesterol 53mg; Calcium 94mg; Fibre 3.2g; Sodium 60mg.

DESSERTS

Thai and South-east Asian cuisine fits perfectly into a healthy diet for, after a spicy meal, a platter of fresh fruits, often carved into the most beautiful shapes, will refresh and cleanse the palate. Impress your guests with an Exotic Fruit Salad with Passion Fruit, Papayas in Jasmine Flower Syrup or Leche Flan. Ices and jellies are popular too, especially when based on fruit or coconut, here in special versions for the low-fat diet. Try a Watermelon Ice or Coconut Cream Diamonds.

COCONUT ICE CREAM ★

ICE CREAM MADE WITH COCONUT MILK AND CONDENSED MILK CAN BE VERY HIGH IN FAT, BUT IN THIS SPECIALLY ADAPTED LOW-FAT, LOW-CHOLESTEROL RECIPE, REDUCED-FAT IS USED TO MAKE THIS DELECTABLE RECIPE SUITABLE FOR ANYONE FOLLOWING A HEALTHY LOW-CHOLESTEROL DIET.

2 Pour the mixture into the frozen freezer bowl of an ice-cream maker (or follow the appliance instructions) and churn till the mixture has thickened. (This will take 30–40 minutes.)

3 Transfer the mixture to a lidded plastic tub, cover and freeze until the consistency is right for scooping. If you do not have an ice-cream maker, pour the mixture into a shallow container and freeze on the coldest setting.

4 When ice crystals form around the sides of the ice cream, beat the mixture, then return it to the freezer. Do this at least twice. The more you do it, the creamier the mixture will be.

5 Make the sauce. Mix the sugar, measured water and ginger in a pan. Stir over medium heat until the sugar has dissolved, then bring the liquid to the boil. Add the pandan leaf, if using, tying it into a knot so that it can easily be removed with the ginger before serving. Lower the heat and simmer for 3–4 minutes. Set aside till required.

6 Serve the ice cream in coconut shells or in a bowl. Sprinkle with the strips of coconut and serve with the gula melaka sauce, which can be hot, warm or cold.

SERVES SIX

INGREDIENTS
   400ml/14fl oz can reduced-fat
     coconut milk
   400ml/14fl oz can reduced-fat
     condensed milk
   2.5ml/1/2 tsp salt
For the sauce
   150g/5oz/3/4 cup palm sugar or
     muscovado (molasses) sugar
   150ml/1/4 pint/2/3 cup water
   1cm/1/2in slice fresh root
     ginger, bruised
   1 pandan leaf (if available)
   coconut shells (optional) and thinly
     pared strips of coconut, to serve

1 Chill the cans of coconut and condensed milk very thoroughly. In a bowl, mix the coconut milk with the condensed milk. Gently whisk together with the salt.

COOK'S TIP
Coconut milk takes longer to freeze than double (heavy) cream, so allow plenty of time for the process.

Energy 291kcal/1242kJ; Protein 7g; Carbohydrate 69.4g, of which sugars 69.4g; Fat 0.3g, of which saturates 0.2g, of which polyunsaturates 0g; Cholesterol 1mg; Calcium 253mg; Fibre 0g; Sodium 175mg.

COCONUT SORBET ★★

DELICIOUSLY REFRESHING AND COOLING, THIS TROPICAL SORBET CAN BE FOUND IN DIFFERENT VERSIONS ALL OVER SOUTH-EAST ASIA. OTHER CLASSIC VIETNAMESE SORBETS ARE MADE WITH LYCHEES, PINEAPPLE, WATERMELON AND LEMON GRASS.

SERVES SIX

INGREDIENTS
175g/6oz/scant 1 cup caster (superfine) sugar
120ml/4fl oz/½ cup reduced-fat coconut milk
50g/2oz/⅔ cup grated or desiccated (dry unsweetened shredded) coconut
a squeeze of lime juice

1 Place the sugar in a heavy pan and add 200ml/7fl oz/scant 1 cup water. Bring to the boil, stirring constantly, until the sugar has dissolved completely. Reduce the heat and simmer for 5 minutes to make a light syrup.

2 Stir the coconut milk into the sugar syrup, along with most of the coconut and the lime juice. Pour the mixture into a bowl or freezer container and freeze for 1 hour.

3 Take the sorbet out of the freezer and beat it with a fork, or blend it in a food processor, until it is smooth and creamy, then return it to the freezer and leave for 30 minutes.

4 Remove the sorbet from the freezer again and beat it with a fork, or blend it in a food processor, until it is smooth and creamy. Then return it to the freezer and leave until completely frozen.

5 Before serving, allow the sorbet to stand at room temperature for 10–15 minutes to soften slightly. Serve in small bowls and decorate with the remaining grated coconut.

COOK'S TIP
This refreshing sorbet is very welcome on a hot day, or as a palate refresher during a spicy meal. You could serve it in coconut shells, garnished with sprigs of fresh mint.

Energy 170kcal/717kJ; Protein 0.7g; Carbohydrate 32g, of which sugars 32g; Fat 5.2g, of which saturates 4.5g, of which polyunsaturates 0.1g; Cholesterol 0mg; Calcium 23mg; Fibre 1.1g; Sodium 26mg.

WATERMELON ICE ★

AFTER A HOT AND SPICY THAI MEAL, THE ONLY THING MORE REFRESHING THAN ICE-COLD WATERMELON IS THIS WATERMELON ICE. MAKING IT IS SIMPLICITY ITSELF.

3 Spoon the watermelon into a food processor. Process to a slush, then mix with the sugar syrup. Chill the mixture in the refrigerator for 3–4 hours.

4 Strain the mixture into a freezerproof container. Freeze for 2 hours, then remove from the freezer and beat with a fork to break up the ice crystals. Return the mixture to the freezer and freeze for 3 hours more, beating the mixture at half-hourly intervals. Freeze until firm.

5 Alternatively, use an ice-cream maker. Pour the chilled mixture into the machine and churn until it is firm enough to scoop. Serve immediately, or scrape into a freezerproof container and store in the freezer.

6 About 30 minutes before serving, transfer the ice to the refrigerator so that it softens slightly. This allows the full flavour of the watermelon to be enjoyed and makes it easier to scoop.

SERVES FOUR TO SIX

INGREDIENTS
90ml/6 tbsp caster
   (superfine) sugar
105ml/7 tbsp water
4 kaffir lime leaves, torn into
   small pieces
500g/1¼lb watermelon

1 Put the sugar, water and lime leaves in a pan. Heat gently until the sugar has dissolved. Pour into a large bowl and set aside to cool.

2 Cut the watermelon into wedges with a large knife. Cut the flesh from the rind, remove the seeds and chop.

Energy 62kcal/263kJ; Protein 0.1g; Carbohydrate 16.3g, of which sugars 16.3g; Fat 0g, of which saturates 0g, of which polyunsaturates 0g; Cholesterol 0mg; Calcium 9mg; Fibre 0g; Sodium 1mg.

EXOTIC FRUIT SALAD ᵂⁱᵀᴴ PASSION FRUIT ★

PASSION FRUIT MAKES A SUPERB DRESSING FOR ANY FRUIT, BUT REALLY BRINGS OUT THE FLAVOUR OF EXOTIC VARIETIES. YOU CAN EASILY DOUBLE THE RECIPE, THEN SERVE THE REST FOR BREAKFAST.

SERVES SIX

INGREDIENTS
    1 mango
    1 papaya
    2 kiwi fruit
    reduced-fat coconut or vanilla ice
      cream, to serve
For the dressing
    3 passion fruit
    thinly pared rind and juice of 1 lime
    5ml/1 tsp hazelnut or walnut oil
    15ml/1 tbsp clear honey

COOK'S TIP
Clear honey scented with orange blossom would be perfect for the dressing.

1 Peel the mango, cut it into three slices, then cut the flesh into chunks and place it in a large bowl. Peel the papaya and cut it in half. Scoop out the seeds, then chop the flesh.

2 Cut both ends off each kiwi fruit, then stand them on a board. Using a small sharp knife, cut off the skin from top to bottom. Cut each kiwi fruit in half lengthways, then cut into thick slices. Combine all the fruit in a large bowl.

3 Make the dressing. Cut each passion fruit in half and scoop the seeds out into a sieve set over a small bowl. Press the seeds well to extract all their juices. Lightly whisk the remaining dressing ingredients into the passion fruit juice, then pour the dressing over the fruit. Mix gently to combine. Leave to chill for 1 hour before serving with scoops of coconut or vanilla ice cream.

Energy 66kcal/278kJ; Protein 1g; Carbohydrate 14.6g, of which sugars 14.5g; Fat 0.8g, of which saturates 0.1g, of which polyunsaturates 0.4g; Cholesterol 0mg; Calcium 26mg; Fibre 2.9g; Sodium 7mg.

Papayas in Jasmine Flower Syrup ★

THE FRAGRANT SYRUP CAN BE PREPARED IN ADVANCE, USING FRESH JASMINE FLOWERS FROM A HOUSE PLANT OR THE GARDEN. IT TASTES FABULOUS WITH PAPAYAS, BUT IT IS ALSO GOOD WITH ALL SORTS OF DESSERTS. TRY IT WITH ICE CREAM OR SPOONED OVER LYCHEES OR MANGOES.

SERVES TWO

INGREDIENTS
105ml/7 tbsp water
45ml/3 tbsp palm sugar or light
    muscovado (brown) sugar
20–30 jasmine flowers, plus a
    few extra flowers, to decorate
    (optional)
2 ripe papayas
juice of 1 lime

COOK'S TIP
Although scented white jasmine flowers are perfectly safe to eat, it is important to make certain that the flowers have not been sprayed with pesticides or any other harmful chemicals. Washing the flowers will not necessarily remove all the residue.

1 Place the water and sugar in a small pan. Heat gently, stirring occasionally, until the sugar has dissolved, then simmer, without stirring, over a low heat for 4 minutes.

2 Pour into a bowl, leave to cool slightly, then add the jasmine flowers. Leave to steep for at least 20 minutes.

3 Peel the papayas and slice in half lengthways. Scoop out and discard the seeds. Place the papayas on serving plates and squeeze over the lime.

4 Strain the syrup into a clean bowl, discarding the flowers. Spoon the syrup over the papayas. If you like, decorate with a few fresh jasmine flowers.

Energy 197kcal/837kJ; Protein 1.6g; Carbohydrate 49.9g, of which sugars 49.9g; Fat 0.3g, of which saturates 0g, of which polyunsaturates 0g; Cholesterol 0mg; Calcium 81mg; Fibre 6.6g; Sodium 17mg.

Jungle Fruits in Lemon Grass Syrup ★

This exotic and refreshing fruit salad can be made with any combination of tropical fruits — just go for a good balance of colour, flavour and texture. You can also flavour the syrup with ginger rather than lemon grass, if you prefer.

SERVES SIX

INGREDIENTS

1 firm papaya
1 small pineapple
2 small star fruit, sliced into stars
12 fresh lychees, peeled and stoned
(pitted) or 14oz/400g can lychees
2 firm yellow or green bananas, peeled
and cut diagonally into slices
mint leaves, to decorate

For the syrup

115g/4oz/generous ½ cup caster
(superfine) sugar
2 lemon grass stalks, bruised and
halved lengthways

1 To make the syrup, put 225ml/
7½ fl oz/1 cup water into a heavy pan
with the sugar and lemon grass stalks.
Bring to the boil, stirring constantly until
the sugar has dissolved, then reduce
the heat and simmer for 15 minutes.
Leave to cool.

2 Peel and halve the papaya, remove
the seeds and slice the flesh crossways.
Peel the pineapple and slice it into
rounds. Remove the core and cut each
round in half. (Keep the core and slice
it for a stir-fry.)

3 Put all the fruit into a bowl. Pour the
syrup, including the lemon grass stalks,
over the top and toss to combine. Cover
and chill for 6 hours, or overnight.
Before serving, remove the lemon grass
stalks and decorate with mint leaves.

Energy 174kcal/742kJ; Protein 1.3g; Carbohydrate 44.2g, of which sugars 43.4g; Fat 0.3g, of which saturates 0g, of which polyunsaturates 0.1g; Cholesterol 0mg; Calcium 38mg; Fibre 2.7g; Sodium 6mg.

COCONUT JELLY WITH STAR ANISE FRUITS ★

*SERVE THIS DESSERT AFTER ANY ASIAN-STYLE MEAL WITH PLENTY OF REFRESHING EXOTIC FRUIT.
THE COMBINATION OF REDUCED-FAT COCONUT MILK WITH FRESH STAR FRUIT AND LYCHEES MAKES
FOR A DELICIOUS AND SURPRISINGLY LOW-FAT DESSERT.*

SERVES FOUR

INGREDIENTS
    250ml/8fl oz/1 cup cold water
    75g/3oz/⅓ cup caster (superfine)
        sugar
    15ml/1 tbsp powdered gelatine
    400ml/14fl oz/1⅔ cups reduced-fat
        coconut milk
For the syrup and fruit
    250ml/8fl oz/1 cup water
    3 star anise
    50g/2oz/¼ cup caster (superfine) sugar
    1 star fruit, sliced
    12 lychees, peeled and stoned (pitted)
    115g/4oz/1 cup blackberries

1 Pour the water into a pan and add the sugar. Heat gently until the sugar has dissolved. Sprinkle over the gelatine and heat gently, stirring, until the gelatine has dissolved. Stir in the coconut milk, remove from the heat and set aside.

2 Grease an 18cm/7in square tin (pan). Line with clear film (plastic wrap). Pour in the milk mixture and chill until set.

3 To make the syrup, combine the water, star anise and sugar in a pan. Bring to the boil, stirring, then lower the heat and simmer for 10–12 minutes until syrupy. Place the fruit in a heatproof bowl and pour over the hot syrup. Cool, then chill.

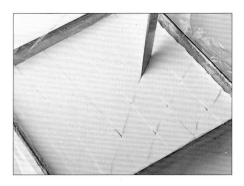

4 To serve, cut the coconut jelly into diamonds and remove from the tin. Arrange the coconut jelly on individual plates, adding a few of the fruits and their syrup to each portion.

COOK'S TIP
Coconut milk is available in cans or cartons. It has a high fat content so look out for the reduced-fat version which can be up to 88 per cent fat free.

Energy 246kcal/1051kJ; Protein 4.4g; Carbohydrate 60g, of which sugars 60g; Fat 0.4g, of which saturates 0.2g, of which polyunsaturates 0.1g; Cholesterol 0mg; Calcium 67mg; Fibre 1.5g; Sodium 114mg.

COCONUT CREAM DIAMONDS ★

DESSERTS LIKE THESE ARE SERVED IN COUNTRIES ALL OVER THE FAR EAST, OFTEN WITH MANGOES,
PINEAPPLE OR GUAVAS. ALTHOUGH COMMERCIALLY GROUND RICE CAN BE USED FOR THIS DISH,
GRINDING JASMINE RICE YOURSELF — IN A FOOD PROCESSOR — GIVES A MUCH BETTER RESULT.

SERVES SIX

INGREDIENTS
  75g/3oz/scant ½ cup jasmine rice,
    soaked overnight in 175ml/6fl oz/
    ¾ cup water
  350ml/12fl oz/1½ cups reduced-fat
    coconut milk
  150ml/¼ pint/⅔ cup reduced-fat
    single (light) cream
  50g/2oz/¼ cup caster
    (superfine) sugar
  raspberries and fresh mint leaves,
    to decorate
For the coulis
  75g/3oz/¾ cup blackcurrants,
    stalks removed
  30ml/2 tbsp caster (superfine) sugar
  75g/3oz/½ cup fresh or
    frozen raspberries

1 Put the rice and its soaking water into a food processor and process for a few minutes until the mixture is soupy.

2 Heat the coconut milk and cream in a non-stick pan. When the mixture is on the point of boiling, stir in the rice mixture. Cook over a very gentle heat for 10 minutes, stirring constantly.

3 Stir the sugar into the coconut rice mixture and continue cooking for a further 10–15 minutes, or until the mixture is thick and creamy.

VARIATION
You could use other soft fruit in the coulis, such as blackberries or redcurrants.

4 Line a rectangular tin (pan) with baking parchment. Pour the coconut rice mixture into the pan, cool, then chill in the refrigerator until the dessert is set and firm.

5 Meanwhile, make the coulis. Put the blackcurrants in a bowl and sprinkle with the sugar. Set aside for about 30 minutes. Tip the blackcurrants and raspberries into a wire sieve set over a bowl. Using a spoon, press the fruit against the sides of the sieve so that the juices collect in the bowl. Taste the coulis and add more sugar if necessary.

6 Carefully cut the coconut cream into diamonds. Spoon a little of the coulis on to each dessert plate, arrange the coconut cream diamonds on top and decorate with the fresh raspberries and mint leaves. Serve immediately.

Energy 146kcal/616kJ; Protein 2g; Carbohydrate 28.5g, of which sugars 18.5g; Fat 3.1g, of which saturates 2g, of which polyunsaturates 0.1g; Cholesterol 8mg; Calcium 50mg; Fibre 0.8g; Sodium 70mg.

TROPICAL FRUIT GRATIN ★★

THIS OUT-OF-THE-ORDINARY GRATIN IS STRICTLY FOR GROWN-UPS. A COLOURFUL COMBINATION OF FRUIT IS TOPPED WITH A SIMPLE SABAYON BEFORE BEING FLASHED UNDER THE GRILL.

SERVES FOUR

INGREDIENTS
2 tamarillos
½ sweet pineapple
1 ripe mango
175g/6oz/1½ cups blackberries
120ml/4fl oz/½ cup sparkling
   white wine
115g/4oz/½ cup caster
   (superfine) sugar
6 egg yolks

VARIATION
Boiling drives off the alcohol in the wine, but children do not always appreciate the flavour. Substitute orange juice if making the gratin for them. White grape juice or pineapple juice would also work well.

1 Cut each tamarillo in half lengthways, then into thick slices. Cut the rind and core from the pineapple and take spiral slices off the outside to remove the eyes. Cut the flesh into chunks. Peel the mango, cut it in half and cut the flesh from the stone (pit) in slices.

2 Divide all the fruit, including the blackberries, among four 14cm/5½in gratin dishes set on a baking sheet and set aside. Heat the wine and sugar in a pan until the sugar has dissolved. Bring to the boil and cook for 5 minutes.

3 Put the egg yolks in a large heatproof bowl. Place the bowl over a pan of simmering water and whisk until pale. Slowly pour on the hot sugar syrup, whisking all the time, until the mixture thickens. Preheat the grill (broiler).

4 Spoon the mixture over the fruit. Place the baking sheet holding the dishes on a low shelf under the hot grill until the topping is golden. Serve the gratin hot.

GRILLED PINEAPPLE WITH PAPAYA SAUCE ★

PINEAPPLE AND STEM GINGER IS A CLASSIC COMBINATION. WHEN COOKED IN THIS WAY, THE FRUIT TAKES ON A SUPERB FLAVOUR AND IS SIMPLY SENSATIONAL WHEN SERVED WITH THE PAPAYA SAUCE.

SERVES SIX

INGREDIENTS
1 sweet pineapple
melted butter, for greasing
   and brushing
2 pieces drained stem ginger in
   syrup, cut into fine matchsticks,
   plus 30ml/2 tbsp of the syrup
   from the jar
30ml/2 tbsp demerara (raw) sugar
pinch of ground cinnamon
fresh mint sprigs, to decorate
For the sauce
1 ripe papaya, peeled and seeded
175ml/6fl oz/¾ cup apple juice

1 Peel the pineapple and take spiral slices off the outside to remove the eyes. Cut it crossways into six slices, each 2.5cm/1in thick. Line a baking sheet with a sheet of foil, rolling up the sides to make a rim. Grease the foil with melted butter. Preheat the grill (broiler).

2 Arrange the pineapple slices on the lined baking sheet. Brush with butter, then top with the ginger matchsticks, sugar and cinnamon. Drizzle over the stem ginger syrup. Grill (broil) for 5–7 minutes or until the slices are golden and lightly charred on top.

3 Meanwhile, make the sauce. Cut a few slices from the papaya and set aside, then purée the rest with the apple juice in a blender or food processor.

4 Press the purée through a sieve placed over a bowl, then stir in any juices from cooking the pineapple. Serve the pineapple slices with a little sauce drizzled around each plate. Decorate with the reserved papaya slices and the mint sprigs.

COOK'S TIP
Try the papaya sauce with savoury dishes, too. It tastes great with grilled chicken and game birds as well as pork and lamb.

Top: Energy 300kcal/1270kJ; Protein 6.2g; Carbohydrate 52.8g, of which sugars 52.7g; Fat 8.7g, of which saturates 2.4g, of which polyunsaturates 1.1g; Cholesterol 302mg; Calcium 119mg; Fibre 4.6g; Sodium 22mg.
Bottom: Energy 97kcal/415kJ; Protein 0.7g; Carbohydrate 24.7g, of which sugars 24.7g; Fat 0.2g, of which saturates 0g, of which polyunsaturates 0.1g; Cholesterol 0mg; Calcium 33mg; Fibre 2.3g; Sodium 19mg.

STEWED PUMPKIN IN COCONUT CREAM ★

FRUIT STEWED IN COCONUT MILK IS A POPULAR DESSERT IN THAILAND. PUMPKINS, BANANAS AND MELONS CAN ALL BE PREPARED IN THIS SIMPLE BUT TASTY WAY.

SERVES FOUR TO SIX

INGREDIENTS
1kg/2¼lb kabocha pumpkin
750ml/1¼ pints/3 cups reduced-fat
   coconut milk
175g/6oz/¾ cup granulated sugar
pinch of salt
4–6 fresh mint sprigs, to decorate

COOK'S TIP
To make the decoration, wash the pumpkin seeds to remove any fibres, then pat them dry on kitchen paper. Roast them in a dry frying pan, or spread them out on a baking sheet and grill (broil) until golden brown, tossing them frequently to prevent them from burning.

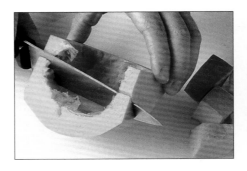

1 Cut the pumpkin in half using a large, sharp knife, then cut away and discard the skin. Scoop out the seed cluster. Reserve a few seeds and throw away the rest. Using a sharp knife, cut the pumpkin flesh into pieces that are about 5cm/2in long and 2cm/¾in thick.

2 Pour the coconut milk into a pan. Add the sugar and salt and bring to the boil. Add the pumpkin and simmer for about 10–15 minutes, until it is tender. Serve warm, in individual dishes. Decorate each serving with a mint sprig and toasted pumpkin seeds (see Cook's Tip).

MANGOES WITH STICKY RICE ★

STICKY RICE IS JUST AS GOOD IN DESSERTS AS IN SAVOURY DISHES, AND RIPE MANGOES, WITH THEIR DELICATE FRAGRANCE AND VELVETY FLESH, COMPLEMENT IT ESPECIALLY WELL.

SERVES FOUR

INGREDIENTS
115g/4oz/⅔ cup white
   glutinous rice
175ml/6fl oz/¾ cup reduced-fat
   coconut milk
45ml/3 tbsp granulated sugar
pinch of salt
2 ripe mangoes
strips of pared lime rind,
   to decorate

1 Rinse the glutinous rice thoroughly in several changes of cold water, then leave to soak overnight in a bowl of fresh cold water.

COOK'S TIP
Like dairy cream, the thickest and richest part of coconut milk always rises to the top. Whenever you open a can or carton, spoon off this top layer and use the thinner, lower fat bottom layer in cooking.

2 Drain the rice well and spread it out evenly in a steamer lined with muslin or cheesecloth. Cover and steam over a pan of simmering water for about 20 minutes, or until the rice is tender.

3 Reserve 45ml/3 tbsp of the cream from the top of the coconut milk. Pour the remainder into a pan and add the sugar and salt. Heat, stirring constantly, until the sugar has dissolved, then bring to the boil. Remove the pan from the heat, pour the coconut milk into a bowl and leave to cool.

4 Tip the cooked rice into a bowl and pour over the cooled coconut milk mixture. Stir well, then leave the rice mixture to stand for 10–15 minutes.

5 Meanwhile, peel the mangoes, cut the flesh away from the central stones (pits) and cut into slices.

6 Spoon the rice on to individual serving plates. Arrange the mango slices on one side, then drizzle with the reserved coconut cream. Decorate with strips of lime rind and serve.

Top: Energy 164kcal/701kJ; Protein 1.7g; Carbohydrate 40.3g, of which sugars 39.4g; Fat 0.7g, of which saturates 0.4g, of which polyunsaturates 0g; Cholesterol 0mg; Calcium 100mg; Fibre 1.7g; Sodium 139mg.
Bottom: Energy 200kcal/846kJ; Protein 3.1g; Carbohydrate 46g, of which sugars 24.3g; Fat 0.8g, of which saturates 0.2g, of which polyunsaturates 0g; Cholesterol 0mg; Calcium 32mg; Fibre 2g; Sodium 51mg.

COCONUT CUSTARD ★★

THIS TRADITIONAL DESSERT CAN BE BAKED OR STEAMED AND IS OFTEN SERVED WITH SWEET STICKY RICE AND A SELECTION OF FRESH FRUIT. MANGOES AND TAMARILLOS COMBINE VERY WELL.

2 Strain the mixture into a jug (pitcher), then pour it into four individual heatproof glasses, ramekins or an ovenproof dish.

3 Stand the glasses, ramekins or dish in a roasting pan. Fill the pan with hot water to reach halfway up the sides of the ramekins or dish.

4 Bake for about 35–40 minutes, or until the custards are set. Test with a fine skewer or cocktail stick (toothpick).

5 Remove the roasting pan from the oven, lift out the ramekins or dish and leave to cool.

6 If you like, turn out the custards on to serving plate(s). Decorate with the mint leaves and a dusting of icing sugar, and serve with sliced fruit.

SERVES FOUR

INGREDIENTS
4 eggs
75g/3oz/6 tbsp soft light
muscovado (brown) sugar
or palm sugar
250ml/8fl oz/1 cup reduced-fat
coconut milk
5ml/1 tsp vanilla, rose or
jasmine extract
fresh mint leaves and icing
(confectioners') sugar,
to decorate
sliced fruit, to serve

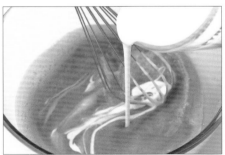

1 Preheat the oven to 150°C/300°F/ Gas 2. Whisk the eggs and sugar in a bowl until smooth. Add the coconut milk and extract and whisk well.

Energy 161kcal/681kJ; Protein 6.5g; Carbohydrate 22.7g, of which sugars 22.7g; Fat 5.7g, of which saturates 1.7g, of which polyunsaturates 0.6g; Cholesterol 190mg; Calcium 57mg; Fibre 0g; Sodium 140mg.

STEAMED CUSTARD ᴵⁿ NECTARINES ★

STEAMING NECTARINES OR PEACHES BRINGS OUT THEIR NATURAL COLOUR AND SWEETNESS, SO THIS IS A GOOD WAY OF MAKING THE MOST OF UNDERRIPE OR LESS FLAVOURFUL FRUIT.

SERVES SIX

INGREDIENTS
    6 nectarines
    1 large (US extra large) egg
    45ml/3 tbsp light
       muscovado (brown) sugar
       or palm sugar
    30ml/2 tbsp reduced-fat
       coconut milk

COOK'S TIP
Palm sugar, also known as jaggery, is made from the sap of certain Asian palm trees, such as coconut and palmyrah. It is available from Asian food stores. If you buy it as a cake or large lump, grate it before use.

1 Cut the nectarines in half. Using a teaspoon, scoop out the stones (pits) and a little of the surrounding flesh.

2 Lightly beat the egg, then add the sugar and the coconut milk. Beat until the sugar has dissolved.

3 Transfer the nectarines to a steamer and carefully fill the cavities three-quarters full with the custard mixture. Steam over a pan of simmering water for 5–10 minutes. Remove from the heat and leave to cool completely before transferring to plates and serving.

Energy 119kcal/507kJ; Protein 3.8g; Carbohydrate 25.2g, of which sugars 25.2g; Fat 1.1g, of which saturates 0.3g, of which polyunsaturates 0.1g; Cholesterol 32mg; Calcium 24mg; Fibre 2.3g; Sodium 20mg.

PUMPKIN PUDDING <u>IN</u> BANANA LEAVES ★

NATIVE TO CAMBODIA, THIS IS A TRADITIONAL PUDDING THAT CAN BE MADE WITH SMALL, SWEET PUMPKINS, OR BUTTERNUT SQUASH WITH DELICIOUS RESULTS. THIS IS A VERY MOREISH DESSERT, OR SNACK, WHICH CAN BE EATEN HOT, AT ROOM TEMPERATURE, OR COLD.

2 In a pan, heat the coconut milk with the sugar and a pinch of salt. Blend the tapioca starch with 15ml/1 tbsp water and 15ml/1 tbsp of the hot coconut milk. Add it to the coconut milk and beat well. Beat the mashed pumpkin into the coconut milk or, if using a blender, add the coconut milk to the pumpkin and purée together.

3 Spoon equal amounts of the pumpkin purée into the centre of each banana leaf square. Fold in the sides and thread a cocktail stick (toothpick) through the open ends to enclose the purée.

4 Fill the bottom third of a wok with water. Place a bamboo steamer on top. Place as many stuffed banana leaves as you can into the steamer, folded side up – you may have to cook them in batches. Cover the steamer and steam parcels for 15 minutes. Unwrap them and serve hot or cold.

SERVES SIX

INGREDIENTS
  1 small pumpkin, about 1.3kg/3lb, peeled, seeded and cubed
  250ml/8fl oz/1 cup reduced-fat coconut milk
  45ml/3 tbsp palm sugar
  15ml/1 tbsp tapioca starch
  12 banana leaves, cut into 15cm/6in squares

VARIATION
You can also try sweet potatoes, cassava or taro root in this recipe.

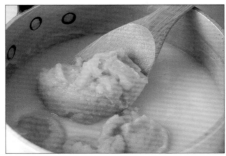

1 Bring a pan of salted water to the boil. Add the pumpkin flesh and cook for 15 minutes, or until tender. Drain and mash with a fork or purée in a blender.

Energy 76kcal/323kJ; Protein 1.7g; Carbohydrate 17g, of which sugars 13.6g; Fat 0.6g, of which saturates 0.3g, of which polyunsaturates 0g; Cholesterol 0mg; Calcium 79mg; Fibre 2.2g; Sodium 46mg.

TAPIOCA PUDDING ★

THIS PUDDING, MADE FROM LARGE PEARL TAPIOCA AND COCONUT MILK AND SERVED WARM, IS MUCH LIGHTER THAN THE WESTERN-STYLE VERSION. YOU CAN ADJUST THE SWEETNESS TO YOUR TASTE. SERVE WITH LYCHEES OR THE SMALLER, SIMILAR-TASTING LONGANS — ALSO KNOWN AS "DRAGON'S EYES".

SERVES FOUR

INGREDIENTS
    115g/4oz/⅔ cup tapioca
    475ml/16fl oz/2 cups water
    175g/6oz/¾ cup granulated sugar
    pinch of salt
    250ml/8fl oz/1 cup reduced-fat
      coconut milk
    250g/9oz prepared tropical fruits,
      such as lychees and papayas
    finely shredded lime rind
      and shavings of fresh coconut
      (optional), to decorate

1 Put the tapioca in a bowl and pour over warm water to cover. Leave to soak for 1 hour so the grains swell. Drain.

2 Pour the measured water in a large pan and bring to the boil over a medium heat. Add the sugar and salt and stir until dissolved.

3 Add the tapioca and coconut milk, reduce the heat to low and simmer gently for 10 minutes, or until the tapioca becomes transparent.

4 Spoon into one large or four individual bowls and serve warm with the tropical fruits. Decorate with the lime rind and coconut shavings, if using.

Energy 324kcal/1384kJ; Protein 1g; Carbohydrate 84.7g, of which sugars 57.2g; Fat 0.4g, of which saturates 0.2g, of which polyunsaturates 0g; Cholesterol 0mg; Calcium 51mg; Fibre 1.8g; Sodium 74mg.

TAPIOCA WITH BANANA AND COCONUT ★

POPULAR IN BOTH VIETNAM AND CAMBODIA, THIS IS THE TYPE OF DESSERT THAT EVERYBODY'S MOTHER OR GRANDMOTHER MAKES. SWEET AND NOURISHING, IT IS MADE WITH TAPIOCA PEARLS COOKED IN COCONUT MILK AND SWEETENED WITH BANANAS AND SUGAR.

SERVES FOUR

INGREDIENTS
   550ml/18fl oz/2½ cups water
   40g/1½oz tapioca pearls
   550ml/18fl oz/2½ cups reduced-fat
      coconut milk
   90g/3½oz/½ cup sugar
   3 ripe bananas, diced
   salt

COOK'S TIP
A pinch of salt added to this recipe enhances the flavour of the coconut milk and counterbalances the sweetness. You can try the recipe with sweet potato, taro root, yellow corn or rice.

1 Pour the water into a pan and bring it to the boil. Stir in the tapioca pearls, reduce the heat and simmer for about 20 minutes, until translucent. Add the coconut milk, sugar and a pinch of salt. Cook gently for 30 minutes.

2 Stir the diced bananas into the tapioca and coconut milk mixture and cook for 5–10 minutes until the bananas are soft but not mushy. Spoon into individual warmed bowls and serve immediately.

Energy 226kcal/964kJ; Protein 1.5g; Carbohydrate 57.2g, of which sugars 45.9g; Fat 0.7g, of which saturates 0.4g, of which polyunsaturates 0.1g; Cholesterol 0mg; Calcium 57mg; Fibre 0.9g; Sodium 154mg.

BAKED RICE PUDDING, THAI-STYLE ★

BLACK GLUTINOUS RICE, ALSO KNOWN AS BLACK STICKY RICE, HAS LONG DARK GRAINS AND A NUTTY TASTE REMINISCENT OF WILD RICE. THIS BAKED PUDDING HAS A DISTINCT CHARACTER AND FLAVOUR ALL OF ITS OWN, AS WELL AS AN INTRIGUING APPEARANCE.

SERVES SIX

INGREDIENTS
175g/6oz/1 cup white or black
glutinous rice
30ml/2 tbsp soft light brown sugar
475ml/16fl oz/2 cups reduced-fat
coconut milk
250ml/8fl oz/1 cup water
3 eggs
30ml/2 tbsp granulated sugar

1 Combine the glutinous rice and brown sugar in a pan. Pour in half the coconut milk and the water.

2 Bring to the boil, reduce the heat to low and simmer, stirring occasionally, for 15–20 minutes, or until the rice has absorbed most of the liquid. Preheat the oven to 150°C/300°F/Gas 2.

3 Spoon the mixture into a large ovenproof dish or individual ramekins. Beat the eggs with the remaining coconut milk and sugar in a bowl.

4 Strain the egg mixture into a jug (pitcher), then pour it evenly over the par-cooked rice in the dish or ramekins.

5 Place the dish or ramekins in a roasting pan. Carefully pour in enough hot water to come halfway up the sides of the dish or ramekins.

6 Cover with foil and bake for about 35–60 minutes, or until the custard has set. Serve warm or cold.

COOK'S TIP
Throughout South-east Asia, black glutinous rice is usually used for sweet dishes, while its white counterpart is more often used in savoury recipes.

Energy 198kcal/834kJ; Protein 5.9g; Carbohydrate 36.2g, of which sugars 14.3g; Fat 3.5g, of which saturates 0.9g, of which polyunsaturates 0.3g; Cholesterol 95mg; Calcium 47mg; Fibre 0g; Sodium 124mg.

CHURROS ★

THESE IRRESISTIBLE FRITTERS, SERVED AT EVERY OPPORTUNITY WITH HOT CHOCOLATE OR COFFEE, CAME TO THE PHILIPPINES WITH THE SPANISH WHO WERE KEEN TO KEEP MEMORIES OF HOME ALIVE.

MAKES ABOUT TWENTY-FOUR

INGREDIENTS
450ml/15fl oz/scant 2 cups water
15ml/1 tbsp olive oil
15ml/1 tbsp sugar, plus extra
  for sprinkling
2.5ml/¹⁄₂ tsp salt
150g/5oz/1¹⁄₄ cups plain
  (all-purpose) flour
1 large (US extra large) egg
sunflower oil, for deep-frying
caster (superfine) sugar,
  for sprinkling

COOK'S TIP
If you don't have a piping (pastry) bag, you could fry teaspoons of mixture in the same way. Don't try to fry too many churros at a time as they swell a little during cooking.

1 Mix the water, oil, sugar and salt in a large pan and bring to the boil. Remove from the heat, and then sift in the flour. Beat well with a wooden spoon until smooth.

2 Beat in the egg to make a smooth, glossy mixture with a piping consistency. Spoon into a piping (pastry) bag fitted with a large star nozzle.

3 Heat the oil in a wok or deep fryer to 190°C/375°F. Pipe loops of the mixture, two at a time, into the hot oil. Cook the loops for 3–4 minutes until they are golden.

4 Lift out the churros with a wire skimmer or slotted spoon and drain them on kitchen paper. Dredge them with caster sugar and serve warm.

LECHE FLAN ★

SERVE THIS TRADITIONAL DESSERT HOT OR COLD WITH CHILLED YOGURT. THE USE OF EVAPORATED MILK REFLECTS THE 50 YEARS OF AMERICAN PRESENCE IN THE PHILIPPINES.

SERVES EIGHT

INGREDIENTS
5 large eggs
30ml/2 tbsp caster (superfine) sugar
few drops vanilla extract
410g/14¹⁄₂oz can reduced-fat
  evaporated (unsweetened
  condensed) milk
300ml/¹⁄₂ pint/1¹⁄₄ cups skimmed milk
5ml/1 tsp finely grated lime rind
strips of lime rind, to decorate
For the caramel
225g/8oz/1 cup sugar
120ml/4fl oz/¹⁄₂ cup water

1 Make the caramel. Put the sugar and water in a heavy pan. Stir to dissolve the sugar, then boil without stirring until golden. Pour into eight ramekins, rotating to coat the sides.

2 Preheat the oven to 150°C/300°F/ Gas 2. Beat the eggs, sugar and vanilla extract in a bowl. Mix the evaporated milk and fresh milk in a pan. Heat to just below boiling point, then pour on to the egg mixture, stirring all the time. Strain the custard mixture into a jug, add the grated lime rind and cool. Pour into the caramel-coated ramekins.

3 Place the ramekins in a roasting pan and pour in enough warm water to come halfway up the sides of the dishes.

4 Transfer the roasting pan to the oven and cook the custards for 35–45 minutes or until they just shimmer when the ramekins are gently shaken.

5 Serve the custards in their ramekin dishes or by inverting on to serving plates, in which case break the caramel and use as decoration. The custards can be served warm or cold, decorated with strips of lime rind.

COOK'S TIP
Make extra caramel, if you like, for a garnish. Pour on to lightly oiled foil and leave to set, then crush with a rolling pin.

Top: Energy 62kcal/257kJ; Protein 0.9g; Carbohydrate 5.7g, of which sugars 0.9g; Fat 4.1g, of which saturates 0.5g, of which polyunsaturates 2.2g; Cholesterol 8mg; Calcium 10mg; Fibre 0.2g; Sodium 3mg.
Bottom: Energy 320kcal/1361kJ; Protein 10.5g; Carbohydrate 65.7g, of which sugars 65.7g; Fat 3.7g, of which saturates 1.1g, of which polyunsaturates 0.4g; Cholesterol 121mg; Calcium 250mg; Fibre 0g; Sodium 139mg.

GLOSSARY

Aduki beans Small, brownish red beans that are often used in sweet recipes.

Agar-agar A gelling and setting agent made from seaweed.

Asian pear One of several varieties of pears with green, russet or yellow skin.

Balachan The Malay term for shrimp paste. An essential ingredient in a wide variety of South East Asian dishes, it is made from tiny shrimps which have been salted, dried and pounded and then left to ferment in hot humid conditions.

Choi sum A mild-tasting brassica.

Chow chow A relish made from pickled vegetables.

Coconut cream A thick cream made from coconut milk

Coconut milk A milk made by soaking grated coconut flesh in hot water and then squeezing it to extract the liquid.

Fermented rice A popular sweetmeat made from fermented cooked glutinous rice.

Galangal Similar to fresh ginger, galangal is a rhizome. The finger-like protruberances of galangal tend to be thinner and paler in colour but the two look similar and are used in much the same way.

Glutinous rice Often referred to as sweet or sticky rice, glutinous rice comes in two varieties, black and white. The grains clump together when cooked.

Above: Thai aubergines are usually small and fairly round in shape.

Hakusai (Chinese cabbage) A vegetable with white stem and green leaves.

Holy basil A pungent variety of basil also known as hot basil.

Jasmine rice A long-grain rice, also known as fragrant or scented rice, with a slightly nutty flavour.

Kabocha A squash with dark green skin and yellow flesh, and a nutty flavour.

Below: Black and white glutinous rice.

Kaffir lime leaves The leaves of an inedible fruit that impart a distinctive citrus flavour to soups, curries, fish and chicken dishes. The rind is also used in some recipes.

Kapi The Thai term for shrimp paste. An essential ingredient in a wide variety of South-east Asian dishes, it is made from tiny shrimps which have been salted, dried and pounded and then left to ferment in hot humid conditions.

Kroeung A Cambodian herb paste made from a blend of lemon grass, galangal, garlic and turmeric.

Lemon basil A variety of basil grown in Thailand used in soups and salads.

Long beans The immature pods of black-eyed beans (peas), also referred to as snake beans.

Lotus root A white-fleshed root from the lotus plant.

Mooli (Daikon) A long, white vegetable of the radish family.

Mung beans A small bean, much used in Vietnam and Cambodia.

Nam pla The Thai term for fish sauce, an essential flavouring in a vast range of savoury dishes.

Nam prik A general term for pungent and hot sauces or dips.

Ngapi The Burmese term for shrimp paste. An essential ingredient in a wide variety of South-east Asian dishes, it is made from tiny shrimps which have been salted, dried and pounded and then left to ferment in hot humid conditions.

Nuoc cham A popular Vietnamese dipping sauce made from chillies.

Nuoc mam The Vietnamese term for fish sauce, an essential flavouring in a vast range of savoury dishes.

Pak choi (bok choy) Loose-leafed brassica with white stems.

Rice flour A flour made by grinding the raw grain to a very fine powder.

Rice sticks These flat, thin dried rice noodles resemble linguine and are available in several widths.

Shimeji Meaty-textured mushroom, similar to oyster mushrooms.

Shiitaki A variety of fungus with a brown cap and white stem.

Sod prik A hot and spicy chilli sauce, originally from China but now popular in Thailand and Vietnam.

Right: Taro is a rough-skinned tuber.

Right: Yam beans look like large brown turnips and are good with spicy dips.

Star anise A star-shaped spice closely resembling anise in flavour.

Star fruit Also known as carambola, this is a bright yellow fruit with a bland, slightly sharp flavour.

Straw mushrooms Delicate, sweet and the most popular variety in Thai cooking.

Tamarind A tart and sour ingredient from the fruit pods of the tamarind tree which is made into a paste or sold in blocks. Tamarind imparts a fruity and refreshing flavour to savoury dishes.

Taro A starchy tuber that tastes rather like a potato.

Terasi The Indonesian term for shrimp paste. It is made from tiny shrimps which have been salted, dried and pounded and then left to ferment in hot humid conditions.

Thai basil A herb with an anise flavour.

Toasted rice flour A speciality of Vietnamese cooking with a coarse texture and a smoky flavour

Tree ear A dried fungi with a crunchy, chewy texture.

Tuk prahoc The Cambodian term for fish sauce, an essential flavouring in a vast range of savoury dishes.

Tuk trey A Cambodian fish sauce mae by fermenting small fish and salt layered in wooden barrels.

Wood ear A dried fungi, also known as cloud ears, with a woody aroma.

MAP OF SOUTH-EAST ASIA

The food of Thailand and South-east Asia is a joy to the senses, combining the refreshing aroma of kaffir lime leaves with the pungency of brilliant red chillies and ginger and the magical flavours of coconut and fresh basil. Throughout the region, the emphasis is on good, freshly cooked food, and every recipe here has been specially adapted for today's low-fat diet.

Rice is the staple diet of the whole region, cultivated in South-east Asia for over five thousand years. Fish forms an important part of the diet in nearly every country from Vietnam and the Philippines to the 13,000 islands of Indonesia. The famous red, yellow and green curries of Thailand are quick and easy to prepare, using reduced-fat coconut milk. Southern India and China influenced Malaysian cooking, and samosas exist side-by side with beef rendang. Ingredients such as lemon grass and galangal are now available worldwide, meaning there has never been a better time to explore Thai and South-east Asian cooking.

Right: Asia is a vast region, from China, Japan and Korea, to Thailand, Vietnam and the South-east Asian islands of Malaysia, Indonesia and the Philippines.

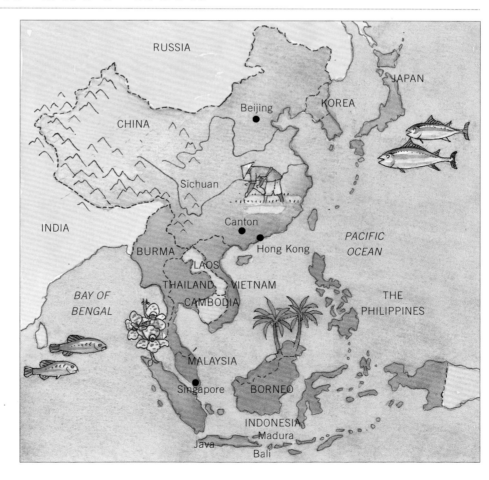

INDEX

A

accompaniments 183, 192,
199, 200, 201, 208,
203, 204, 205, 207,
209, 211, 226
almonds 16
anchovies 78
appetizers
chicken satay with peanut
sauce 130
corn fritters 60
fish cakes with cucumber
relish 64
lamb saté 153
popiah 74–5
pork pâté in a banana
leaf 61
soft-shell crabs with chilli
and salt 68
aromatics 72
Asian pears 16
asparagus
asparagus and crab soup 33
stir-fried asparagus with
chilli, galangal and lemon
grass 202
Thai asparagus 201
aubergines 14, 15
aubergine and sweet potato
stew with coconut milk 98–9
aubergine curry with coconut
milk 86
aubergine salad 220
green beef curry with Thai
aubergines 174

B

baked rice pudding,
Thai-style 247
balachan 226
bamboo 45
bamboo shoots 14–15
red chicken curry with
bamboo shoots 138–9
bamboo steamer 9
barbecuing
barbecue chicken 133
Thai marinated sea
trout 127
bananas
jungle fish cooked in banana
leaves 118
pumpkin pudding in banana
leaves 244
tapioca with banana and
coconut 246
basil
chicken and basil coconut
rice 143
jasmine rice with prawns and
Thai basil 184
lotus stem salad with
shallots and shredded
fresh basil 219
spicy tofu with basil and
peanuts 93
stir-fried chicken with basil
and chilli 134

beans
nutrition 27
snake beans with tofu 89
stir-fried long beans with
prawns, galangal and
garlic 105
tofu and green bean red
curry 88
beansprouts 15
soya beansprout herb
salad 216
beef 23
beef noodle soup 54–5
beef stew with star anise 172
chilli and honey-cured dried
beef 168
fried rice with beef 175
green beef curry with Thai
aubergines 174
seared beef salad in a lime
dressing 169
stir-fried beef in oyster
sauce 173
Thai beef salad 170–1
beer
lobster and crab steamed
in beer 115
bok choy see pak choi
braised black pepper
pork 161
braising 13
broccoli 14
broiling see grilling
broth with stuffed cabbage
leaves 37
brown rice with lime and
lemon grass 183
buns 21

C

cabbage
broth with stuffed cabbage
leaves 37
cabbage salad 221
chicken and shredded
cabbage salad 227
carambola see star fruit
cardamom 94
carp 24
cashew nuts
corn and cashew nut
curry 85
cellophane noodle soup 31

catfish
catfish cooked in a clay
pot 121
cereals: nutrition 27
cha gio and nuoc
cham 67
cha shao 155
cheese
lemon grass skewers with
lime cheese 236
chestnuts 16
chicken 13, 23
barbecue chicken 133
chicken and basil coconut
rice 143
chicken and lemon grass
curry 141
chicken and shredded
cabbage salad 227
chicken rice soup with lemon
grass 48–9
chicken satay with peanut
sauce 130
chicken with chillies and
lemon grass 135
chicken with lemon sauce 132
fragrant grilled chicken 131
fragrant rice with chicken,
mint and nuoc cham 136
ginger, chicken and coconut
soup 46–7
green chicken curry 142
larp of Chiang Mai 170–1
mixed meat noodles 194–5
red chicken curry with
bamboo shoots 138–9
southern chicken curry 140
spicy chicken with young
ginger and coriander 137
steamboat 191
stir-fried chicken with basil
and chilli 134
yellow chicken curry 145
chillies 17, 111, 135
chilli and honey-cured dried
beef 168
pineapple with ginger and
chilli 206
Saigon southern-spiced chilli
rice 181
soft-shell crabs with chilli
and salt 68
steamed fish with chilli
sauce 119
stir-fried asparagus with
chilli, galangal and lemon
grass 202
stir-fried chicken with basil
and chilli 134
sweet-and-sour cucumber
with chillies, coriander
and mint 218
Thai tempeh cakes with
sweet chilli 63
trout with tamarind and
chilli sauce 125
Chinese broccoli 14
Chinese chestnuts 16

Chinese chives
Thai noodles with Chinese
chives 187
Chinese duck curry 146
Chinese leaves 14
Chinese-style scallops and
prawns 110
choi sum 14
churros 248–9
cholesterol 11
cilantro see coriander
cinnamon meat loaf 166–7
clams
mussels and clams with lemon
grass and coconut milk 71
coconut 133, 240, 230
aubergine and sweet potato
stew with coconut milk 98–9
chicken and basil coconut
rice 143
coconut and seafood soup 39
coconut cream diamonds 237
coconut custard 242
coconut ice cream 230
coconut jelly with star anise
fruits 236
coconut rice 178
coconut sorbet 231
curried seafood with coconut
milk 108–9
fish in coconut custard 120
ginger, chicken and coconut
soup 46–7
glazed pumpkin in coconut
milk 87
Indonesian coconut rice 179
mussels and clams with
lemon grass and coconut
milk 71
noodles and vegetables in
coconut sauce 188
pork and pineapple coconut
curry 162
prawn and cauliflower 114
pumpkin and coconut soup 40
stewed pumpkin in coconut
cream 240–1
cooking
dumplings 20–1
pickles 211
rice 153
coriander
garlic and ginger rice with
coriander 180

sweet-and-sour cucumber
with chillies, coriander
and mint 218
tofu soup with mushrooms
and tomato 35
corn
corn and cashew nut
curry 85
corn fritters 60
crab 24
asparagus and crab soup 33

lobster and crab steamed in
beer 115
soft-shell crabs with chilli
and salt 68
crispy Shanghai spring
rolls 77
crispy wonton soup 52
cucumber 122
cucumber relish with fish
cakes 64
sambal nanas 226
sweet-and-sour cucumber
with chillies, coriander and
mint 218
curry
chicken and lemon grass
curry 141
Chinese duck curry 146
corn and cashew nut
curry 85
curried pork with pickled
garlic 164
curried seafood with coconut
milk 108–9
curry pastes 107
green beef curry with Thai
aubergines 174
green chicken curry 142
green curry puffs 65
green prawn curry 106
jungle curry of guinea
fowl 144
northern fish curry 116
pork and pineapple coconut
curry 162
prawns with yellow curry
paste 107
red chicken curry with
bamboo shoots 138–9

southern chicken curry 140
Thai vegetable curry
with lemon grass
rice 94–5
tofu and green bean red
curry 88
tofu and vegetable Thai
curry 90–1
yellow chicken
curry 145

D
daikon *see* mooli
dairy products: nutrition 27
dark soy sauce 175
deep-frying
basil leaves 134
desserts 229
baked rice pudding,
Thai-style 247
churros 248–9
coconut cream
diamonds 237
coconut custard 242
coconut ice cream 230
coconut jelly with star anise
fruits 236
exotic fruit salad with passion
fruit 233
grilled pineapple with papaya
sauce 238–9
leche flan 248–9
lemon grass skewers with
lime cheese 236
mangoes with sticky
rice 240–1
papayas in jasmine flower
syrup 234
steamed custard in
nectarines 243
stewed pumpkin in coconut
cream 240–1
tapioca pudding 245
tropical fruit gratin 238–9
watermelon ice 232
duck 23
aromatic broth with roast
duck, pak choi and egg
noodles 50–1
Chinese duck curry 146
crispy roast duck 148
duck and spicy orange
sauce 147
duck with pineapple and
ginger 149

E
eggplants *see* aubergines
eggs
fried vegetables with nam
prik 209
leche flan 248–9
nutrition 27
omelette soup 32
steamboat 191
escabeche 117
exotic fruit salad with passion
fruit 233

F
fat-free cooking methods 13
fats 9, 10–11
cutting down on
11, 12
monounsaturated 11
nutrition 27
polyunsaturated 11
role in the diet 10
saturated 9, 10–11
types of 10
fenugreek 114
festive rice 182
firecrackers 66
fish 13, 24–5
Cambodian bamboo, fish
and rice soup 45
catfish cooked in a clay
pot 121
charcoal-grilled fish with
mung beansprouts and
herbs 123
escabeche 117
fish cakes with cucumber
relish 64
fish in coconut custard 120
hot and fragrant trout 124
hot-and-sour fish soup 43
jungle fish cooked in banana
leaves 118
northern fish curry 116
nutrition 26
spicy pan-seared tuna with
cucumber, garlic and
ginger 122
steamboat 191
steamed fish with chilli
sauce 119
Thai fish broth 44
Thai marinated sea trout
127
Thai-style trout 126
trout with tamarind and
chilli sauce 125
flavourings 17
fragrant grilled chicken 131
fragrant mushrooms in lettuce
leaves 208
fried rice
fried rice with beef 175
jasmine rice with prawns
and Thai basil 184
Thai fried rice 185
fried vegetables with nam
prik 209
fritters
corn fritters 60
fruit 16
exotic 12
exotic fruit salad with
passion fruit 233
jungle fruits in lemon
grass syrup 235
nutrition 26–7
Thai fruit and vegetable
salad 215
tropical fruit
gratin 238–9

G
galangal 105
stir-fried asparagus with
chilli, galangal and lemon
grass 202
stir-fried long beans with
prawns, galangal and
garlic 105
garlic 17
curried pork with pickled
garlic 164
garlic and ginger rice with
coriander 180
morning glory with garlic and
shallots 204
potato, shallot and garlic
samosas with green peas 58
spicy pan-seared tuna with
cucumber, garlic and
ginger 122
stir-fried long beans with
prawns, galangal and
garlic 105
Thai prawn salad with garlic
dressing and frizzled
shallots 224–5
ginger 17, 35, 122, 111
garlic and ginger rice with
coriander 180
ginger, chicken and coconut
soup 46–7
pineapple with ginger and
chilli 206
spicy chicken with young
ginger and coriander 137
stir-fried baby squid
with ginger, garlic and
lemon 112

stir-fried pineapple with
ginger 205
green beef curry with Thai
aubergines 174
green chicken curry 142
green curry puffs 65
green papaya salad 212
green peppercorns 144
green prawn curry 106
grey mullet 24
grilled pineapple with papaya
sauce 238–9
guinea fowl curry 144

H
herbs 72, 190
  pan-steamed mussels with
    lemon grass, chilli and
    Thai herbs 70
  rice noodles with fresh
    herbs 190
honey 168, 233
hot and fragrant trout 124
hot and sour prawn soup 46–7
hot and sour soup 53
hot and sweet vegetable and
  tofu soup 34
hot Thai pickled shallots 211

I
ice cream
  coconut ice cream 230
Indonesian coconut rice 179

J
jaggery *see* palm sugar
jasmine flower syrup and
  papayas 234
jasmine rice with prawns and
  Thai basil 184
jungle curry 97
jungle curry of guinea fowl 144
jungle fruits in lemon grass
  syrup 235

K
kaffir lime 85
kumquats 16

L
lamb 23
  lamb saté 153
larp of Chiang Mai 170–1
leche flan 248–9
lemon grass 17, 111, 202
  brown rice with lime and
    lemon grass 183
  chicken and lemon grass
    curry 141
  chicken rice soup with lemon
    grass 48–9
  chicken with chillies and
    lemon grass 135
  grilled prawns with lemon
    grass 73
  jungle fruits in lemon grass
    syrup 235

lemon grass pork 159
lemon grass skewers with
  lime cheese 236
lemon grass snails 80–1
mussels and clams with
  lemon grass and coconut
  milk 71
northern fish curry 116
pork on lemon grass
  sticks 152
spicy tofu with basil and
  peanuts 93
Thai vegetable curry with
  lemon grass rice 94–5
lemons
  lemon sauce with chicken 132
lettuce
  lettuce leaves and fragrant
    mushrooms 208
  Vietnamese table salad 217
light soy sauce 175
lime 114
  brown rice with lime and
    lemon grass 183
  kaffir lime leaves 85
  pak choi with lime dressing 200
  seared beef salad in a lime
    dressing 169
lobster and crab steamed in
  beer 115
lotus
  lotus stem salad with
    shallots and shredded
    fresh basil 219
low-fat spreads 13
lychees 16

M
mackerel 24, 26
mangoes 16
  green mango salad 213
  mangoes with sticky rice 240–1
marinades 13
meat 23; *see* beef; *see* lamb;
  see pork
  cha shao 155
  lean cuts 12
  meat dishes 151, 152, 155–7,
    159, 162–4, 173–4
  nutrition 26
microwaved foods 13
mint
  fragrant rice with chicken,
    mint and nuoc cham 136
  sweet-and-sour cucumber
    with chillies, coriander and
    mint 218
mirin 63
mixed vegetable soup 36
mooli 14, 15
morning glory with garlic and
  shallots 204
mushrooms 15, 22
  fragrant mushrooms in lettuce
    leaves 208
  hot and sour soup 53
  tofu soup with mushrooms
    and tomato 35

mussels
  mussels and clams with lemon
    grass and coconut milk 71
  pan-steamed mussels with
    lemon grass, chilli and Thai
    herbs 70
  steamed mussels with chilli
    and ginger 111

N
noodles 8, 18
  aromatic broth with roast
    duck, pak choi and egg
    noodles 50
  beef noodle soup 54–5
  cellophane noodle soup 31
  egg noodles 66
  mixed meat noodles 194–5
  noodles and vegetables in
    coconut sauce 188
  plain noodles with four
    flavours 186
  rice noodles with fresh
    herbs 190
  rice noodles with pork 197
  steamboat 191
  stir-fried noodles in seafood
    sauce 193
  sweet and hot vegetable
    noodles 189
  Thai noodles with Chinese
    chives 187
  wheat noodles with stir-fried
    pork 196
northern fish curry 116
northern prawn and squash
  soup 42
nuoc cham 136
nutrition chart 26–7
nuts 16
  nutrition 27

O
oils 13
  nutrition 27
omelette soup 32
orange sauce 147
oyster mushrooms 207
oyster sauce
  stir-fried beef in oyster
    sauce 173

P
pak choi 14
  aromatic broth with roast
    duck, pak choi and egg
    noodles 50–1
  pak choi with lime
    dressing 200
palm sugar 243
pan-steamed mussels with
  lemon grass, chilli and
  Thai herbs 70
pancakes 18–19
  Nonya spring roll
    pancakes 18
  popiah 74–5
  reheating 18

papayas
  green papaya salad 212
  papaya sauce 238–9
  papayas in jasmine flower
    syrup 234
party foods 57–9, 62, 63,
  65–7, 77–9
pastes
  curry pastes 107
  magic paste 36
peanuts
  chicken satay with peanut
    sauce 130
  spicy tofu with basil and
    peanuts 93
peas
  potato, shallot and garlic
    samosas with green
    peas 58
peppers
  stuffed sweet peppers 84
phoenix prawns *see* fantail
  prawns
pineapple
  duck with pineapple and
    ginger 149
  grilled pineapple with papaya
    sauce 238–9
  pineapple with ginger and
    chilli 206
  pork and pineapple coconut
    curry 162
  sambal nanas 226
  stir-fried pineapple with
    ginger 205
piquant prawn laksa 38
plain noodles with four
  flavours 186
poaching 13
pomelo salad 222
popiah 74–5
pork 23
  baked cinnamon meat
    loaf 166–7
  braised black pepper
    pork 161
  broth with stuffed cabbage
    leaves 37
  cha shao 155
  curried pork with pickled
    garlic 164
  dry-cooked pork strips 154
  hot and sour soup 53

lemon grass pork 159
mixed meat noodles 194–5
pork and pineapple coconut
    curry 162
pork and prawn soup with
    rice sticks 41
pork on lemon grass
    sticks 152
rice noodles with pork 197
rice rolls stuffed with
    pork 158
saeng wa of grilled
    pork 160
steamboat 191
stir-fried pork and butternut
    curry 165
stir-fried pork with dried
    shrimp 157
sweet and sour pork
    stir-fry 156
sweet and sour pork, Thai
    style 163
wheat noodles with stir-fried
    pork 196
potatoes
    potato, shallot and garlic
        samosas with green
        peas 58
poultry; *see* chicken; *see* duck;
    see guinea fowl
    poultry dishes 129, 131–4,
        138–42, 144–6, 149
prawns 25; *see also* shrimp
    broth with stuffed cabbage
        leaves 37
    Chinese-style scallops and
        prawns 110
    firecrackers 66
    green prawn curry 106
    grilled prawns with lemon
        grass 73
    hot-and-sour prawn
        soup 46–7
    jasmine rice with prawns and
        Thai basil 184
    mixed meat noodles 194–5
    northern prawn and squash
        soup 42
    piquant prawn laksa 38
    pork and prawn soup with
        rice sticks 41
    prawn and cauliflower
        curry 114
    prawns with yellow curry
        paste 107
    sambal goreng with
        prawns 104
    seafood salad with fragrant
        herbs 223
    sinigang 102
    stir-fried long beans with
        prawns, galangal and
        garlic 105
    stir-fried prawns with
        tamarind 103
    Thai prawn salad with garlic
        dressing and frizzled
        shallots 224–5

preparation
    chicken 140
    mushrooms 22
    prawns 224
    spring rolls 19
    tamarind 72
    turmeric 145
pumpkin
    glazed pumpkin in coconut
        milk 87
    pumpkin and coconut soup 40
    pumpkin pudding in banana
        leaves 244
    stewed pumpkin in coconut
        cream 240–1

R
red chicken curry with bamboo
    shoots 138–9
rice 18
    baked rice pudding, Thai-style
        247
    brown rice with lime and
        lemon grass 183
    Cambodian bamboo, fish and
        rice soup 45
    chicken and basil coconut
        rice 143
    chicken rice soup with lemon
        grass 48–9
    coconut rice 178
    festive rice 182
    fragrant rice with chicken,
        mint and nuoc cham 136
    fried rice with beef 175
    garlic and ginger rice with
        coriander 180
    Indonesian coconut rice 179
    jasmine rice with prawns and
        Thai basil 184
    mangoes with sticky rice
        240–1
    pork pâté in a banana leaf 61
    rice noodles with pork 197
    rice rolls stuffed with pork 158
    Saigon southern-spiced chilli
        rice 181
    Singapore rice vermicelli 192
    Thai fried rice 185
    Thai vegetable curry with
        lemon grass rice 94–5
rice vinegar 17

S
saeng wa of grilled pork 160
salads
    aubergine salad 220
    cabbage salad 221
    green papaya salad 212
    larp of Chiang Mai 170–1
    pomelo salad 222
    saeng wa of grilled pork 160
    seafood salad with fragrant
        herbs 223
    sweet and sour salad 214
    Thai beef salad 170–1
    Thai fruit and vegetable
        salad 215
    Thai prawn salad with garlic
        dressing and frizzled
        shallots 224–5
salmon 24, 25
salt and pepper
    prawns 69
sambals
    sambal goreng with
        prawns 104
    sambal nanas 226
samosas 59
    potato, shallot and garlic
        samosas with green
        peas 58
sardines 12
sauces
    chicken satay with peanut
        sauce 130
    chicken with lemon sauce 132
    fried vegetables with nam
        prik 209
    grilled pineapple with papaya
        sauce 238–9
    noodles and vegetables in
        coconut sauce 188
    pork pâté in a banana
        leaf 61
    soy 17
    steamed fish with chilli
        sauce 119
    stir-fried beef in oyster
        sauce 173
    stir-fried noodles in seafood
        sauce 193
    Thai tempeh cakes with
        sweet chilli 63
    trout with tamarind and chilli
        sauce 125
scallions *see* spring onions
scallops 25
    Chinese-style scallops and
        prawns 110
sea bass 25
seafood *see also* shellfish
    coconut and seafood
        soup 39
    curried seafood with coconut
        milk 108–9
    stir-fried noodles in seafood
        sauce 193
seaweed 15
seeds
    nutrition 27

shallots
    hot Thai pickled shallots 211
    lotus stem salad with shallots
        and shredded fresh
        basil 219
    morning glory with garlic and
        shallots 204
    northern fish curry 116
    potato, shallot and garlic
        samosas with green
        peas 58

Thai prawn salad with garlic
    dressing and frizzled
    shallots 224–5
shellfish; *see also* seafood;
    see prawns
    Chinese-style scallops and
        prawns 110
    curried seafood with coconut
        milk 108–9
    green prawn curry 106
    mussels and clams with
        lemon grass and coconut
        milk 71
    nutrition 26
    pan-steamed mussels with
        lemon grass, chilli and
        Thai herbs 70
    prawns with yellow curry
        paste 107
    salt and pepper prawns 69
    sambal goreng with
        prawns 104
    sinigang 102
    stir-fried baby squid with
        ginger, garlic and
        lemon 112
    stir-fried prawns with
        tamarind 103
shrimp; *see also* prawns
    stir-fried pork with dried
        shrimp 157
side dishes 183, 192, 199–201,
    203–5, 207–9, 211, 226
Singapore rice vermicelli 192
sinigang 102
snacks 57–9, 62–3, 65–7, 77–9
snails
    lemon grass snails 80–1
snake beans
    snake beans with tofu 89

soft-shell crabs with chilli
    and salt 68
soups 29
    asparagus and crab soup 33
    cellophane noodle soup 31
    coconut and seafood
        soup 39
    crispy wonton soup 52
    ginger, chicken and coconut
        soup 46–7
    hot and sour prawn
        soup 46–7
    hot and sour soup 53
    hot and sweet vegetable
        and tofu soup 34
    mixed vegetable soup 36
    northern prawn and squash
        soup 42
    omelette soup 32
    piquant prawn laksa 38
    pumpkin and coconut
        soup 40
    spicy green bean soup 30
    squash and prawn soup 42
    Thai fish broth 44
southern chicken curry 140
southern-style yam 207
soy sauce 175
soya milk
    soya beansprout herb
        salad 216
spices 73
    baked cinnamon meat
        loaf 166–7
    pork pâté in a banana leaf 61
    steamed vegetables with
        Chiang Mai spicy dip 203
spicy green bean soup 30
spicy pan-seared tuna with
    cucumber, garlic and
    ginger 122
spicy tofu with basil and
    peanuts 93
spring onions 15
spring rolls
    cha gio and nuoc cham 67
    crispy Shanghai spring
        rolls 77
    Nonya spring roll pancakes 18
    spring rolls with mushrooms
        and pork 72
    Thai spring rolls 78–9
    tung tong 62

squash and prawn soup 42
squashes
    stir-fried pork and butternut
        curry 165
squid 25
    griddled squid and tomatoes
        in a tamarind dressing 113
    stir-fried baby squid with
        ginger, garlic and lemon 112
star anise
    beef stew with star anise 172
    coconut jelly with star anise
        fruits 236
star fruit 16
steamboat 191
steaming 8, 13, 27
    morning glory with garlic
        and shallots 204
    steamed custard in
        nectarines 243
    steamed fish with chilli
        sauce 119
    steamed vegetables with
        Chiang Mai spicy dip 203
stewed pumpkin in coconut
    cream 240–1
stir-frying 8–9, 13
    chicken with chillies and
        lemon grass 135
    stir-fried asparagus with
        chilli, galangal and lemon
        grass 202
    stir-fried baby squid
        with ginger, garlic and
        lemon 112
    stir-fried beef in oyster
        sauce 173
    stir-fried chicken with basil
        and chilli 134
    stir-fried long beans with
        prawns, galangal and
        garlic 105
    stir-fried noodles in seafood
        sauce 193
    stir-fried pineapple with
        ginger 205
    stir-fried pork with dried
        shrimp 157
    stir-fried prawns with
        tamarind 103
    wheat noodles with stir-fried
        pork 196
storage
    mushrooms 22
stuffed sweet peppers 84
sweet and hot vegetable
    noodles 189
sweet and sour pork
    stir-fry 156
sweet and sour pork,
    Thai style 163
sweet and sour salad 214
sweet and sour vegetables
    with tofu 92
sweet potatoes
    aubergine and sweet
        potato stew with coconut
        milk 98–9

T
tamarind
    griddled squid and tomatoes
        in a tamarind dressing 113
    stir-fried prawns with
        tamarind 103
    trout with tamarind and chilli
        sauce 125
tapioca
    tapioca pudding 245
    tapioca with banana and
        coconut 246
tempeh
    Thai tempeh cakes with
        sweet chilli 63
Thai asparagus 201
Thai beef salad 170–1
Thai fish broth 44
Thai fragrant rice 126, 182
Thai fried rice 185
Thai fruit and vegetable
    salad 215
Thai marinated sea trout 127
Thai noodles with Chinese
    chives 187
Thai prawn salad with garlic
    dressing and frizzled
    shallots 224–5
Thai spring rolls 78–9
Thai tempeh cakes with sweet
    chilli 63
Thai vegetable curry with
    lemon grass rice 94–5
Thai-style baked rice
    pudding 247

Thai-style trout 126
tofu 23
    hot and sweet vegetable
        and tofu soup 34
    nutrition 27
    snake beans with
        tofu 89
    spicy tofu with basil and
        peanuts 93
    sweet and sour vegetables
        with tofu 92
    tofu and green bean red
        curry 88
    tofu and vegetable Thai
        curry 90–1
    tofu soup with mushrooms
        and tomato 35

tomatoes
    griddled squid and
        tomatoes in a tamarind
        dressing 113
tropical fruit gratin 238–9
trout
    hot and fragrant trout 124
    Thai marinated sea trout 127
    Thai-style trout 126
    trout with tamarind and chilli
        sauce 125
tuna 25
    spicy pan-seared tuna with
        cucumber, garlic and
        ginger 122
tung tong 62
turmeric 145

V
vegetables 14–15, 83
    aubergine and sweet potato
        stew with coconut milk 98–9
    cooking 13
    corn and cashew nut curry 85
    crunchy summer rolls 76
    fried vegetables with nam
        prik 209
    hot and sweet vegetable and
        tofu soup 34
    jungle curry 97
    mixed vegetable soup 36
    noodles and vegetables in
        coconut sauce 188
    nutrition 27
    pickled vegetables 210
    snake beans with tofu 89
    spicy green bean soup 30
    steamed vegetables with
        Chiang Mai spicy dip 203
    stuffed sweet peppers 84
    sweet and hot vegetable
        noodles 189
    sweet and sour vegetables
        with tofu 92
    Thai fruit and vegetable
        salad 215
    Thai vegetable curry with
        lemon grass rice 94–5
    tofu and green bean red
        curry 88
    tofu and vegetable Thai
        curry 90–1
    vegetable forest curry 96
    Vietnamese table salad 217

W
water chestnuts 15
watermelon ice 232
woks 8–9, 13
wontons
    crispy wonton soup 52
    green curry puffs 65
    wrappers 8, 18–19

Y
yams
    southern-style yam 207
yellow chicken curry 145